MW01487073

SPEAK DATA

Artists, Scientists, Thinkers, and Dreamers on How We Live Our Lives in Numbers

SPEAK DATA

Giorgia Lupi and Phillip Cox

PA PRESS

PRINCETON ARCHITECTURAL PRESS · NEW YORK

Published by
Princeton Architectural Press
A division of Chronicle Books LLC
70 West 36th Street
New York, NY 10018
papress.com

Printed and bound in China

28 27 26 25   4 3 2 1   First edition

Editor: Jennifer N. Thompson
Designers: Giorgia Lupi and Britt Cobb
Typesetting: Natalie Snodgrass

Library of Congress Cataloging-in-Publication Data
Names: Lupi, Giorgia author | Cox, Phillip author
Title: Speak data : artists, scientists, thinkers, and dreamers on how we live our lives in numbers / Giorgia Lupi and Phillip Cox.
Description: First edition | New York : Princeton Architectural Press, [2025] | Summary: “Essays and interviews examining the intersection of data and the various fields and sectors that define our society today” –Provided by publisher
Identifiers: LCCN 2025001764 | ISBN 9781797230276 paperback | ISBN 9781797230283 ebook
Subjects: LCSH: Information behavior | Communication in information science | Information visualization | LCGFT: Essays | Interviews
Classification: LCC ZA3075 .L87 2025 | DDC 025.5/24–dc23/eng/20250324
LC record available at https://lccn.loc.gov/2025001764

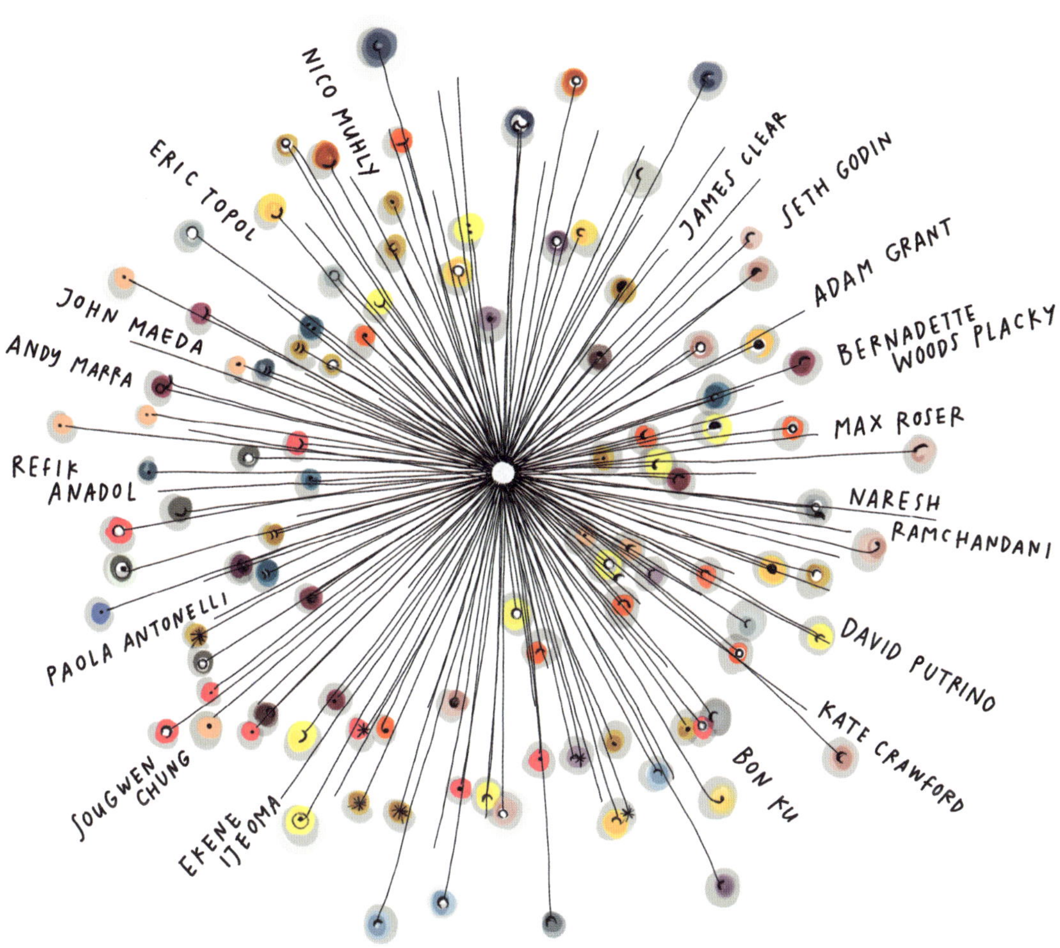
NICO MUHLY
ERIC TOPOL
JAMES CLEAR
SETH GODIN
ADAM GRANT
JOHN MAEDA
ANDY MARRA
BERNADETTE WOODS PLACKY
MAX ROSER
REFIK ANADOL
NARESH RAMCHANDANI
PAOLA ANTONELLI
DAVID PUTRINO
SOUGWEN CHUNG
KATE CRAWFORD
BON KU
EKENE IJEOMA

Introduction

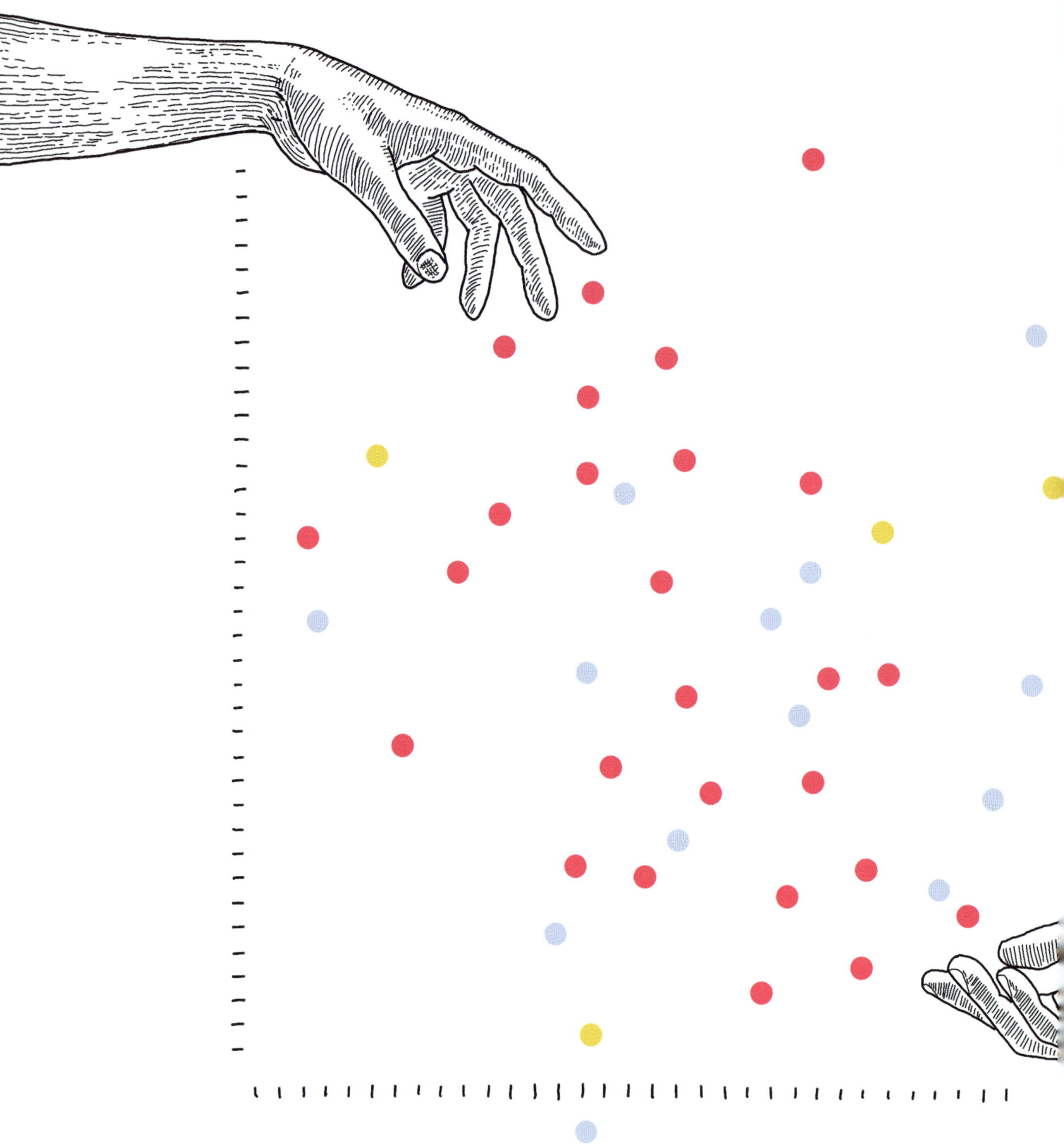

Introduction

Data is the most powerful force in society today. It's hardly an exaggeration. Data is everywhere—present in every moment, every event, every transaction or interaction with someone else. Every time you send a text, call a friend, fill out a form, hail a taxi, stream a movie, surf the web, pay a bill, buy groceries, buy *anything*, take your temperature, count your steps, swipe right (or left), you generate data. There's data in the weather, in the air, in the ground, in outer space. If you own a smartwatch, you carry data on your body. If you have a cardiac pacemaker, you carry data *in* your body. The sheer quantity of data available at one's fingertips is enough to make your head spin. In 2023, the internet topped out at 123 *zettabytes* of data. That's approximately 123 trillion gigabytes, and growing every day.

We are surrounded by an invisible ecosystem of data, and it's becoming harder and harder to ignore. For many, the COVID-19 pandemic was a rude awakening to the world of data. How high were case counts? Was the number of infections rising or falling? Or, more practically: Was it safe to go outside? Were the vaccines working? Were we "flattening the curve"? All of these questions revolved around understanding numbers, interpreting statistics, parsing graphs, and reading charts. For maybe the first time ever, basic human survival was a test of data literacy. It's safe to say we failed.

Of course, our dependency on data goes far beyond the pandemic. From the rise of artificial intelligence to the specter of global climate change, today data makes and shapes our lives. But what is data, really? It's a question that is surprisingly hard to answer. To some, data means numbers: figures on a screen, dots on a graph. It's also often (falsely) equated with facts, an invariable form of concrete knowledge that always tells the truth. But in reality, data is hardly so incontrovertible. Data is an abstraction of reality, a useful but imperfect representation of real life. Like life, it's full of nuance, imprecision, and ambivalence. It's quantitative *and* it's qualitative. And, as we'll strongly see in the pages to come, it's made by us—humans. There is no data without we humans creating it. No surprise, then, that data is often riddled with human bias.

This book is our attempt to explore what data is today, and what it might mean for our collective future. Both of us have particular histories with data. For Giorgia, it's an obsession that began in childhood, counting and sorting the contents of her grandmother's tailor shop in Italy. Data helped bring logic to chaos, even if the nebulous taxonomies she used to organize the shop's buttons and ribbons were only in her head. In college, she discovered architecture, an entire profession rooted in numbers, and became infatuated with urban mapping: how one could visualize, through data, the spatial and social footprint of a city. The more sophisticated your map became—the more data it took into account—the more true to life it was.

Unlike Giorgia, Phillip did not start life as a "data person" per se. He came to data through a side door: music. Grade-school piano lessons revealed music's quantitative underbelly, a mathematical system of progressions and relationships, minor fifths and major thirds. Data wasn't just functional; through music it could communicate intangible things like ideas and emotions. When he joined his high school's string orchestra, he discovered that he wasn't the only one who could understand this system—everyone could. Data, expressed through music, brought people together and helped them speak in one voice. Like the perfect ticking of a metronome, it kept everyone in time.

Today, through our work at the design agency Pentagram, we help companies and individuals communicate data to the wider world (you can see some of our team's work on the following pages). While most designers use color, shape, or typography to express ideas, we use data. Sometimes this looks like a traditional graph or a chart, but more often it takes unconventional forms: a sculpture, a website, a mural, even an article of clothing. Our team has had the pleasure of collaborating with both massive corporations and tiny start-ups in figuring out how to communicate their data. But really, anyone can use data as a lens through which to understand the world. You just need to know how.

Akin to a pair of glasses that can be taken on and off, data is a filter to find pattern, structure, and ultimately meaning in the visual cacophony of modern life, one subject at a time. We call this superpower Data Humanism, and it's a radically different way to think about, understand, and engage with numbers.[1] As the name suggests, Data Humanism centers people, rather than numbers, in its conception of data. Just as the humanist movement during the Renaissance sought to emphasize individuals rather than God as the ultimate source of meaning, Data Humanism underscores the

foundational role of people—us—in data's collection, analysis, and communication. Despite how it may sometimes appear, data is always the product of human hands.

In our hyper-complex, ever-changing world, we don't believe there's just one definition of data. There can't be. Data's pervasiveness means that there are multiple definitions—multiple meanings—that must be contended with if we are to truly understand the full potential of data in our lives. The seventeen individuals interviewed here each provide their own, singularly insightful (and sometimes surprising) perspective on what it means to work, live, or communicate through data today. They are scientists, artists, writers, researchers, and activists. Few would describe themselves as data experts, but that's what makes their points of view so valuable. As data becomes further entrenched in society, all of us will need to think more critically about the data we produce, consume, interpret, and manipulate daily.

These interviews show us where to start. In chapter 1, we explore the ways data can (and can't) describe human identity with writer James Clear, organizational psychologist Adam Grant, and activist Andy Marra. In chapter 2, we discuss data communication and visualization with marketer Seth Godin, writer Naresh Ramchandani, meteorologist Bernadette Woods Placky, and economist Max Roser. In chapter 3, neuroscientist and physical therapist David Putrino, physician and design researcher Bon Ku, and cardiologist and scientist Eric Topol illuminate the data of our health. In chapter 4, we tackle urgent topics around technology and data with AI scholar Kate Crawford, tech pioneer John Maeda, and new-media artist Refik Anadol. Finally in chapter 5, we look to the future of data and creativity with curator Paola Antonelli, artists Sougwen Chung and Ekene Ijeoma, and composer Nico Muhly.

Of course there are many more perspectives to consider, far more than could fit in a single book. Think of this volume as only the beginning of a much larger conversation. But after talking to each of these individuals, we're inspired by data's positive potential for our shared future. Our personal belief is that data is language. It's a lexicon for accessing the full complexity of human ideas, stories, and behaviors. It's a vocabulary that anyone can use, and that anyone can understand. And if we learn to truly "speak data," we can open up new worlds of meaning about ourselves, others, and everything around us.

MethaneSAT

Home Satellite Press About Us Team Contact

FOSSIL FUELS ARE A MAIN SOURCE OF METHANE

The oil and gas industry emits 80 million tonnes of methane every year.

It is the second largest source of human-caused methane emissions after agriculture. As the world's largest oil and gas producer, the United States has both an opportunity and a responsibility to lead the way on reducing methane emissions.

↑
MethaneSAT: a data storytelling website for the Environmental Defense Fund about methane emissions, 2022

NOTES

1 See Giorgia Lupi, "Data Humanism: The Revolutionary Future of Data Visualization," *Print* magazine, January 30, 2017, https://www.printmag.com/article/data-humanism-future-of-data-visualization/. This philosophy was honed with Gabriele Rossi and Simone Quadri of Accurat, the data visualization company Giorgia cofounded in 2011.

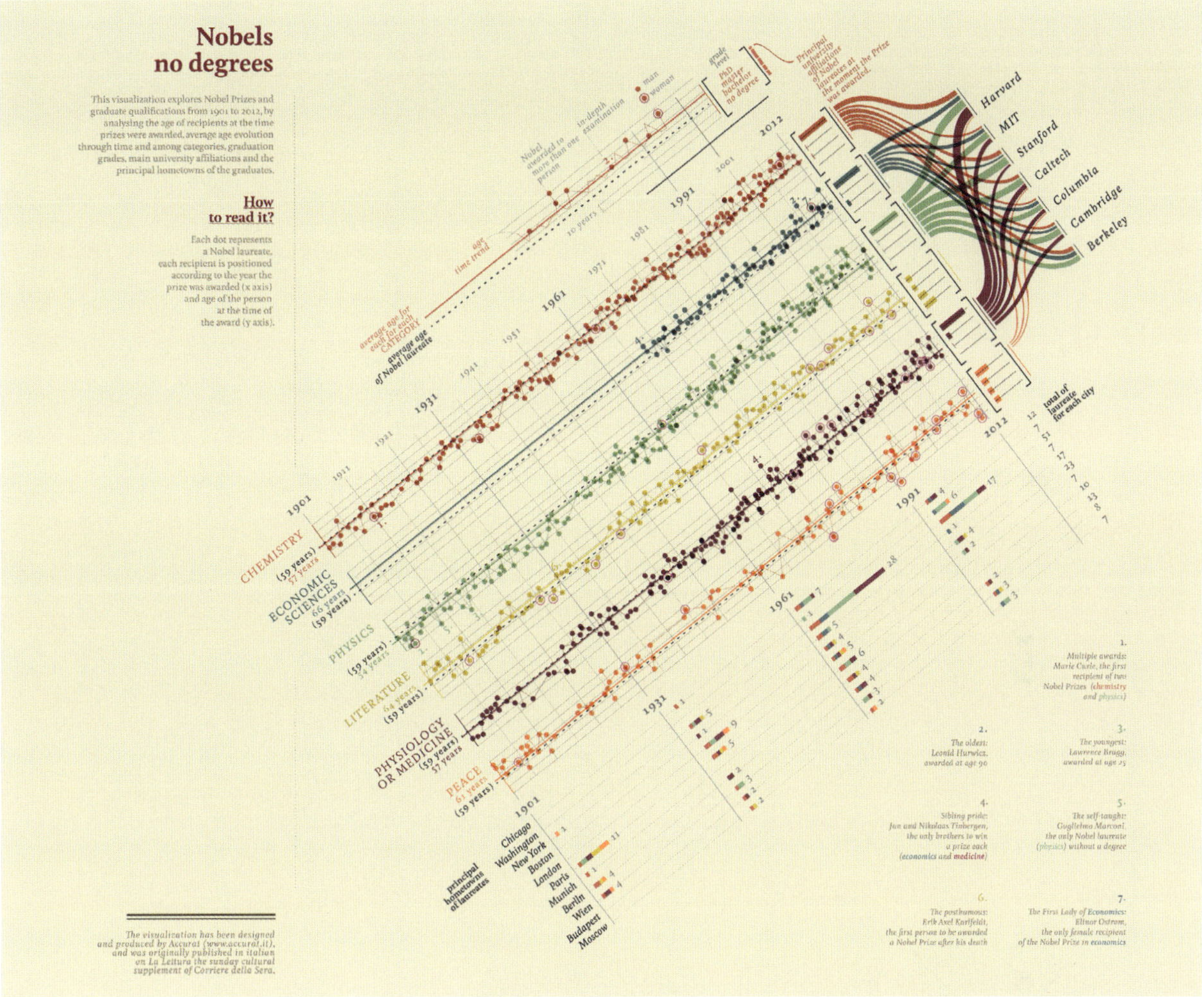

Nobels no degrees

This visualization explores Nobel Prizes and graduate qualifications from 1901 to 2012, by analysing the age of recipients at the time prizes were awarded, average age evolution through time and among categories, graduation grades, main university affiliations and the principal hometowns of the graduates.

How to read it?

Each dot represents a Nobel laureate, each recipient is positioned according to the year the prize was awarded (x axis) and age of the person at the time of the award (y axis).

CHEMISTRY (59 years) 57 years

ECONOMIC SCIENCES 66 years (59 years)

PHYSICS (59 years) 54 years

LITERATURE 64 years (59 years)

PHYSIOLOGY OR MEDICINE (59 years) 57 years

PEACE 61 years (59 years)

average age for each CATEGORY

average age of Nobel laureate

age time trend

Harvard

MIT

Stanford

Caltech

Columbia

Cambridge

Berkeley

total of laureate for each city

principal hometowns of laureates

Chicago

Washington

New York

Boston

London

Paris

Munich

Berlin

Wien

Budapest

Moscow

1. Multiple awards: Marie Curie, the first recipient of two Nobel Prizes (chemistry and physics)

2. The oldest: Leonid Hurwicz, awarded at age 90

3. The youngest: Lawrence Bragg, awarded at age 25

4. Sibling pride: Jan and Nikolaas Tinbergen, the only brothers to win a prize each (economics and medicine)

5. The self-taught: Guglielmo Marconi, the only Nobel laureate (physics) without a degree

6. The posthumous: Erik Axel Karlfeldt, the first person to be awarded a Nobel Prize after his death

7. The First Lady of Economics: Elinor Ostrom, the only female recipient of the Nobel Prize in economics

The visualization has been designed and produced by Accurat (www.accurat.it), and was originally published in italian on La Lettura the sunday cultural supplement of Corriere della Sera.

↑

Nobels, No Degrees: one of a series of intricate data visualizations for the Italian newspaper *Corriere della Sera*, 2012

→

Data ITEMS: A Fashion Landscape: a wall-drawn data visualization for an exhibition about fashion at the Museum of Modern Art, New York, 2019

→
Counting Inequality: a data visualization sculpture about income inequality for the research institute RAND, 2019

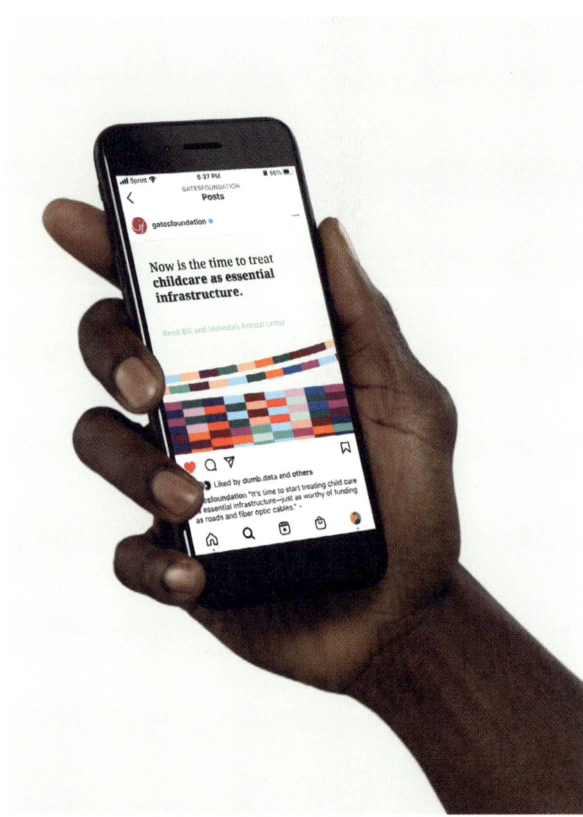

↓
Equal Is Greater: a data visualization design system about gender equality for the Gates Foundation, 2020

→
Data Humanism manifesto, 2017

DATA HUMANISM

SMALL ~~big~~ data

data ~~bandwith~~ QUALITY

imperfect ~~infallible~~ data

subjective ~~impartial~~ data

inspiring ~~descriptive~~ data

serendipitous ~~predictive~~ data

data ~~conventions~~ POSSIBILITIES

data ~~to simplify complexity~~ / DEPICT

data ~~processing~~ DRAWING

data driven design

spend ~~save~~ time with data

data is ~~numbers~~ PEOPLE

data will make us more ~~efficient~~ HUMAN.

↑
Mindworks: The Science of Thinking: a physical data visualization exhibition for the University of Chicago, 2020

↑
Peninsula Talks: an interactive data visualization magazine exploring Italian craftsmanship, 2015

→
Triennale Milano: data-driven branding for the Italian design museum, 2025

Bruises: The Data We Don't See: a data visualization and music composition about a personal health journey, 2018

Giorgia Lupi and Kaki King

1

Counting Ourselves: Data and Identity

CENSUS - U.S. - 20XX -

Counting Ourselves

A slim envelope arrives in your mailbox sometime in late spring. You open it, and out tumbles a banal-looking form. On it are nine simple questions. Some of them appear innocuous: How old are you? What is your telephone number? Others are oddly more pointed: Do you live in a house, apartment, or mobile home? How many people were living with you on April 1? Are you of Hispanic, Latino, or Spanish origin?

You take a moment to carefully think through your responses. After all, lying on this form would be a federal crime.

This is the United States census, and it may be one of the most powerful—but least recognized—examples of data's impact on our lives. Mandated by Article I of the US Constitution, the census strives to give an accurate count of the country's population every ten years. So much rests on its tabulations: the apportionment of seats in the House of Representatives; the allocation of trillions of dollars in federal spending; the definition of electoral districts. In the United States, data is power, and the census tells us who gets more of it. As Dan Bouk, a historian who studies the US census, has written, "Our democracy is only as good as our data, and our data is only as good as our democracy."[1]

In 2019, the Museum of the City of New York approached our team at Pentagram to create an original artwork about the census. Any other year it might have felt like an odd topic to tackle, but that year we immediately grasped the timeliness of their request. The 2020 census was looming, and all was not well. President Donald Trump and his administration had been accused of repeatedly pressuring census officials to institute new survey questions or skew the count for political gain. A normally mundane function of government bureaucracy had been embroiled in political controversy. Against this backdrop, the museum was putting together an exhibition exploring the profound questions at the heart of the census and its mandate: What does it mean to count people? And how can we as a country do it better?

We took the museum's brief as a chance to rethink the census entirely. Reviewing the questionnaire the US Census Bureau used for the 2010 edition (the most recent version available at the time), we were struck by the shallowness of the questions and the responses they encouraged. How could the fullness of human identity be captured in such a bland questionnaire? How could our government really know us without asking about our personalities, our values, our greatest hopes or our deepest fears? The census questions might give a broad sense of our country's demographic makeup, but they hardly explained who a person really was.

Our frustration with the census perhaps stemmed from a larger realization: Numbers, on their own, are notoriously boring. They're empirical, stable, resolute. They say what they mean. One is not two is not three; five plus five always equals ten. Humans, on the other hand, rarely say what we mean. We are complex, contradictory, and nuanced. Characteristically human domains like emotion, belief, or imagination can barely be pinned down in words, much less in quantification. So when numbers are used to *describe* humans—really, when humans are reduced to numbers—things tend to go awry.

History is littered with such blunders, the most notorious in recent memory being the 2016 US presidential election. On November 8, 2016, pollsters at *The Economist* / YouGov declared, based on a survey of 3,677 likely voters, that Hillary Clinton would clinch the election by a margin of 4 percentage points.[2] On November 9, Trump was declared the winner. What happened? The numbers had been so clear—but when they collided with human behavior, the results were less than predictable.

Data's seductive simplicity is part of the problem. Like a forty-ton pneumatic press, quantification can render the messiness of human experience down to just a single number, essentialized to the extreme. This process has obvious benefits, but, as the 2016 election showed, it also carries with it considerable risk. What would it look like to take a different approach? To use data to *embrace* human complexity rather than whittling it away?

Considering the museum's brief, we thought back to one of Giorgia's previous projects that wrestled with these same ideas. *Dear Data* was an experiment that would likely make the analysts at the US Census Bureau shudder. Each week, for a year, Giorgia sent a transatlantic postcard to her friend Stefanie Posavec covered in analog data visualizations describing what had happened to her during the past week. Each week Stefanie also sent one in return, covered in her own beautiful data

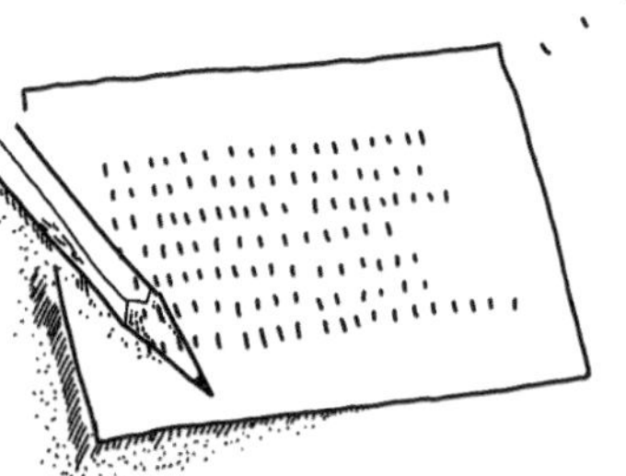

drawings. It was like a piece of durational performance art, and over twelve months and fifty-two postcards, the two were brought closer, using data as their primary mode of communication.

Counting the mundanity of daily life is nothing new. Since the early 2000s, the quantified self (QS) movement, with its roots in Silicon Valley, has been perfecting ways to use technology to record nearly every aspect of human behavior. In 2010, QS was featured in a blockbuster cover story in *The New York Times Magazine*, accompanied by a fitting illustration of a stick figure made out of tape measures. While QS is perhaps less prevalent today, the movement's data-tracking principles live on in the Fitbits, Apple Watches, and WHOOPs millions of us carry around every day. But *Dear Data* differed from these previous examples in an important manner. While most data trackers strive to be as focused and efficient as possible, Giorgia and Stefanie wanted to make sure to include all the messy bits of human experience as well. Their visualizations weren't polished pie charts, but elaborately hand-drawn doodles, each custom conceived for the topic at hand and filled with annotations, qualifications, and commentary. They captured not just quantitative information but qualitative and emotional context, like what the two friends thought about something, or a small story that explained why a number was the way it was.

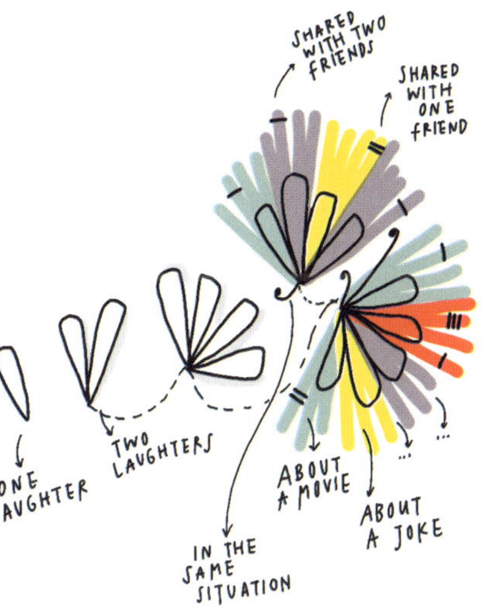

The census project gave us the chance to apply the lessons of *Dear Data* to a slightly more real-world application. How could we make the census more human—a richer encapsulation of human identity and experience? We called the final artistic piece *What Counts*, and it became a poetic meditation on census taking and government quantification. Subverting the normal census questionnaire, our survey instead posed far more intimate questions, like "How do you define home?," "Compared to your actual age, do you feel young or old?," and "Do you feel that what you currently have in life is 'enough'?" Our favorite question was the last one: "Do you believe the future is bright or grim?"

Museum visitors entered their answers to our questionnaire on an iPad in the gallery. As they did, their responses created a unique graphic symbol that we called a data portrait. Colorful and hand-drawn, each data portrait was an imperfectly

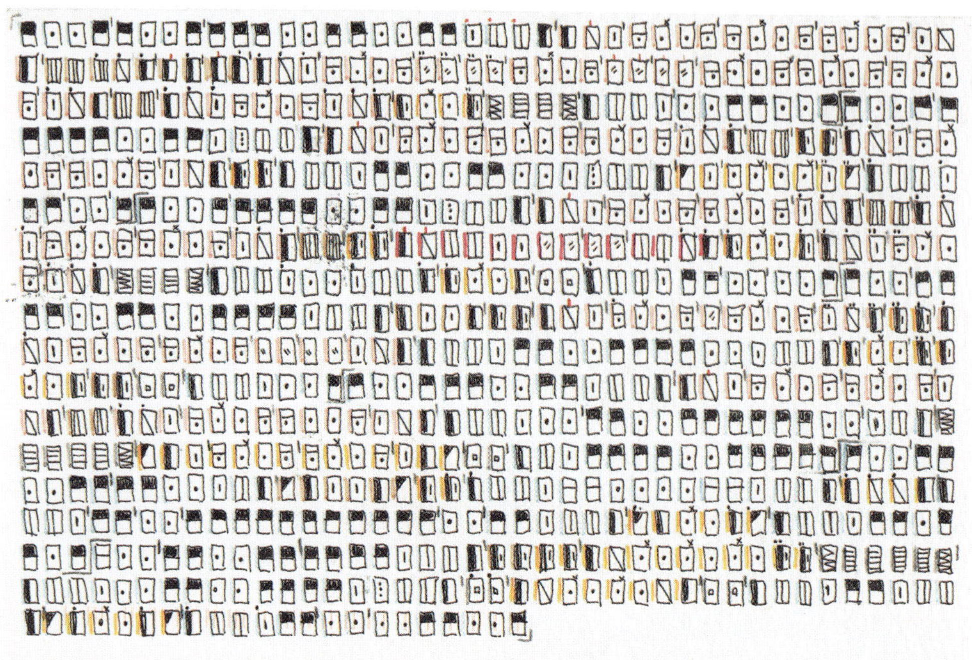

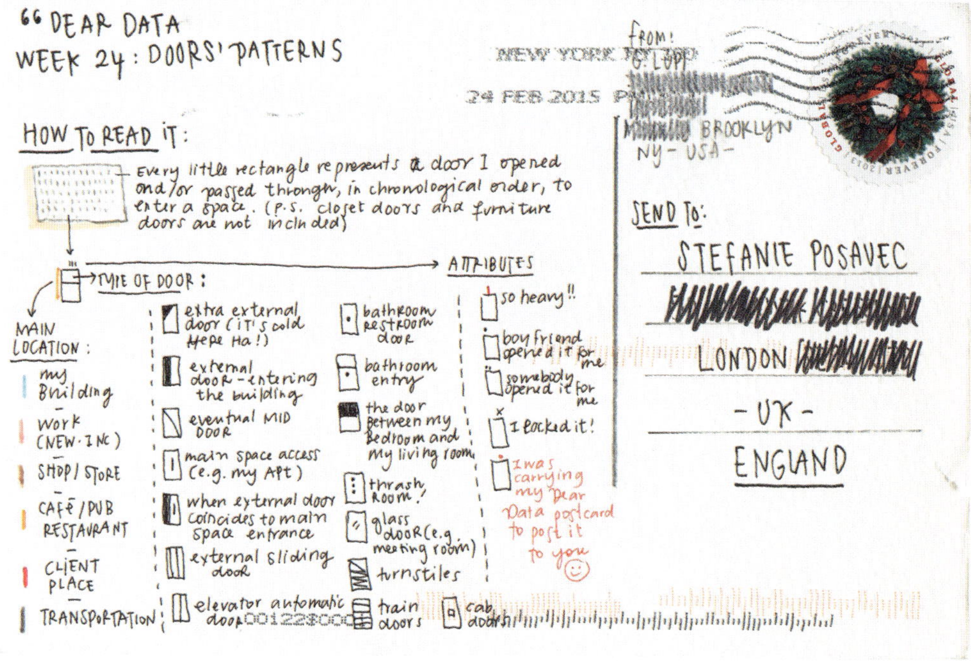

↑

Dear Data: Week 24–A
Week of Doors
(front and back)

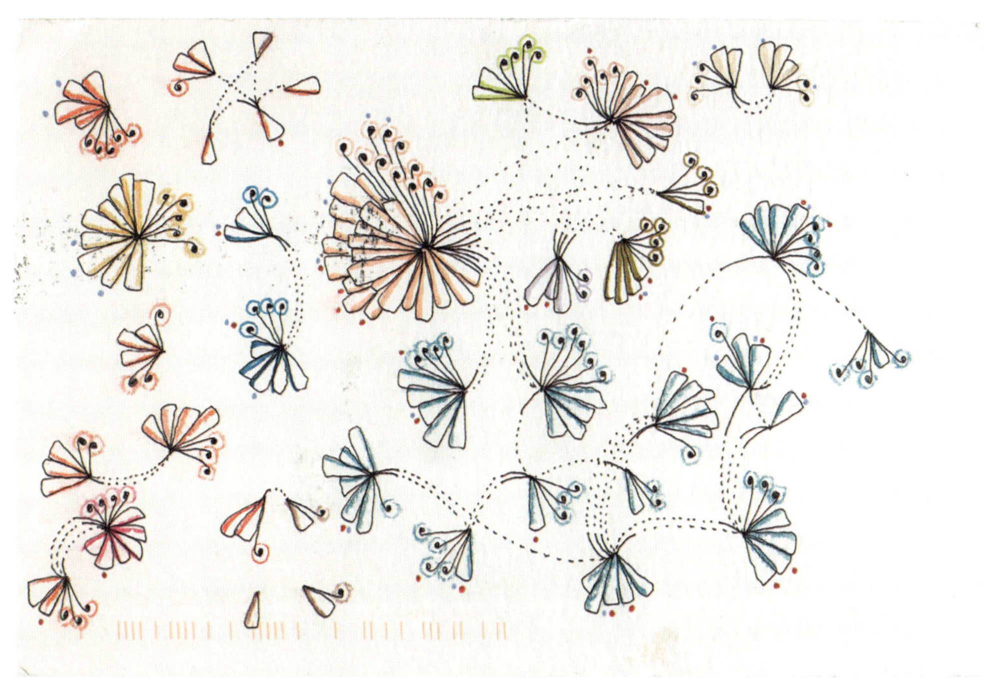

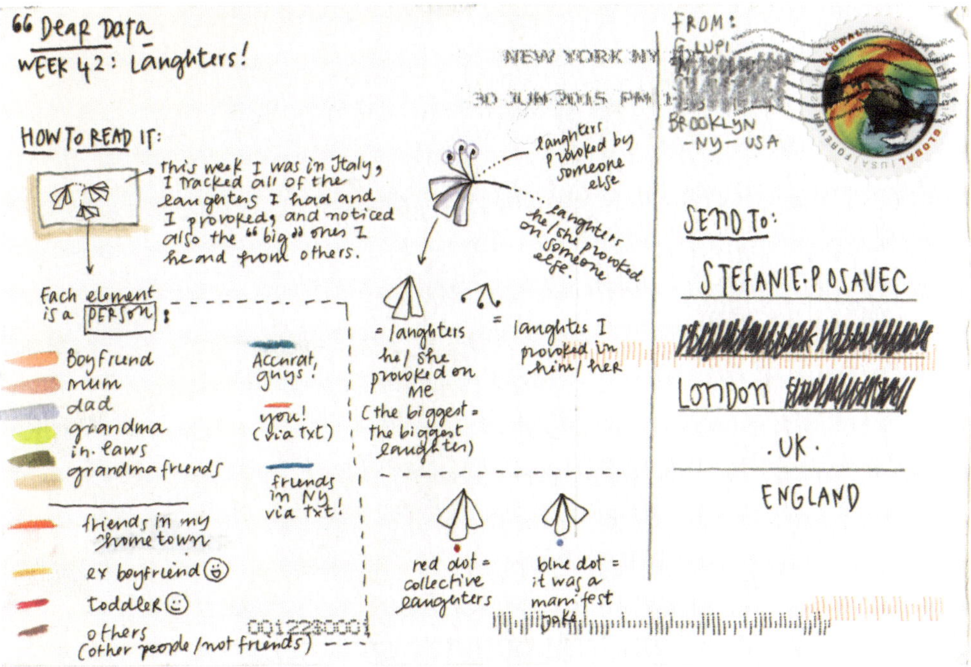

↑

Dear Data: Week 42–
A Week of Laughter
(front and back)

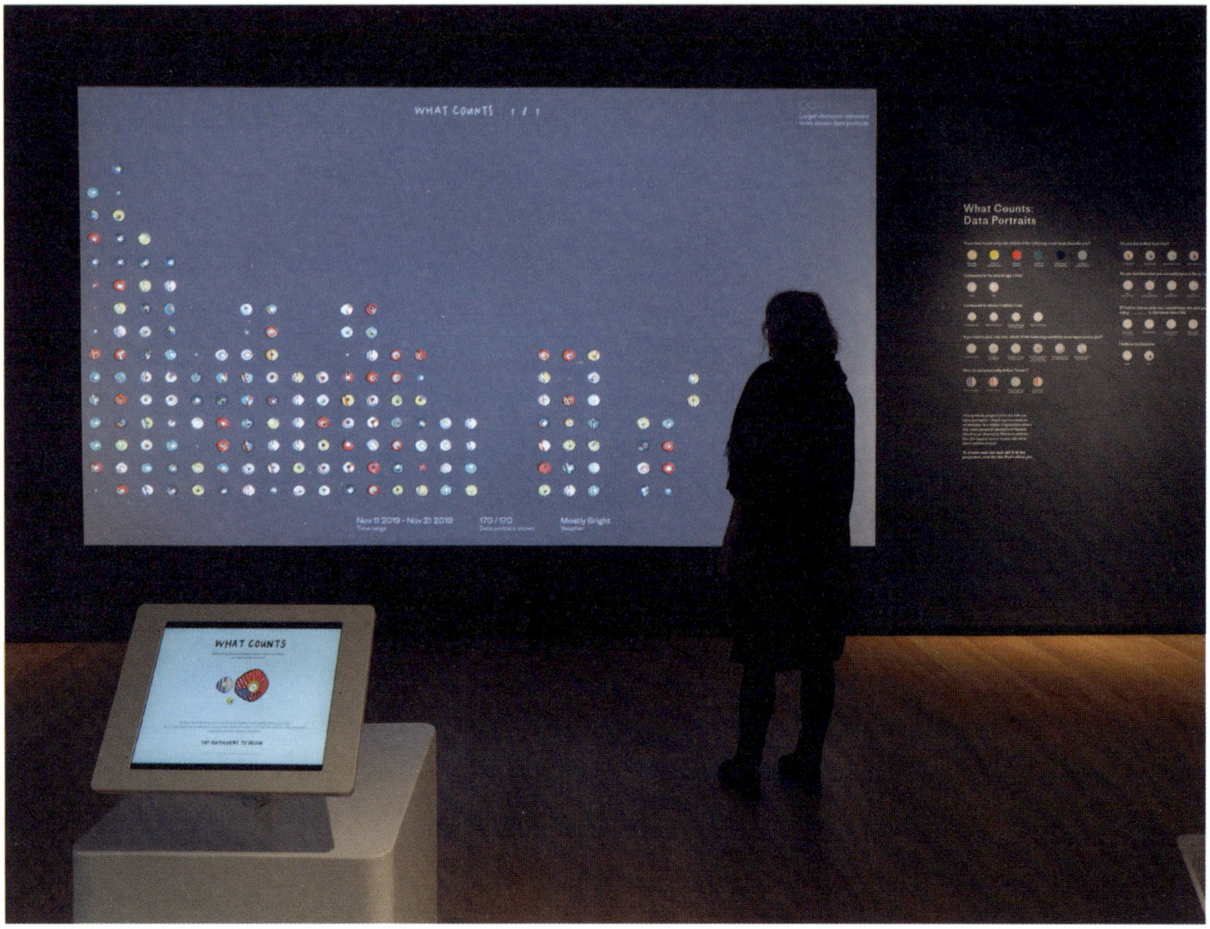

↑
Installation view,
What Counts, 2020

→
Data portraits
printed as wearable
buttons with legend,
What Counts, 2020

↑
Data portrait,
What Counts, 2020

perfect representation of the person in question. The multiplicity of discrete elements, and the nearly exponential number of combinations possible within each portrait, underscored the intersectional nature of human identity. Human preferences, emotions, and ideas were given graphic form in a way we rarely expect of conventional data visualization. With the data portrait complete, the user could add their creation to a projection of all the portraits generated over the course of the show. It was a beautiful sight: hundreds of unique insignias, a rich and dynamic collective of individuation.

Although one can fantasize about our government adopting a more humanistic approach to data representation, it's unlikely that the Census Bureau will be embracing our proposal anytime soon. Instead, *What Counts* remains an idealistic but hopeful provocation for rethinking how data shapes our lives, and for reminding all of us that identity is complex and nuanced. What makes you *you* can hardly be reduced down into nine simple questions.

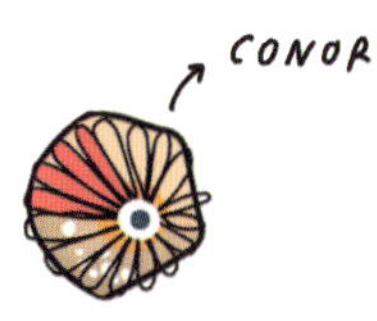

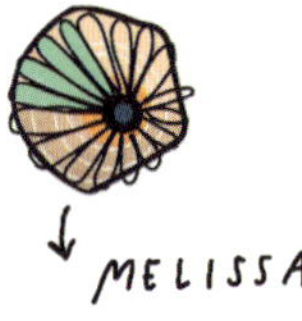

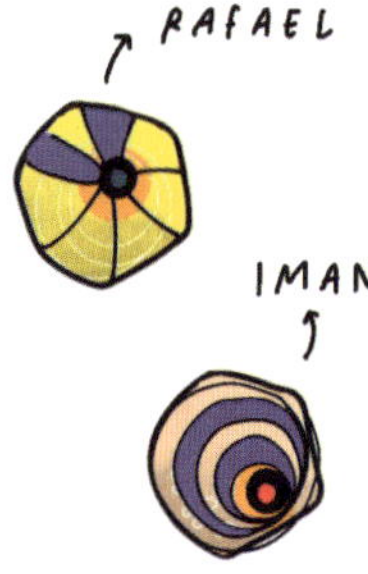

NOTES

1 Dan Bouk, *Democracy's Data: The Hidden Stories in the US Census* (MCD Farrar, Straus and Giroux, 2022), 20.

2 YouGov, "*The Economist* / YouGov Poll (Likely Voters)," November 8, 2016, available at https://d25d2506sfb94s.cloudfront.net/cumulus_uploads/document/95dcxi5lfl/econToplines_lv.pdf.

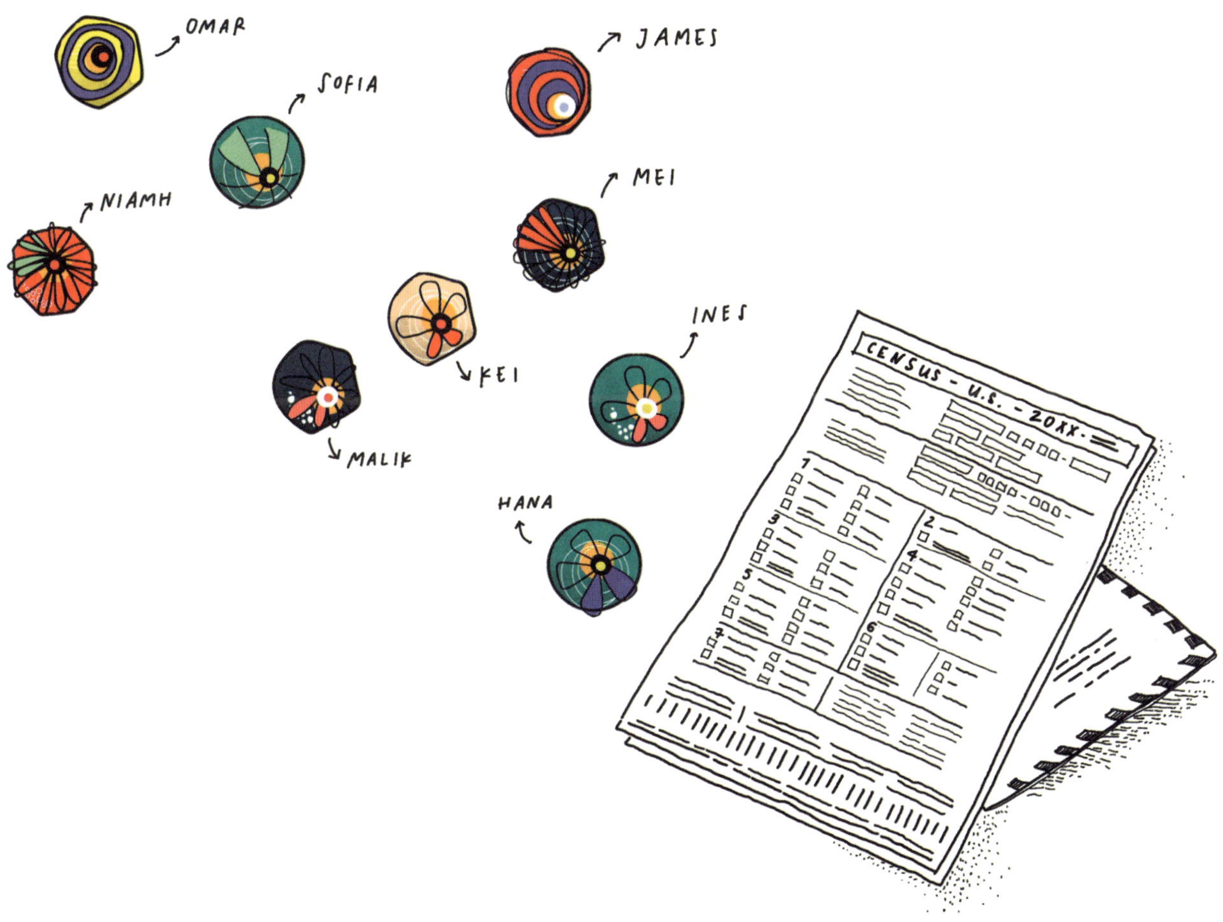
OMAR
SOFIA
JAMES
NIAMH
MEI
KEI
INES
MALIK
HANA
CENSUS - U.S. - 20XX

James Clear

James Clear is a writer obsessed with habits: how we make them, how we break them, and how we can leverage them to live healthier and more fulfilling lives. The author of New York Times *bestseller* Atomic Habits: An Easy and Proven Way to Build Good Habits and Break Bad Ones, *James has educated millions on the "tiny changes" that are key to lasting behavioral change. In high school, he was a star baseball player—until a bat to the face, and half a dozen facial fractures along with it, threatened to end his promising athletic career. A grueling six-year recovery compelled him to formulate his own refreshingly logical approach to habits, one rooted in clearheaded analysis and rational goal setting. In this conversation, James talks about personal data tracking; the paradoxes of Goodhart's law; and the tricky relationship between data and control.*

As a former athlete, we imagine you're a person who tracks their data. Are you? And if so, how do you decide what to track?

Generally speaking, I think it's probably not worth it to track most things. Time is limited and attention is limited. But there are some really important things that *are* worth tracking. The motivation that you can get from tracking those most important or high-leverage activities pays off in an enormous way.

There's a lot of tracking that can happen passively. But if you think about it from the lens of habits, when you ask somebody to track a habit, you're actually asking them to build *two* habits, because they have to do the thing they were originally going to do, and they have to build the habit of tracking it. So you're adding a layer of complexity that wasn't there previously. For that reason, I only try to track the highest-leveraged habits in my life. Some things pass that test and are worth it, but a lot of things are not. That doesn't necessarily mean that I don't measure them. I'm making a distinction between tracking and measurement. I view tracking as an active process, while measurement can be happening in the background.

For example, my calendar is a record of my travel throughout the year. At the end of each year, I do an annual review: How many new states did I visit? How many countries? How many cities was I in? How many nights away from home? Does it feel like I was away from family too much? Or does it feel like not enough, and would I like to get out on the road a little bit more next year? I get all that without doing any active tracking, but my calendar measures it. That's a form of measurement that doesn't require much active participation on my side.

Meanwhile, my workouts are at the opposite end of the spectrum. In that case, I find it very helpful to actively track my behavior. I prefer manual tracking in a notebook for this. I physically write down each set that I do. If I have a particularly hard workout, the act of tracking even helps get me through the workout. Sometimes I'll play this little trick on myself where I'll write down the next step and think, "Well, I don't really feel like doing this, but I already wrote it down, so I guess I have to do it." And then I do it, and I write the next step down right away. So I kind of inch my way through my workout in that fashion.

The active tracking and measurement is a motivator. From a habit-building standpoint, this is one of the biggest benefits that tracking and measurement can provide, in that you have signals of progress. A signal of progress is one of the most motivating feelings to the human mind. Even if it's smaller than you ultimately hoped, even if it's less than what you wish you had done, it feels good to be moving forward.

So much of life is living in this gray zone where you don't really know if you're getting better or not. Am I a better parent than I was yesterday? Am I a better friend? Am I kinder? It's very hard to measure a lot of things we care about in life. So when you *do* have some form of measurement that you can tangibly track, it feels great to have undeniable proof. To say, yes, I did that to move the ball forward a little bit today. I find that really helpful for workouts, but it can be utilized in many different ways.

Video games are masterful at this. There are so many different signals of progress in a video game. There is your score, which is usually in one of the corners of the screen, so you can see it going up through the level. That's a form of tracking. There are little musical notes or audio features that happen when you pick up a weapon or grab a ruby or a bag of gold or whatever. That little jingle feels good. It's a bit of feedback. Even the pitter-patter of your steps as you run through the level is an audio signal that you're advancing or moving forward. The collective power of all those little pieces of feedback makes video games incredibly motivating, gets users to move through the levels.

Absolutely. We approach data collection from the standpoint of asking the right questions: What is it that actually matters? You're talking about rewards. Seeing progress in your stats or in your spreadsheet definitely is a motivator. Sometimes the tracking itself is the reward—to the point that tracking makes one feel so in control that the resulting data is irrelevant. The data is there to look at if desired, but it's secondary to the satisfaction derived from the act of tracking itself. This is like data hoarding.

It's interesting—this connection between data and control, or tracking and control. Most of the big areas of my life where I have made significant progress, to my mind, have had some form of measurement associated with them. For instance the backbone of my business is my newsletter subscriber email list. I have been tracking the size of my email list from day one. But I've realized it's not useful to track total subscribers. As long as my net new number of subscribers is growing steadily over time, I'm going to end up in an awesome spot.

But there is a potential pitfall of data tracking, which is that you can get so focused on the number itself that you lose sight of what you were trying to do originally. You've probably heard of Goodhart's law: Once the target becomes the measure, it ceases to be a good measure.[1] It's like getting a good score on a test; that's

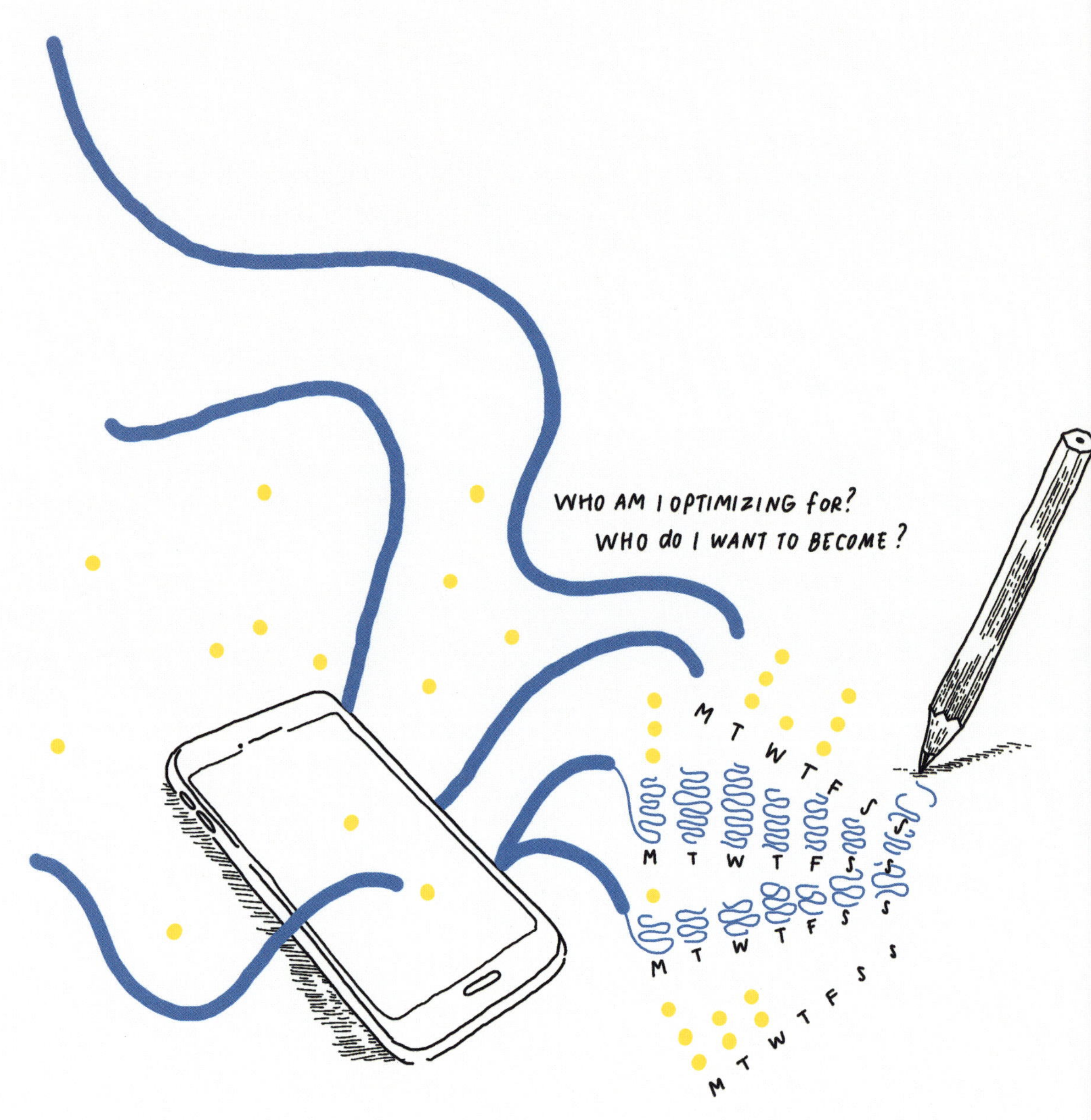
WHO AM I OPTIMIZING FOR?
WHO DO I WANT TO BECOME?

"A SIGNAL OF PROGRESS IS ONE OF THE MOST MOTIVATING FEELINGS TO THE HUMAN MIND.

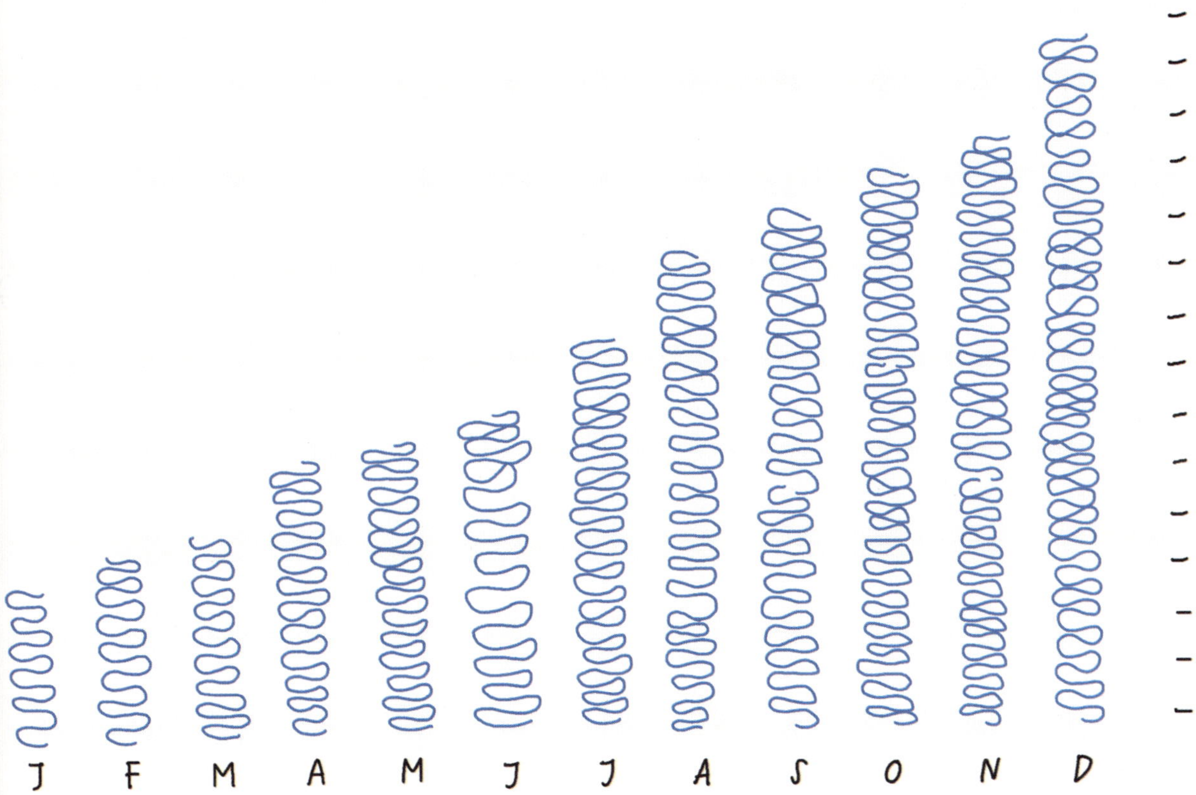

J F M A M J J A S O N D

—JAMES CLEAR

not necessarily about learning. This can become a problem in a lot of forms of tracking. Yet I find it less of an issue if you identify the right thing to track. If I only tracked the overall size of the email list, well, then I could start doing all kinds of stuff. I could buy subscribers from other people, or pump in a dead list that isn't even active or paying attention. I'd be optimizing for the wrong thing. But net new subscribers per day—that's interesting to me because it means a lot of things. It means that word of mouth is growing. I think a lot of good data collection encourages you to focus less on the result and more on the trajectory. Or maybe I should say, less on your current position and more on your current trajectory. If I'm just collecting as much data as I can, and it will be there if I need it but I probably won't check it, it's actually about feeling more in control.

The more you count something and you observe something, you name it.

Words like *notice* and *observe* and *collecting* are interesting to me. As a writer, one of the backbones of my creative process is "broad funnel, tight filter." I try to collect a huge range of examples of something, and then get very, very strict about what I let through that filter. It's funny to me sometimes when people say, "I love your book! You have such great ideas." They wouldn't say that if they'd seen the original ideas that I came up with! I had 10,000, and then I cut 9,500 of them, and the only ones I published were the 500 good ones. Having this willingness to collect a very broad dataset, or in a creative act maybe generate a very broad dataset and then have a strict or high standard for what I let through the filter, leads to a much better outcome—or at least a much more unique outcome.

For a while I had this little rule for myself where whenever I wrote an article, I would brainstorm twenty-five titles. The title I ended up picking would always be, like, number seventeen or twenty-one. It always came later in the process. It was the act of generating a lot of options that led to an interesting one. Almost always, your first idea or the first thing you collect or the first thing you generate is top of mind. Meaning, it's obvious—it's the same thing most other people would think of.

I heard the singer Ed Sheeran put it one time as "turning on a sink and letting the water run out." At first it's kind of muddy, but if you run it long enough, the water will get clear. A lot of things in life are like that. You need to collect enough examples or generate enough options to get to the clear water.

So you do this huge data collection, and then you filter. By deciding what the filter is or where it's set, you're already categorizing in your mind. You have to come up with macro categories of what is good, what is bad, what success looks like. To us, it means you're looking for qualifiers for the data—qualitatively describing things that were on a list before.

Would you call these qualifiers? That's how you would define the filter?

In this case, yes!

I have a couple of questions that I always talk about and return to in my work. The first is: What am I optimizing for? People optimize for totally different things. Sometimes you optimize for money. Sometimes you optimize for free time or time with family or creative freedom. All kinds of stuff. It's a very personal answer. But you need to decide what you're optimizing for before you can figure out what data to seek out in the first place, then how to filter it and refine it.

The second question is: What do I want my days to look like? A lot of people sit down and think about what they want their business to look like: how much revenue they want to make, how many people they want to reach, what kind of impact they want to have, what kind of company they're willing to create, how many employees they'd like to have. But I think you need to start by asking: How do I want to live my days? And then, inside of *that* box: How can I build the biggest company? Or: How can we make the most impact?

And then a final question: Who do I wish to become? And then inside that: What kind of outcome do I want? What goal do I want to achieve, or what result will I like? I think it's better to think about who I'm trying to be and then figure out which habits reinforce that. To use it in the context of this conversation: What data can help me become that kind of person? What information or insight would help lead me down that path? What set of statistics or images or knowledge would be useful in facilitating that kind of identity? It's only by having good answers to questions like that that you're in a position to pay attention to the right things in the first place. Otherwise you just kind of go off on this wild goose chase where you're collecting data because you feel like you're supposed to, or because it's better to have more information, or because more knowledge is good. No one wants to feel uncertain. But you actually need more of a North Star.

Do you have a personal definition of data?

Recorded feedback. A lot of feedback happens and then vanishes. But if it gets recorded, then it becomes data. Of course, if you start thinking about data that way, well then, shoot, data is almost anything, because almost anything can get recorded. But it's kind of a magical thing—potentially one of the most powerful things humans have ever done.

With wearable devices like the Apple Watch and Fitbit, everybody can more easily track personal data. Overall, do you think that's a good thing?

It's like an *Inception* moment, where your data plants a seed in your mind: "Oh, the number is off. Maybe I don't feel that great." Probably the most classic example of this is stepping on a scale. How many people set out on a journey of weight loss, then they step on the scale the next day and the number is not moving in the right direction, and they feel like a failure? So, what's the right cadence of tracking? I have a friend who's losing weight right now. He told me when he started out that he was only going to weigh himself once a month. I think that's great. That is both frequent enough—he gets to see progress—and infrequent enough—he's not going to notice if his weight fluctuates from day to day even though he's doing the right things, and get disheartened.

That said, generally speaking, the tighter the feedback loop, the quicker you learn. This is more or less how we get through all of life. If you touched a hot stove and didn't feel the sensation of burning until three minutes had passed, your hand would be on fire by the end. It's too late. But since the feedback is instantaneous, you pull away before you even touch the stove because you can feel the heat. Rapid feedback leads to quicker learning, as a general rule.

> **Your ideas of cadence trajectory, and using inputs as signals as opposed to letting them be in control, paints a beautiful picture.**

You need a resilient mindset with all of this. You are the one in control. The numbers are not in control. It's very easy to let the numbers drive your life, or to think they are. But they're not. They're just a signal.

NOTES

1 Goodhart's law was theorized by the British economist Charles Goodhart. See Charles Goodhart, "Problems of Monetary Management: The UK Experience," in *Inflation, Depression, and Economic Policy in the West*, ed. Anthony S. Courakis (Mansell, 1981), 116.

Data is

RECORDED feedback. IT'S KIND of A MAGICAL THING

—JAMES CLEAR—

Adam Grant

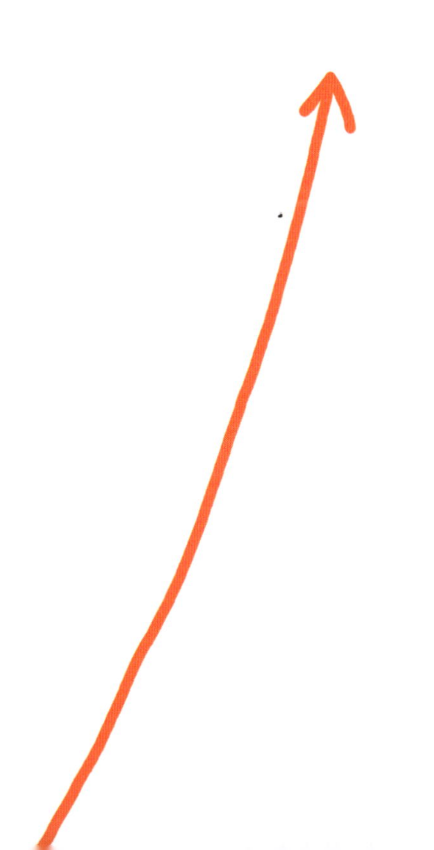

Adam Grant is the Saul P. Steinberg Professor of Management and Professor of Psychology at the Wharton School of the University of Pennsylvania. Yet that impressive title barely covers the full breadth of his activities. Adam is an academic researcher, an award-winning teacher, a podcaster, and a public intellectual. He's interested in big human topics like motivation, generosity, rethinking, and potential. He's also the author of six books, including the bestselling Think Again: The Power of Knowing What You Don't Know. *In this conversation, Adam talks about learning lessons from the pandemic;* datum *versus* data*; and how abstract numbers can lead to very real human outcomes.*

As a psychologist studying organizational behavior, data is a tool that you use every day. What do you think people get wrong about data the most?

People often have a very hard time accepting data that challenge their intuition or experience. I always want to tell them that if the evidence disagrees with your experience, you shouldn't immediately say the data are wrong. It might be that *you're* an outlier, that your experience is not representative, and the data are actually revealing a trend that you simply don't fit.

A lot of my work relates to how people interpret social science research, because that's where I confront the general public. One thing I see a lot is people reading a study and then figuring, well, that study was done with a sample of only a few thousand people in this industry or that country, and dismissing the results because of that. This is basic confirmation bias and desirability bias. You shouldn't trust your personal opinion over rigorous evidence gathered across many people.

In an article you wrote for *The Guardian*, you describe arguing with a friend on the efficacy and safety of the COVID-19 vaccine. You wrote, "I had fallen victim to what psychologists call binary bias. It's when we take a complex spectrum and oversimplify it into two categories. If we want to have better arguments, we need to look for the shades of grey."[1] This is more or less what you're talking about. With all that in mind, what is the utility of data?

The analogy I use is medicine. Today we have evidence-based medicine, but once upon a time, medical professionals tried to solve problems via bloodletting and lobotomies. Thanks to randomized controlled trials and careful longitudinal studies, we now have much safer and more reliable treatments. With evidence-based medicine, people are living longer and are healthier.

So now look at how we interpret data from medicine. If you were to summarize all the randomized controlled trials of the average effect of ibuprofen on pain reduction and express the findings in the form of a correlation from -1 to +1, most people would think the correlation would be 0.7 or 0.8. After all, we have a lot of Advil in the world. But in actuality, an analysis showed that the average correlation was 0.14. That's shockingly low to a lot of people, but the fact that it's a small effect doesn't mean it's insignificant. That's the first lesson: Patterns in data do not have to be large to be consequential. You play that effect out over millions and millions of people, and a lot of people will benefit. And that benefit will be widely distributed.

Secondly, the treatment doesn't have the same effect on everyone. There are contingencies. So instead of asking whether Advil is effective, we want to ask: For whom is it effective? When is it effective? This question of when and for whom allows us to look at the data and say: This is real, but only under certain circumstances. Now we need to know how widespread those circumstances are. This is real for some people. What are the commonalities of those people?

Exactly. What's the context? What are the nuances? Data is a snapshot in time. Tomorrow, or in a month, things might be different. Especially when we see data represented in a very definite and defined way, we assume it has absolute power to always represent a situation. This became a problem during the pandemic, of course.

The last lesson from medicine is that what's effective evolves over time. The problems we're trying to treat can change. We need to update our evidence and ask: What are the best available data on any given question or for solving a given problem? Is there a reason why what was true ten, twenty, thirty years ago may not apply today? I would still rather base my opinions on strong evidence that's old than no evidence at all, but we need to keep an eye on how things evolve as our contexts change.

I think the biggest pandemic takeaway regarding the role of data is that experts and public officials did a remarkably terrible job communicating about uncertainty and contingency. I should have known it was going to happen. Chapter 8 in my book *Think Again*, which I wrote before the pandemic, was about how you don't lose trust when you say, "More research needs to be done," or "Here are the initial conclusions, but there are conditions under which they may not hold," or "Here is what our initial trials suggest. Once we've done more trials, we'll update our conclusions." And let people know what that process looks like and how the scientific research is not only done, but accumulated.

This is probably the most useful thing I've said to a friend of mine who is very skeptical about vaccines after three-plus years of debate. He would say to me, "One study says this and one study says the opposite!" My response is that you shouldn't weigh both sides equally. You should weigh strong evidence more heavily than weak evidence.

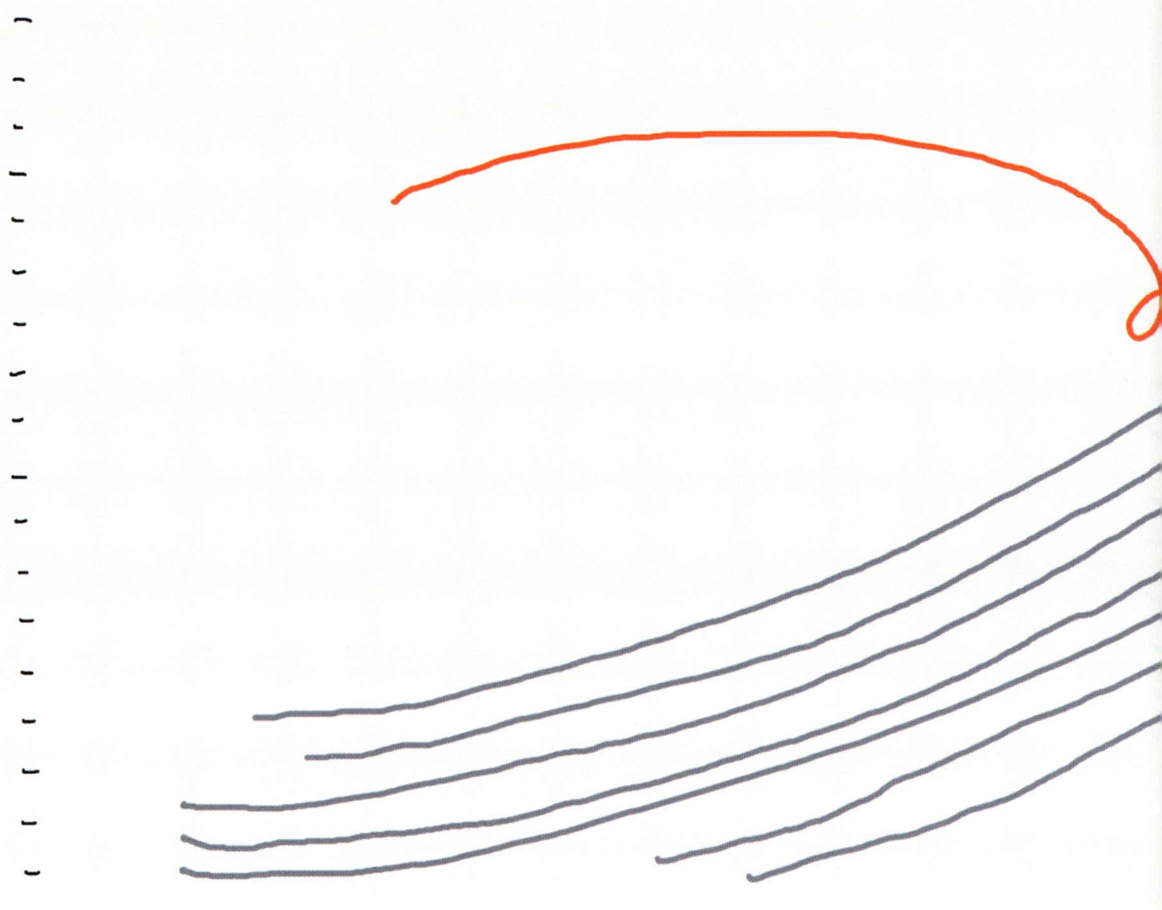

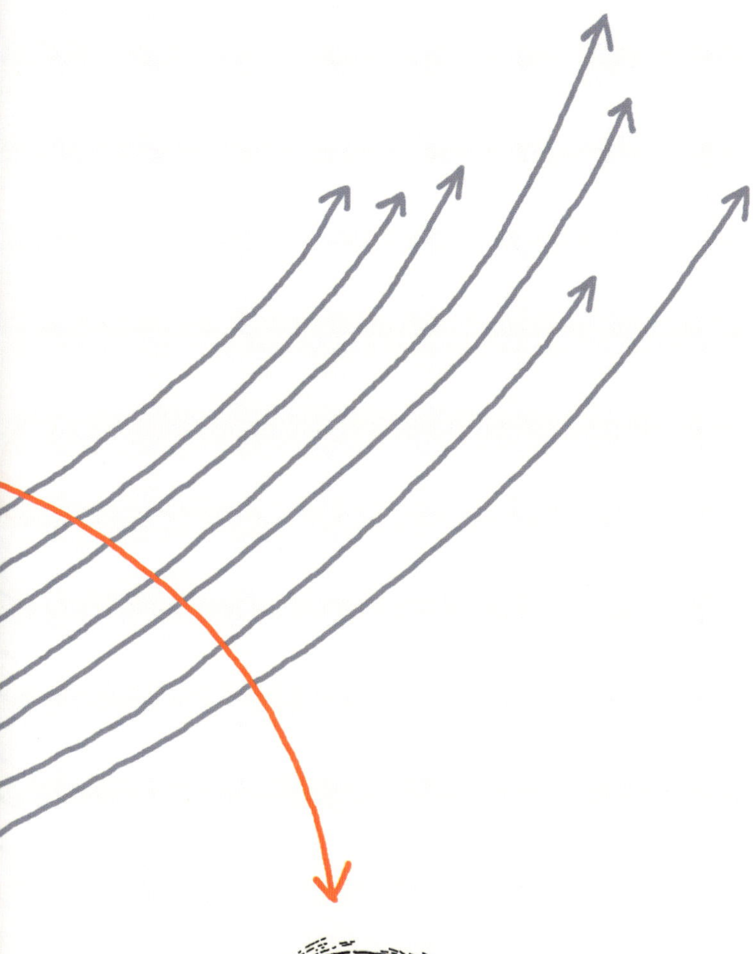

“IF EVIDENCE DISAGREES WITH YOUR EXPERIENCE, YOU SHOULDN'T IMMEDIATELY SAY THAT THE DATA ARE WRONG. IT MIGHT BE THAT YOU ARE AN OUTLIER, THAT YOUR EXPERIENCE IS NOT REPRESENTATIVE AND THE DATA ARE ACTUALLY REVEALING THE TREND, AND THAT YOU DON'T FIT THE TREND.

—ADAM GRANT

We need to be much more nuanced in how we communicate. We need to clarify where there's uncertainty. We need to highlight where there are contingencies. We need to be as open about what we don't know as about what we do know. One of the things we saw during COVID-19 is that source credibility dominates message credibility. People will believe a weak argument from someone they trust much more readily than a strong argument from someone they don't trust. One of the ways you become a trusted source is by very clearly admitting your uncertainty, showing intellectual humility, and expressing doubt where appropriate. I hope we don't have to keep relearning that lesson over and over again.

What's your personal definition of data?

Data are information gathered through systematic and rigorous observation.

We love that you say data *are*. To us as well, *data* is plural.

A datum, or a data point, is one piece of information. Data are the collections of those observations.

To change the subject slightly, you've spoken in the past about the relative power of data versus stories to influence people and change minds. This is also something we think a lot about in our work. When do you think a really powerful statistic is appropriate, versus when a human story is going to be more effective? And when can they be combined?

It's a false dichotomy to say they can't be combined. My point of view on the responsible use of stories is that we should start with the data and then find stories that illuminate the data.

Stories are often more effective at evoking emotion. They allow us to distance ourselves from our own perspectives a bit. In addition to immersing ourselves in the narrative, they immerse us in a character. We get transported into stories, and we tend to experience them more than we evaluate them. Sometimes that can make people less rigorous in scrutinizing data, and that becomes a problem when the stories aren't guided by data.

The more surprising data are, the more likely they are to capture attention. If you have data that challenge people's intuition, you're much more likely to pique their curiosity. But you have to be careful, because, as the sociologist Murray Davis wrote in his classic paper "That's Interesting!," people are intrigued when you challenge their weakly held intuitions, whereas they get defensive when you question their strongly held intuitions. So there's nuance there.[2]

> **From a visual perspective, we try to anchor stories in more aggregated data, but then disaggregate them by pulling out a couple of data points that can explain the context. By doing this in a narrative way, it can become more accessible, like a plot of a book. That's really fascinating.**

Another way to tell a story about data is to start with what people would expect, then lead them to overturning their assumptions. People often find that journey revealing and enlightening, and it can become an emotional arc.

Yet another thing I've learned is to present a surprising result and then ask people how they would explain it. It opens their minds quite a bit: they generate reasons they find persuasive, and thus become active participants in the dialogue. Instead of preaching your view or prosecuting theirs, you engage them in the process of thinking like a scientist and generating hypotheses. I quite enjoy that.

NOTES

1 Adam Grant, "'You Can't Say That!': How to Argue, Better," *The Guardian*, July 30, 2022, https://www.theguardian.com/lifeandstyle/2022/jul/30/you-cant-say-that-how-to-argue-better.

2 Murray S. Davis, "That's Interesting!: Towards a Phenomenology of Sociology and a Sociology of Phenomenology," *Philosophy of the Social Sciences* 1, no. 4 (December 1971): 309-44.

~~Data is~~ are

INFORMATION GATHERED THROUGH SYSTEMATIC AND RIGOROUS OBSERVATION

— ADAM GRANT —

Andy Marra

Andrea "Andy" Hong Marra is a civil rights activist and CEO of Advocates for Trans Equality, a national nonprofit fighting for the legal and political rights of trans people in the United States. At A4TE, Andy oversees a team of lawyers, policy experts, and community organizers dedicated to ensuring that all people in US society are treated equally. A4TE also produces the US Trans Survey, the largest survey of trans people, by trans people, in the United States. A longtime leader in the LGBTQ+ movement, Andy is one of the country's most salient voices on civil rights today. In this conversation, Andy discusses the role of data in advocacy work; the pros and cons of categorization; and why visibility does not necessarily lead to acceptance.

What has been the impact of data and data-based evidence on the LGBTQ+ movement?

It's a good question. I think it's worth naming up front that the trans rights movement and the broader LGBTQ+ rights movement have made progress at breakneck speed in comparison to the vast majority of other social justice movements in the United States. In a little more than fifty years, we have seen marriage equality, nondiscrimination protections for LGBTQ+ folks in the workplace, and a number of other protections, including access to trans health care and making sure that LGBTQ+ young people are treated well in schools and have access to resources and support. We can point to several moments and markers that demonstrate how quickly the LGBTQ+ and trans rights movements have made progress.

For the broader LGBTQ+ rights movement, data collection has been incredibly important—a leading factor in making the case for policy and legal protections for trans people. In 1990, President George H. W. Bush signed the Hate Crime Statistics Act, which required the FBI to collect data on sexual orientation as it pertains to hate violence in the country. That opened the door for activists to be able to say, "Now you can't deny that we exist. You have data that actually demonstrates that we exist. And not only do we exist, but we are disproportionately targets for hate violence in this country."

You're counting something that was never counted before.

Right. Data collection is incredibly important in that respect, and is an increasingly important subject more broadly among LGBTQ+ policy advocates. That said, the reality that we are currently living in and grappling with is that visibility does not translate into acceptance. We've seen cultural markers of progress with, say, celebrities like Laverne Cox on the small and big screens. We've seen more and more LGBTQ+ or trans-specific storylines in entertainment. There are issues being talked about openly in the news in a way that we have never seen before. But that visibility doesn't necessarily serve as an indicator of acceptance. We are also witnessing an incredible amount of scrutiny and demonization of trans people across the country.[1]

I think this has a lot to do with marriage equality, meaning marriage for same-sex couples in this country. Those who oppose equality and justice learned a lot from the marriage equality movement, in which LGBTQ+ activists told very personal stories of loving, committed couples who simply wanted to be treated like everybody else. Instead of changing minds by talking about the thousands of rights that were being denied them, it was the stories about everyday folks next door who want to be able to get married and live lives very similar to their neighbors in their own communities. That is what moved this country toward unprecedented acceptance of marriage equality across the political spectrum, across faith and religion. To this day, overwhelming majorities support marriage equality.

The problem is that opponents to LGBTQ+ rights learned about what we call "hearts and minds" work—the changing-of-narratives work and the culture work—that they were woefully behind on. Today, opponents to trans rights use almost the same playbook that LGBTQ+ activists used to advance marriage equality. They are using stories. They are finding spokespeople from different identities, from different backgrounds, to propagate a narrative of vitriol and demonization. They are also using junk science to enable state legislatures to pass bills intended to criminalize various aspects of our lives. This has become the centerpiece of many political conversations in this country. As a result, trans people have become the latest scary monster. Trans people are now having to say, "We're not monsters. We're just everyday people like you."

When you say *data*, how would you define that?

Data serves as a language. It's a common language for a diverse number of stakeholders to consume and understand.

So much of this relates to how we define identity as individuals, as a culture, as a government, and then how we *communicate* that sense of identity to others. For better or for worse, that's usually through a binary categorization: You are X or you are Y. What are the pros and cons of categorizations of this type?

Categorization is a helpful tool to indicate a person's identity. It doesn't tell the full story, but rather serves as a quick reference point or marker to give context to a person's lived experience. And it tells us who they are in a legal context. To be legally recognized as your gender identity is incredibly important for trans people. It says, "Hey, this is who I am and how I identify, and here is a state-sanctioned document that demonstrates that." Many people don't ever give it much thought. But think about providing identification with your debit or credit card at the grocery store, or filling out an employment form, or filling out an intake form when you go to a medical facility. If a person encountering your identification sees your gender marker not aligning with how you are presenting to the world, it can create uncomfortable and even discriminatory conditions for you, or, worse, put you at actual risk of violence.

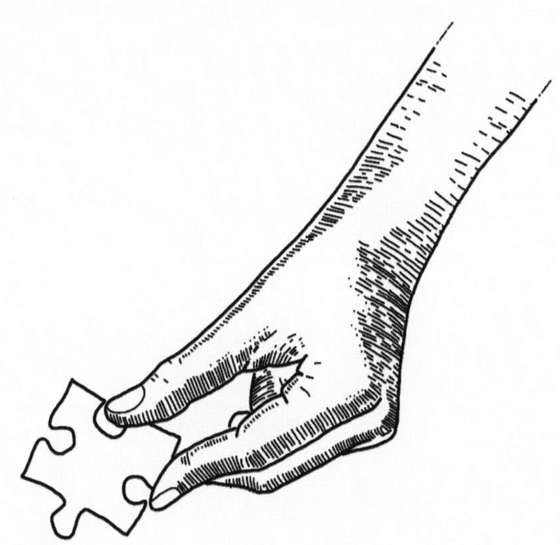

“CATEGORIZATION IS A HELPFUL TOOL TO INDICATE A PERSON'S IDENTITY. IT DOESN'T TELL THE FULL STORY.

—ANDY MARRA

Also, when we say *trans people*, that encompasses a number of gender identities—for instance folks who are nonbinary. We are seeing more and more people come out and identify as nonbinary: Either they do not identify within the gender spectrum at all, or they identify with one or more aspects of identities within it. As a result, we're seeing increasing numbers of states and jurisdictions honoring and recognizing those gender identities. The federal government and states across the country are introducing the X marker on government identification to honor folks who are either nonbinary or folks who do not identify as either male or female. We are making progress on the legal and political fronts to make sure we're recognizing the full spectrum of folks who may or may not identify within the gender binary.

This pertains to even something like your US passport. Many people don't think much of their passport, but it is a government ID and it allows you to leave and enter the country. People aren't able to freely move around the world unless they have a passport. If a trans person travels to another country where the climate is more conservative or hostile, and a government official there deems the gender marker on their passport as not corresponding with their gender identity, it puts them at a greater risk.

Again, categorization is just a starting point. It is almost the first part or the preface to a much larger story to tell. When we look at something like government identification and see "male" or "female," we think that's a checkmark and the end-all be-all. But who I am is more than just what's on my government identification.

Right. There's two aspects here. There's the legal aspect, which obviously has a lot of important implications for health and safety, government services, and more. But then there's the more personal aspect, when one can say, "My government sees me how I see myself." Which feels incredibly powerful and gratifying for anyone.

Data helps us make the case for advancing legal and policy protections in a number of areas. Take the Youth Risk Behavior Survey, a national survey distributed across the country to students and schools. It asks a number of questions to better understand the school and student experience. It wasn't until approximately ten years ago that the survey started to include questions explicitly about gender identity so as to encompass the experiences of trans students, which in turn demonstrated that trans students are at greater risk of being harassed or bullied in school settings.

We've had to fight for the progress we've had, and to make the case stronger, we've often collected our own bodies of research. I think the US Trans Survey, which our organization produces, is a great example. It is the country's largest body of research on the trans experience, and one of the top cited. We frequently refer to the US Trans Survey in amicus briefs and in actual lawsuits. I would say it is a hallmark body of research for the trans rights movement.

The US Trans Survey is also a survey *about* trans people *created* by trans people. Why is that important?

There is real utility for data—not just data collected by government agencies but also research that originates from the community itself. It's not a body of research that I would say is owned by any one organization; rather it is a reflection of the entirety of the trans rights movement. And what makes this research so compelling and visionary is that it asks a diverse array of questions about not just the identity of trans people, but also how identity impacts a multitude of aspects of their lives—everything from health insurance to experiences of accessing medical care, applying for a job, going to school and walking down the hallway there. This research is the collective reflection of the trans experience in this country. The latest report secured almost one hundred thousand respondents, so it is a massive dataset. And we expect to be releasing more specialized reports from it.

But really, it legitimizes the trans experience. And it also, I think, encourages and inspires and challenges researchers across fields to further diversify, and drill down, in their own practices.

You said before that visibility does not necessarily lead to acceptance. How can we use data to build both visibility and acceptance for trans people? Do we need to think about data in a different way?

I've talked a lot about quantitative data, but qualitative data is incredibly important to the equation for social change and progress. The story behind data is always the starting point for me. But what is missing from the equation is the vehicle and the infrastructure to communicate that story effectively. So, yes, we have the stories, but are we reaching people in the right ways? And if not, how can we adapt so as to create the kind of impact we want?

We have made exceptional gains when it comes to data and technology, but I see a need for progressive movements broadly to grapple with how we apply these latest developments, including things like generative AI, to our work. A heightened segmentation or hyper-understanding of who your audience is and how to reach them is the secret sauce for having cultural impact, making a cultural or social change. We have the stories. We just need to figure out the best way to reach the people.

NOTES

1 "Youth Risk Behavior Surveillance System (YRBSS)," US Centers for Disease Control and Prevention, https://www.cdc.gov/yrbs/index.html.

Data is

A COMMON LANGUAGE FOR A DIVERSE NUMBER OF STAKEHOLDERS TO CONSUME AND UNDERSTAND

— ANDY MARRA —

2

Making Meaning: Data and Communication

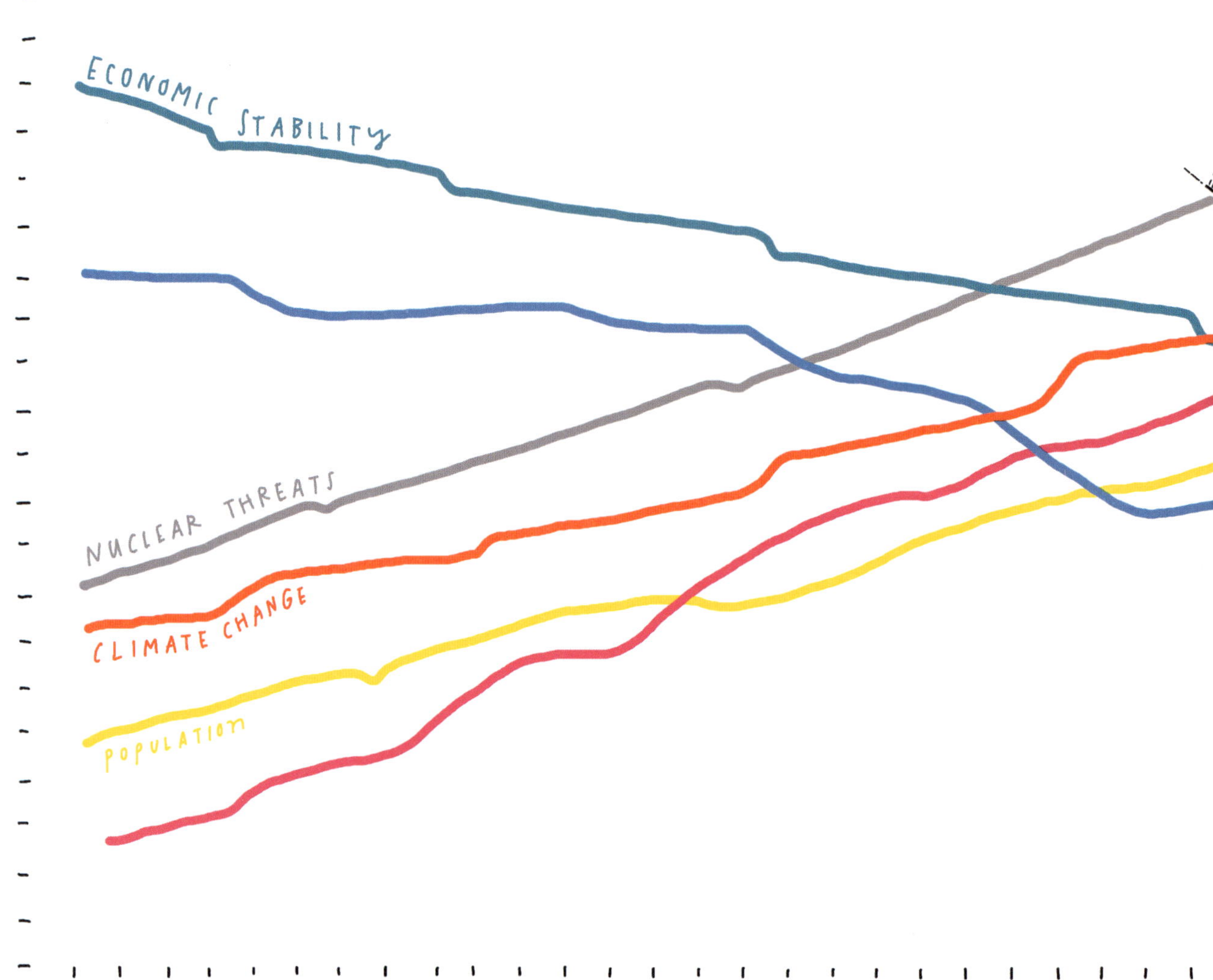
ECONOMIC STABILITY
NUCLEAR THREATS
CLIMATE CHANGE
POPULATION

Making Meaning

On an unassuming winter day, in an unassuming conference room in downtown Chicago, the end of the world is being counted down. Welcome to the reading of the Doomsday Clock, presented annually without fail since 1947 by the Bulletin of the Atomic Scientists. The clock itself isn't much to look at—a rudimentary drawing of four dots and two lines—but its simplicity is deceiving. Like any good abstraction, it communicates a whole range of ideas with both powerful immediacy and ruthless efficiency.

Every year, the Bulletin convenes a panel of expert scientists and analysts to determine the clock's movement. They make their determination based on a range of statistical indicators—data—which measure our world. Are we moving closer to global annihilation? The clock moves forward toward proverbial midnight; time is running out. Or, alternatively, are things improving and humanity has managed to work toward solving our most pernicious problems? The clock moves backward, away from midnight; for now, we've bought ourselves a bit more time. When the Bulletin began this ritual, on the eve of the Cold War, they set the clock at seven minutes to midnight. A lot has happened in the world since. As of 2024, the clock stands at 90 seconds to midnight.[1]

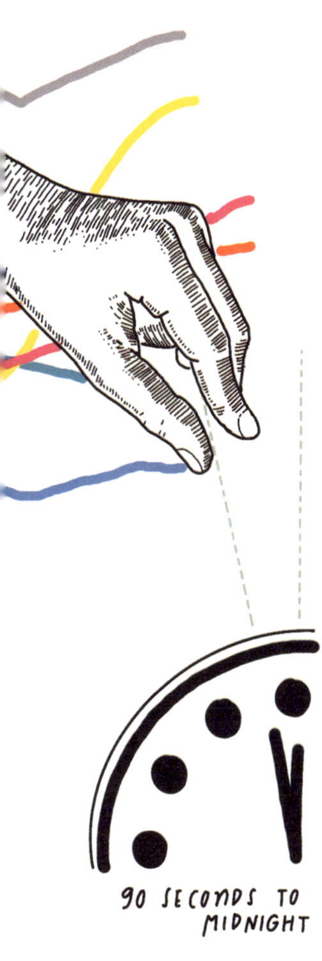

The Doomsday Clock was designed in the 1940s by the painter Martyl Langsdorf (who often went by just her first name, Martyl) and has since gained broad resonance in our culture, appearing in literature, television, and film. It's a symbol, but also a surprisingly effective example of data visualization. In a few straightforward marks, the clock summarizes reams of quantitative knowledge about science, politics, economics, technology, demographics, and more, and then synthesizes that knowledge into a familiar graphic metaphor. But importantly, the clock is also *emotional*. It tells a story that everyone can understand: Time is limited, so we'd better get our act together. The reactions it elicits are visceral. Like the shot clock in the last moments of a championship basketball game, you just can't look away.

The graphic designer (and our colleague at Pentagram) Michael Bierut has called the Doomsday Clock the "most powerful piece of information design of the twentieth century," and we're inclined to agree.[2] But what makes a good data visualization? It's a hard question to answer. Is it the most accurate explanation of a number's meaning? The ease with which the reader understands? A sort of graphic elegance that makes the most complex numbers easy to understand and beautiful to look at? Data visualization expert Edward Tufte has written persuasively about what he calls the data–ink ratio: Expend the least amount of effort communicating the greatest amount of data.[3] Is it about efficiency, speed, or power?

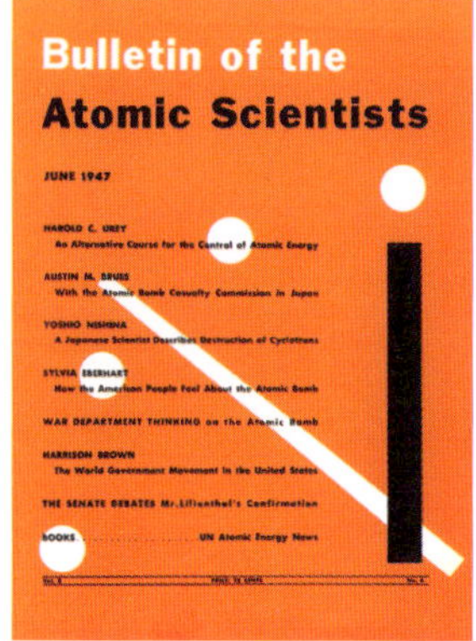

↑
Cover of the *Bulletin of the Atomic Scientists*, 1947

Maybe. Considerations like these might well be appropriate depending on the situation. After all, a pilot needs a ruthlessly simple elevation gauge to steer their craft safely; a financial analyst wants a basic chart to plot investments strategically. We live in an image-driven world where visual literacy is low but the need to access information is high. But what such a zero-sum game often misses is fundamental to data visualization's ultimate purpose: to convey a record of reality. Data encodes meaning, and visualization gives us access to that meaning in legible form. Instead of asking what makes a good data visualization, what if we asked a bigger question, free of past conventions or constraints: What is the most effective way to *communicate meaning*? And to answer that question, we need a fundamentally different approach.

A few years ago, the staff of the Bulletin approached our team with an intriguing request related to their upcoming clock reading. They didn't want to change the iconic Doomsday Clock—who could improve on it?—but were seeking a way to better contextualize it. For outside observers, the Bulletin works under a shroud of secrecy. To maintain impartiality, its deliberations are confidential until the clock's reading is revealed. Unsurprisingly, this leads to a barrage of questions each year about why the clock's hands moved forward or back. For their latest announcement, the Bulletin wanted to offer an idea of the amount of research and discussion that goes into the decision to reposition the clock. Could we help?

We launched into a process that has become a hallmark of our information design practice, a tested methodology that, we believe, yields valuable and exciting results. Every project begins with research and a deep immersion into the content at hand—in this case, no easy task. From nuclear risk to climate change to disruptive technology, unless you're a PhD scientist, the Bulletin's work is not for the faint of heart. We pored over research papers; interviewed prizewinning experts; and were even allowed to listen in on meetings with the Bulletin's Science and Security Board, the primary group of world-renowned experts who determine the clock's reading each year.

Most importantly, we also were led by our own curiosity, asking "where," "when," and "why" at every turn. It soon became clear that to do justice to this information, we would need to leave behind the shopworn canon of conventional data visualization. Bar charts, pie charts, line graphs, histograms—in our tech-driven world, this standard lexicon is ubiquitous, showing up everywhere from news reports to phone bills to video games. Software like Microsoft Excel allows anyone to be a dataviz designer. But to us, this approach represented nothing more than blindly throwing technology at the problem. Instead, we were determined to let the data define the right design solution rather than the other way around. New meanings necessitated new models.

Data visualization pioneers like Charles Joseph Minard, Florence Nightingale, and W. E. B. Du Bois knew this well. Take Minard's famous 1869 map of Napoleon's 1812 Russian campaign: an undulating, layered diagram illustrating the movements of thousands of French soldiers over time. To track the advance and retreat of Napoleon's troops, Minard devised an unconventional map that communicates six different variables—geography, path, direction, population, temperature, and

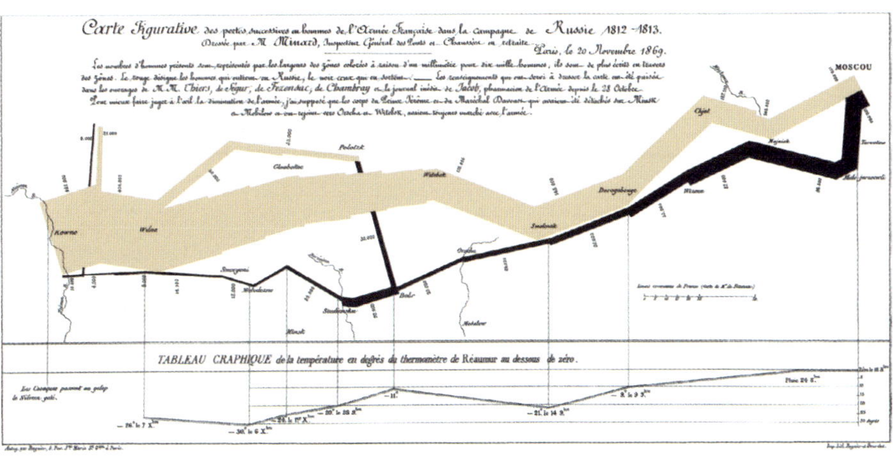

→
Charles Joseph Minard, *Figurative Map of the Successive Losses of Men of the French Army During the Russian Campaign 1812-1813*, 1869

Nuclear Risk

An Expanding Concern

The number of nuclear warheads has fallen from Cold War highs and nuclear testing has all but ceased. Still, nuclear risk is rising as arms control treaties wither and die, the potential for accidental nuclear war remains under-appreciated despite decades of nuclear mishaps, and nuclear weapons countries devote billions of dollars to nuclear modernization. Has the world come full circle and begun a new nuclear arms race?

Information on nuclear warheads, countries possessing or seeking nuclear weapons, nuclear testing, and nuclear diplomatic agreements is arrayed on a circular timeline that starts in 1940 (lower left) and moves clockwise toward the present.

WEAPONS

- Country with nuclear weapons
- New country gains weapons
- Country pursuing nuclear weapons
- New country pursuing weapons
- × Nuclear weapon accident

NUCLEAR TREATIES

In the last few years, Russia and the United States withdrew from the landmark Intermediate-range Nuclear Forces Treaty, both countries announced withdrawal from the Open Skies Treaty, and the United States withdrew from the landmark Iran Nuclear Deal. This dismantlement of much of the world's arms control regime raises the real possibility of a renewed nuclear arms race.

1970
India
1966 Palomares B-52 crash, Spain
Israel
China
USA
1962 Cuban Missile Crisis
1960
France
1958 Tybee Island mid-air collision, USA
UK
Russia
1950
USA
1947 Doomsday Clock created and Cold War begins
1945 Bombing of Hiroshima and Nagasaki
1942 Manhattan Project authorized by President Roosevelt

Nuclear Risk: An Expanding Concern data visualization, 2020

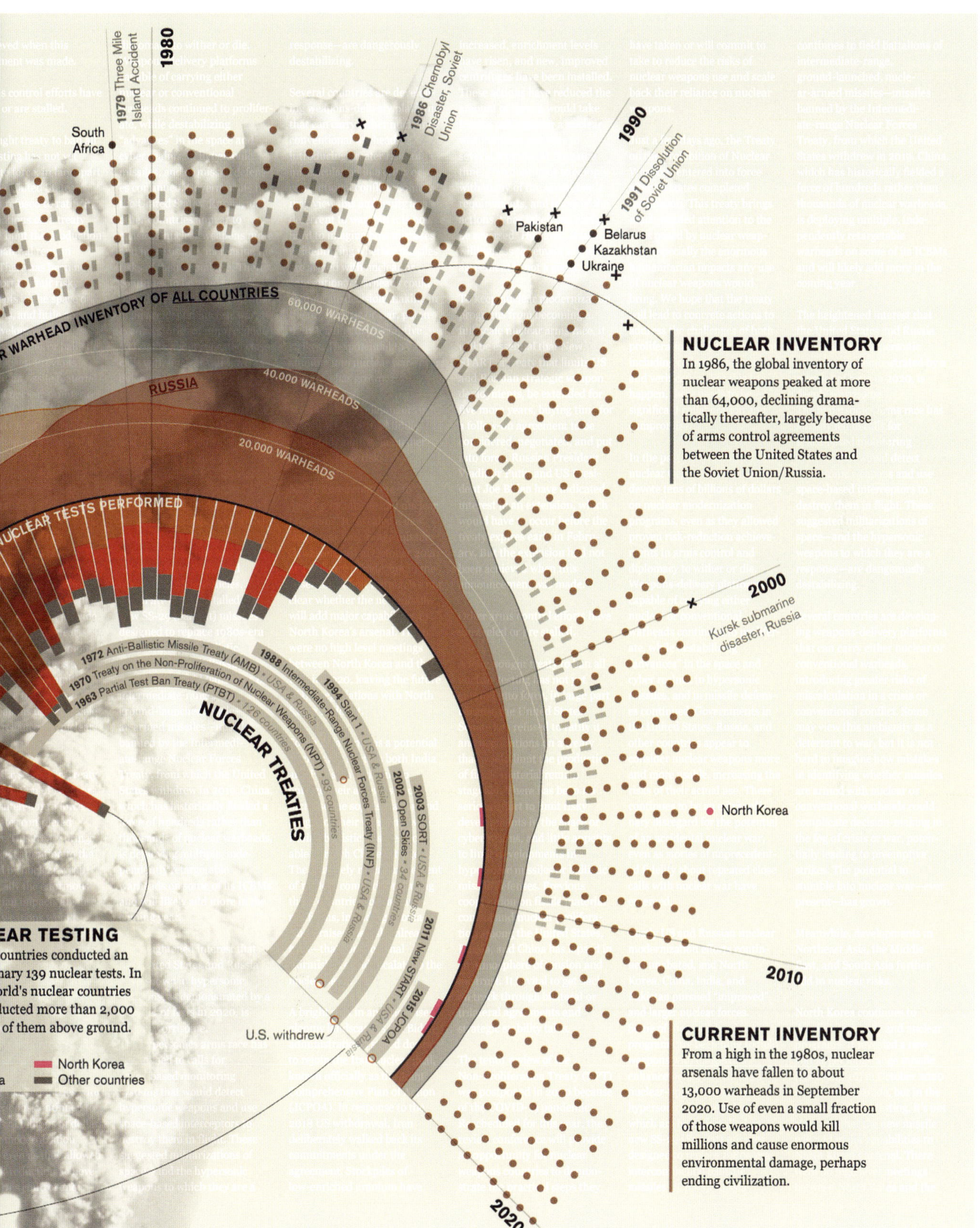

NUCLEAR INVENTORY

In 1986, the global inventory of nuclear weapons peaked at more than 64,000, declining dramatically thereafter, largely because of arms control agreements between the United States and the Soviet Union/Russia.

EAR TESTING

ountries conducted an ary 139 nuclear tests. In rld's nuclear countries ducted more than 2,000 of them above ground.

CURRENT INVENTORY

From a high in the 1980s, nuclear arsenals have fallen to about 13,000 warheads in September 2020. Use of even a small fraction of those weapons would kill millions and cause enormous environmental damage, perhaps ending civilization.

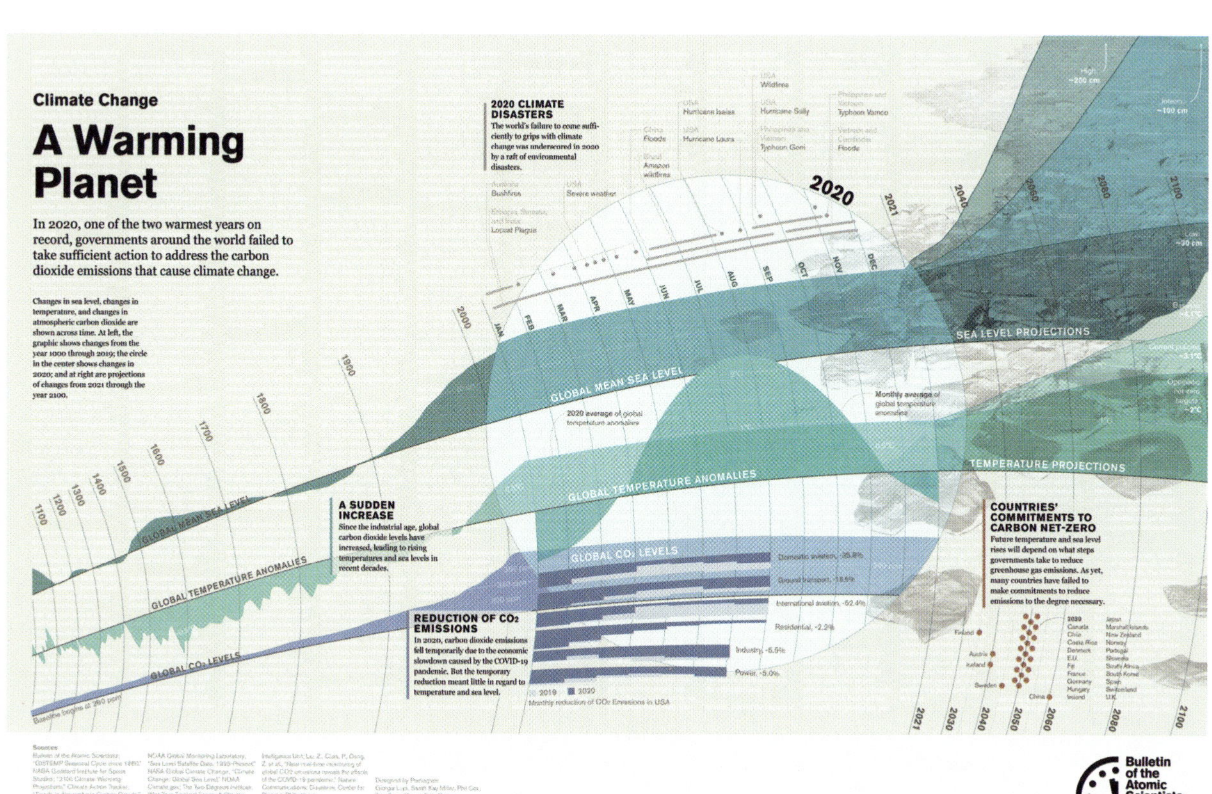

↑

Climate Change: A Warming Planet data visualization, 2020

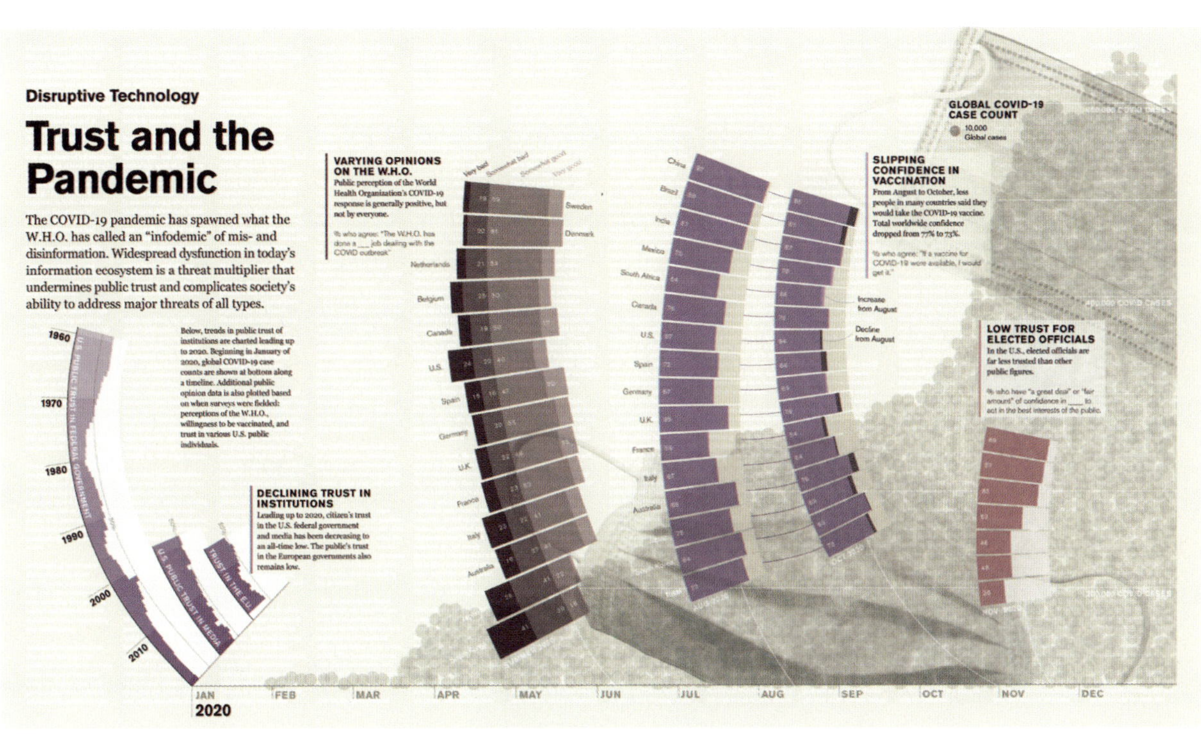

↑
Disruptive Technology:
Trust and the Pandemic
data visualization, 2020

time—in a single image, a feat that would never be possible with a traditional flowchart. The result is a striking portrait of these soldiers' trials, analytically precise but just as emotionally evocative as the Doomsday Clock. It's a complete story, and it rewards deep and lingering examination.

For the Bulletin visualizations, we took a similar tack. To illuminate the expanding concern of nuclear proliferation, we imagined an unusual radial data visualization, mimicking the combustion of a nuclear warhead, and arrayed data about nuclear inventories, tests, and treaties around it. To represent the accelerating threat of climate change, we organized data about temperature, sea levels, and carbon emissions—often treated as isolated trends—along a single, curvilinear timescale. For a final visualization about trust in public institutions during the COVID-19 pandemic, we created bespoke graphs of public opinion sentiment data, which we then plotted on top of COVID-19 case counts.

Like Minard's map from 1869, our three visualizations embrace new forms for communicating their meaning. They serve up information in layers, with strong visual hierarchies that lead the viewer's eye through the content. For those with limited time (or attention spans), takeaways are structured and clear, but there are also intricate, detailed graphics with which the more intrepid reader can spend time if they wish. We believe that whenever the main purpose of data visualization is to open people's eyes to fresh knowledge, it is not only impractical, but actually misleading, to avoid a certain level of visual complexity. Visualizing data is about providing access to our reality, not just simplifying it. We can write rich and dense stories with data and celebrate the true depth of complex realities. While some may find these visualizations unconventional to look at, we hope they encourage careful reading, and therefore a more invested engagement in the meaning behind the numbers.

Another pillar of our approach to data visualization is context. Data is never only what we see on a spreadsheet, and hiding below the surface of any single data point is a whole world of contextual information. This context is vital for telling richer, fuller, and ultimately truer stories. Augmenting hard data with layers of "softer" and more qualitative information is the only way to present this larger picture. For the Bulletin visualizations, we peppered each graphic with annotations, callouts, and tangents that provided context for what the statistics were telling us. This secondary gloss provided a first-person narration to what could otherwise have been a rather cold and impenetrable story. It helped the data make sense.

As a final flourish, behind each graphic we collaged in text from transcripts of the real deliberations of the Bulletin's Science and Security Board. This subtle textual layer alluded to the amount of behind-the-scenes analysis that went into the clock's reading, underscoring the essential human component often overlooked in data visualization. It's a reminder that data is always human made: collected, analyzed, evaluated, and communicated by people.

Martyl's original Doomsday Clock design is one way to use visual communication to convey meaning. Our three data visualizations discussed here are another. Both are valid responses to the same brief, albeit born of very different eras and design philosophies. But as the world becomes more and more complex, and its problems more and more urgent, it may be time to embrace new methods of information design that can fully speak to the issues we face. Ecological crises, global pandemics, artificial intelligence, economic inequality, political instability: such knotty topics demand data visualizations that prioritize complexity over simplification; contextualization over reduction; and customization over convention. And there's no time to lose. The clock is ticking.

NOTES

1 John Mecklin, "A Moment of Historic Danger: It Is Still 90 Seconds to Midnight," *Bulletin of the Atomic Scientists*, January 23, 2024, https://thebulletin.org/doomsday-clock/current-time/.

2 Michael Bierut, "Designing the Doomsday Clock," *The Atlantic*, November 5, 2015, https://www.theatlantic.com/entertainment/archive/2015/11/doomsday-clock-michael-bierut-design/412936/.

3 Edward Tufte, *The Visual Display of Quantitative Information*, 2nd ed. (Graphics Press, 2001), 93.

2,005

54.57

8,587

3.14

2,157

37,679

5,050

26,843

111,616

839,002

.8333

624

1202

45,082

227

1.618

0.7734

704,347

27,488

Seth Godin

Seth Godin hardly needs introduction. A prolific writer on business and marketing topics, he is the author of more than twenty books. He is a virtuosic public speaker, and his TED talk on how ideas spread has received more than seven million views. For years, Seth has been obsessed with how humans think—and what might get them to change their behavior. His 2022 book The Carbon Almanac: It's Not Too Late *trains his formidable brain on how we can get the world to care more about the globe's most urgent topic: climate change. In this conversation, Seth talks about the crucial differences between data, information, and truth; how absolute confidence in numbers is an ideal, but never a reality; and why* USA Today *might be to blame for society's misunderstanding of quantitative information.*

552

2,369,082

101

33

.999

Over the years, you've written a fair bit about data and the communication of data from a marketer's perspective. How do you wrap your head around this topic?

Let's start with three words, because if we don't understand them, it's going to get confusing. The three words I'm going to pick are *data*, *information*, and *truth*. Data is a bunch of numbers that we choose to highlight. It's a mass of verifiable numbers that have no information in them—yet. There is a sampling that goes on, as we cannot acquire all the data ever. Information is when a human being turns data into knowledge or understanding. And truth is impossible. When we present data in an attempt to create information, it always has a point of view.

Do you feel like the world has misunderstood what data is?

I think we don't even understand the question. We should ask ourselves: Are we in the information business, or are we simply delivering data? If you just give me data, it's boring. I won't read it. But if you want to help me turn it into information, please own the fact that information always has a point of view, especially when it's backed up by data. Giorgia and Phillip, you're in the information business. You're not in the data business. The magic of your work is that you're very clear about that. Putting the word *human* in Data Humanism is really important. Because you're saying: Here is *one* way to look at a bunch of data that can be verified.

I'll give you another example. My wife and I recently listened to Robert Caro's book *The Power Broker* on a long road trip. It's sixty-six hours long. There's a chapter in which the book's subject, Robert Moses, lists all the traffic on the Long Island Expressway every year for ten years. The audiobook narrator just reads his chart. It's as boring as it sounds. That's data, not information.

All data is subjective, in that a human being decided what to collect and how to collect it. Yet when the general public sees a chart, too often they automatically trust it. Why have we all been trained to trust so blindly?

Since the Industrial Age, we have pushed people not to talk about their feelings. Instead, we have pushed people to talk about facts. The challenge is that as things get more complicated, people tend to feel stupid. And if you feel stupid, you don't want to talk about it.

This happens for example with sunk costs and the simple truths of statistics. If the poll says there is a 60 percent chance that someone is going to get elected, most people think that means that 60 percent of people are going to vote for that person, and thus there's a 100 percent chance that they're going to get elected. When that isn't what happens, they get angry. There isn't a deep understanding of what the stuff on the screen even means. Then the media has an incentive to try to turn things that people don't understand into things that will emotionally resonate because we are emotionally starved. My point is: If you don't really understand, that's what the system wants.

At the same time, people blindly trust data about say, an election, but when it comes to climate change, they are more suspicious. Why?

Forty years ago, Exxon's chief engineer wrote a memo in which he described, in extraordinary detail, exactly what the climate was going to be like in 2022. And he was right. But Exxon decided, with a trillion dollars of resources in the ground, that they would sow disinformation instead. It's much, much easier to sow disinformation than to sow understanding. It's not that people don't care about the climate. It's that they don't understand. There are a whole bunch of reasons for that: Human beings are bad at predicting the future. Human beings are bad at statistics. And human beings are bad at discerning between good charts and bad charts.

I can't help but think about Jerry Siegel and Joe Shuster's original Superman origin story. Superman's dad figured out that Krypton was going to explode. He had a plan for all the people on Krypton to leave before it was too late. But none of the people in power wanted to look at his data. None of them wanted to understand what was happening. But when the earthquakes began, they understood. And then it was too late.

The challenge we have as communicators is not to create a stampede or a panic, because those don't yield resilient results, but to create a body of work that isn't political. There are people who want it to be political because political means, "Don't talk about it!" There are other things in our world that it's okay to talk about. It's okay to talk about the rate of acceleration due to gravity, which is 32 feet per second squared. That's not a political issue. With climate data, we need to just keep coming back to these first principles of explaining what it is, so people have a foundation for actual understanding.

What's your personal definition of data?

Data is a mass of verifiable numbers that have no information in them—yet.

That puts the onus on us as designers—and, more broadly, anyone creating representations of data—to get it right.

My problem with the data visualizations published by outlets like *The Washington Post* and *The New York Times* is that they pretend they're telling you something that is true—but they're not. What they're doing is capturing a bunch of data and trying to turn it into information, but it always carries with it some point of view. If we're going to do a good job with data visualization, we'd better be clear about what the so-called alt text says for the chart or the graph we're making. Editors at major newspapers don't like having to use alt text honestly because they put up a picture of a firefighter and a four-year-old boy, and they think that a picture is worth a thousand words. But I think they should tell us why they chose that picture. Is it because the boy looks like this and is wearing these sorts of clothes? Is it because the firefighter is a woman? Editors should say those things, because they picked that photograph for a purpose.

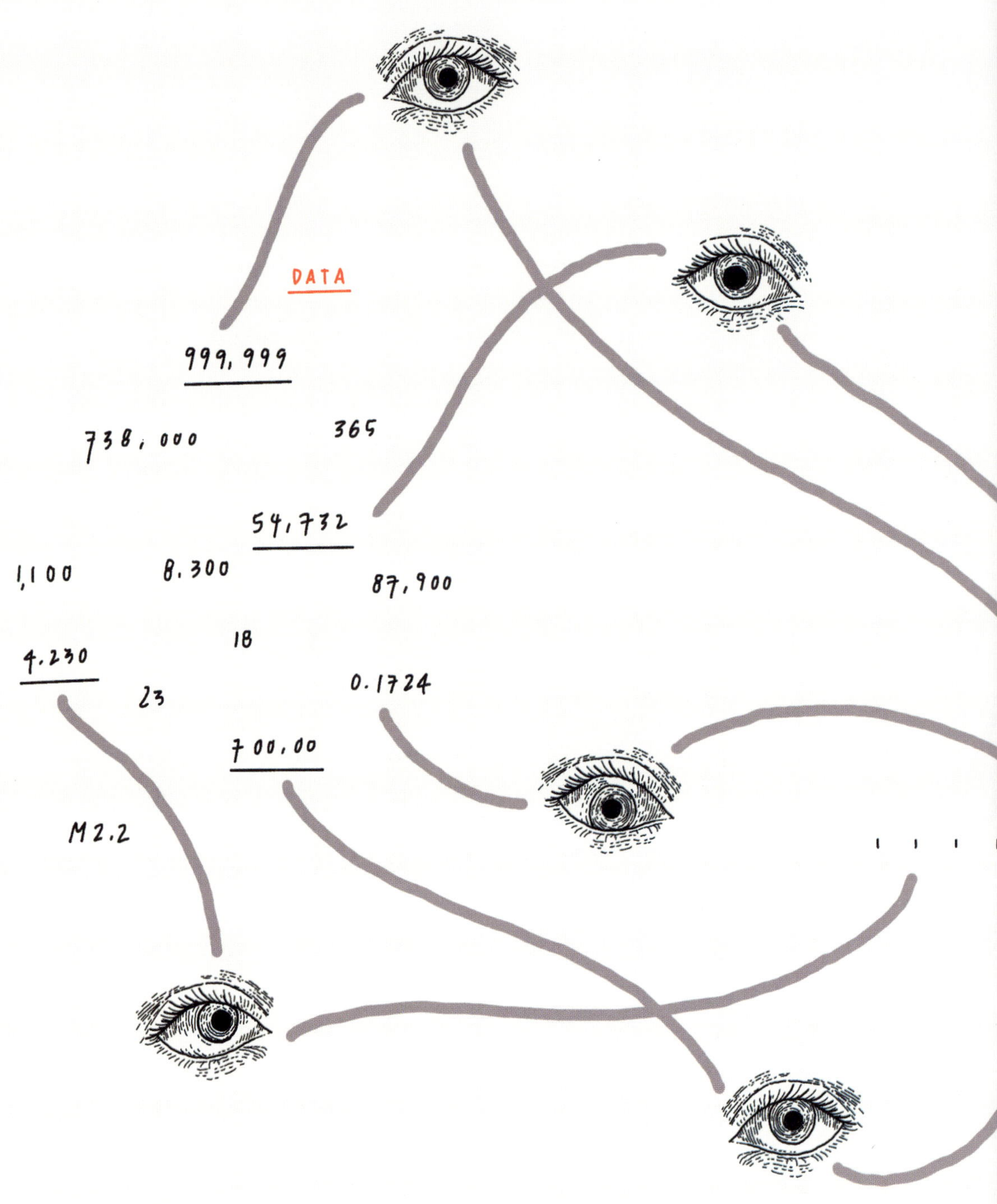
DATA
999,999
738,000
365
54,732
1,100
8,300
87,900
18
4,230
23
0.1724
700,00
M2.2

TRUTH

INFORMATION

"DATA IS A BUNCH OF NUMBERS THAT WE CHOOSE TO HIGHLIGHT. (...) INFORMATION IS WHEN A HUMAN BEING TURNS DATA INTO KNOWLEDGE OR UNDERSTANDING. AND TRUTH IS IMPOSSIBLE. WHEN WE PRESENT DATA IN AN ATTEMPT TO CREATE INFORMATION, IT ALWAYS HAS A POINT OF VIEW.

—SETH GODIN

I have never seen *The New York Times* run a correction that says, "The chart we ran didn't honestly express what we wanted to say." They have to run corrections all the time for mistakes made in text-based stories, but if you see a chart in *The New York Times* that's banal or ineffective or poorly done, there's no place to even comment on it. It's viewed like the weather—you can't do anything about it. But this is not the weather. It's reporting. And if you are a reporter, you should own your work.

We need to be clear with one another before we make any graph or chart. What's it for? What is the point that we are trying to make? Because it is not okay to say, "Well, it's true." There's lots of ways that you can present information. If there's more than one way, then you're no longer dealing with what's true, you're dealing with: *This* is the point that I'm trying to make. *This* is the information that I think you should be willing to verify.

We saw people use and misuse data countless times during the pandemic. Has COVID-19 shifted your thinking on this?

Demagogues always misuse data to put forward invalid information. The very nature of being a demagogue is that you cannot sustain rational criticism and discourse. If you could, you wouldn't be a demagogue. There aren't any particularly vivid examples that come to me around COVID-19, but I can name plenty from the 1930s, 1940s, and 1950s—a peak moment of propaganda. Or, think about how North Korea is so good at manipulating imagery, using something that looks like data to make something that feels like information. Many people who have the power to do this in public have no training, understand nothing about statistics, and think what's pretty is what's important. I'll blame a lot of that on *USA Today*, and some of that on Microsoft.

You should need to have a license and some basic training. It should be harder to successfully publish a data visualization than it is to drive a car. Yet we let people drive around in cars that could injure a few people, while there are plenty of people who are busy making charts and graphs that are deceiving people into making bad decisions that cost lots of lives.

Can you point to anyone who is doing it well?

There are only two fields: fields where people having access to data will help them make better decisions, and fields where it won't. And it seems to me, in both cases, that teaching people about information and doing a better job of delivering it will help us make better decisions. It's an obligation in a field where people are counting on it, and it's an opportunity in a field where they're not.

Let me give you an example that you might not have leapt to. It's what Michael Lewis wrote about in the book *Moneyball*.[1] The magic of *Moneyball* wasn't that the A's had secret data. The data was available to everybody. The magic of *Moneyball* was that the A's had *useful* information—information that had been hiding in plain sight but that no one had ever explained before.

There's also this tyranny of simplicity. We're constantly led to believe that a simple chart is a better chart. What's the role of simplicity in clear communication?

I believe that a useful representation of data is 100 percent about the light bulb moment. If you can't make that light bulb turn on, don't show it to me. Minard's chart of Napoleon's battle is only useful to a hundred people who are deeply involved in understanding what happened to Napoleon. But it is impossible for someone who didn't know anything about the topic beforehand to look at that chart and have that light bulb illuminate.

Do not say, "This is all the data," or "Make your own decision." No, it's not all the data! And you don't really want me to make my own decision. What are you trying to show me? If you're going to use a bar chart instead of a line chart, and if you're going to manipulate the axes so it looks like there's a huge difference between 80 and 84 percent when there's not, tell us what you did and why you did it. If you can't say that honestly, then I don't want to believe anything else you did when you built your chart.

When you take this approach, people get it. For instance, if you want to teach people about plastics recycling, showing them how much plastic gets recycled in a way that is verifiable and visual helps them get it. Turn on a bright light and say, "Did you see that? Because we don't want you to unsee it." People don't need all the extra nuance of the amount of plastic burned, or the amount of plastic that was appropriately recycled because it was sorted. All that is more and more analog truth. What we're trying to say to you is that most plastic doesn't get recycled, and that plastic recycling is basically a myth and a fraud.

Once you see that and you can verify it, you're going to make different decisions.

NOTES

1 Michael Lewis, *Moneyball: The Art of Winning an Unfair Game* (W. W. Norton, 2003).

Data is

A MASS OF
VERIFIABLE NUMBERS
THAT HAVE NO
INFORMATION IN
THEM... YET

—SETH GODIN—

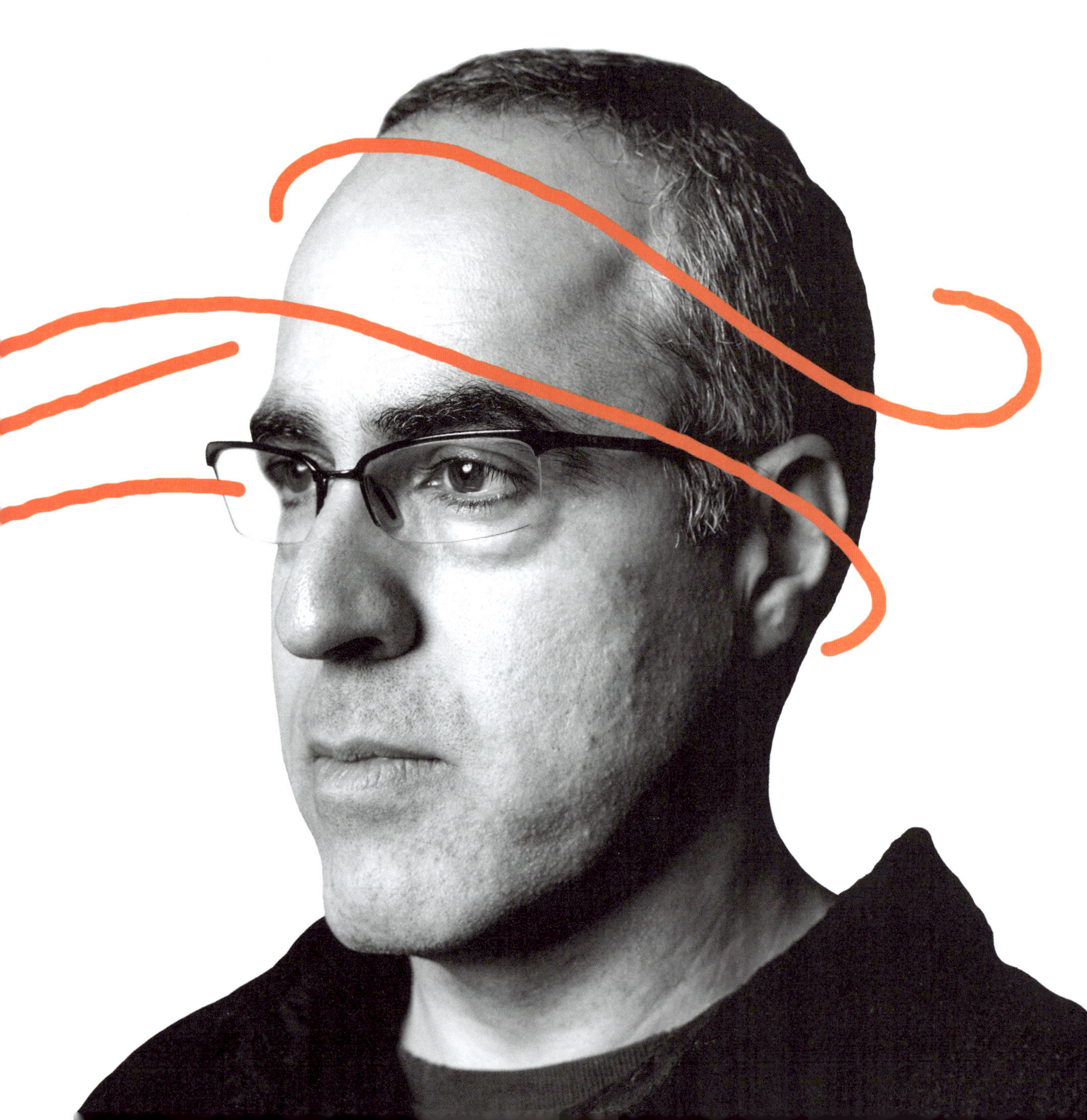

Naresh Ramchandani

Naresh Ramchandani is one of the most insightful thinkers on the climate crisis today. A copywriter by training, he began his career in the world of advertising, creating groundbreaking campaigns for the likes of Maxell tapes, IKEA, and YouTube, and writing about consumer behavior for The Guardian. *Along the way he began to model a refreshingly new method of communicating the urgency of climate change, using smarts and wit to reach audiences in a profoundly tangible way. In 2007 Naresh cofounded Do the Green Thing, a "creativity-versus-climate-change" charity that has inspired more than fifty million people in two hundred countries to live a greener life. We met him when he was a partner at Pentagram, and we've had the pleasure of collaborating several times on projects marrying data visualization with his unique mastery of language. In this conversation, Naresh explains why climate change is everyone's problem; the beauty of the "hockey stick"; and what it takes to tell a really good story.*

You've stated that "climate change has been the most challenging brief I've ever worked on and resulted in the work I've been most proud of—and I hope the best is yet to come."[1] Why is it so challenging? And what have you seen fail versus succeed?

The climate crisis is a by-product of all the ways we live our lives, and to combat the climate crisis, we have to change the ways we live. It's that simple, and that complex. How do we persuade or incentivize the execs of fossil fuel companies, construction firms, and fast-fashion manufacturers to look beyond next year's profits? How do we ask farmers to prioritize the long-term health of the soil and the broader rural ecosystem over this year's yield? How do we encourage policymakers to look beyond the next election? How do we ask citizens to look beyond the fast fashion they can buy and wear today, the hardware they can upgrade to this week, the holiday they can get off to this summer, the food they can afford this month?

And in the more affluent sections of the Global North, arguably the principal perpetrators of the climate crisis: How do we ask those people to reduce their profits, power, and style, and buy more expensive energy or less tasty food when the main beneficiaries are not their communities, not their countries, and, as so-called delayers would argue, not even their generation?

That's the scale of the challenge. It's a beast. It's a "hyperobject," as the philosopher Timothy Morton described it, which was this idea of something so big that you can't hold it.[2] It takes numerous perspectives to even understand it. It cannot be solved by one person, or even lots of people. It needs everyone. Yet we as humans like simple things, and we act for ourselves. I'd argue that all this makes the challenge fascinating.

But it's also easy to see why so many young people are falling into climate despair. For this challenge to be met, we need to deconstruct the values, the frameworks, the ideas and actions that make our world about me, and the here and now, and construct the alternative values, frameworks, ideas, and actions that can power a sustainable future. We'll need to innovate, imagine, reimagine, exemplify, protest, expose, advocate, simplify. And do it all with the highest levels of creativity so no one can ignore it, and with inexhaustible energy because we're not creating a case study but making the future. I think a full response to the climate crisis should speak to the full range of human motivations. Scientific evidence and moralizing campaigns are great for some, but until the palette gets richer, we'll struggle to bring a critical mass of people into the movement.

Let's talk then about creativity, and how we can get more effective about communicating the climate crisis. Of course, we always start with data. One of the more famous examples of data visualization in the public imagination was Al Gore's famous hockey-stick graph in *An Inconvenient Truth*.[3] But we'd wager that such a technical graph would never even move the needle in today's conversation. Everything now feels like it needs to be "bite sized" and "snackable" to be taken up by the general public, which is difficult for a topic that's as complex as climate.

I'm no data designer, but I've actually got a lot of time for the hockey-stick visual. I'd say it looks technical but communicates very quickly. In one glance it tells me the world's getting a lot hotter, and really fast, and that this conclusion is scientifically indisputable. I've always thought it looks like a lie detector graph, with the volume of lies climbing as the temperature climbs, which of course is painfully true. "The crisis isn't happening." Lie. "It's not our fault." Lie. "It's everyone's responsibility." Lie. "Everyone suffers the crisis equally." Lie. "My country's doing its bit." Possibly. "My company's doing its bit." Maybe. "My family or community are doing our bit." Often that's wishful thinking, which is different from the truth.

The problem with the hockey stick is that the story it tells is too old and too big. Most of us know there's a climate crisis. Now we need to know the specifics—precisely what industries, technologies, processes, and behaviors are causing it—so we can figure out how to act effectively upon it, know how to reverse it. We need to know precisely who it's impacting—territories, communities, time frames—so we can apply the remedies with accuracy and justice. Precisely what's being done, so we can take hope and know what else to do.

I often hear people talking about "doing my bit" or "playing my part" in relation to the climate crisis, and so it often means feeling a responsibility and doing something, anything, in response. If each of us could be strategic and precise about what our part is within an overall theory of change, we'd have a chance with this thing. For me, that's where sharp data, data design, and data storytelling could really help right now.

You likely also know the famous "warming stripes" cover of *The Economist*, which has been enormously influential as a case study in mainstream data visualization.[4]

The warming-stripes visualization tells exactly the same story as the hockey stick—and has the same problems. It tells us that the world's getting a lot hotter, fast, but that's not new enough or precise enough. What it has over the hockey stick is that it's a modern and striking piece of design. You could argue that its beauty is important because the visualization has been published and shared around the world, and there's nothing wrong with restating the problem powerfully every now and then. At the same time, I worry that its beauty glosses over the need for action. I saw a few people wearing it as a T-shirt this summer like this year's *Unknown Pleasures*, but it can't be *Unknown Pleasures*, an attractive design worn for its aesthetic.[5] It has to mean you're doing something.

It's also inherently abstract. That's not good or bad per se, but it's important to realize that it's an abstract visualization about a global statistic. It's pretty divorced from the day-to-day reality of most people.

The philosopher Roman Krznaric writes about the "climate gap," in which empathy fails to travel "across space and through time"—in other words, a failure of people in one part of the world to change behavior that's impacting people in another part of the world or impacting a future generation in their own part of the world because they cannot feel for them.[6] This is why local stories are so important. The global stories can tell us the extent of the problem, the horrendous tally of species going extinct, the appalling scale of climate injustice, the cycle of extreme weather, the unthinkable profits made by industries that are most at fault. But do the global stories get us to act? Can we cross the empathy gap? When *our* city is battered by a flood or a hurricane, when *our* woods are ravaged by fire, when *our* farmers' crops are failing because of drought, when *our* neighbors die from a heat wave, when we don't see that butterfly in *our* garden anymore, then sadly (if you're an optimist) or understandably (if you're a pessimist), that's when the crisis gets too close for comfort, and we act.

Now, I'm a data optimist, and I can see data-pointed stories closing Krznaric's empathy gap in many areas. For instance, in the United States and the United Kingdom, we've lived through several years of increasing political polarization, with the UK bitterly divided on multiculturalism, liberalism, and globalization, and in 2020 a US president who interfered in election results that went against him in seven states. With bipartisan channels and extreme rhetoric making ideological differences increasingly extreme, could data stories close the gap? Could they express the gentler views, portray the don't-knows, show people enjoying a debate without hate, bring alive the many voters who curate their views from different sides of the divide, and explain the policies that bring bipartisan benefit despite being lionized or villainized? I'd argue that powerful stories with data at their center have a chance of helping both sides understand both sides.

Part of the problem is that so much of this climate data, usually produced by governments and multilaterals like the IPCC [United Nations Intergovernmental Panel on Climate Change], is dense and inscrutable to the layperson. Yet the implications are critically important for everyone. How do we make these important studies more intelligible and widely understood? Should data or data visualization play a role?

Climate science gives the climate movement its moral legitimacy. In the coldest and most unemotional terms, it supplies the current truths and assured predictions that create headlines, set intergovernmental agendas, direct government policies, and fuel all climate-positive action. That's a big role, and maybe that's enough. But when I look over climate science reports, I wonder what would happen if the data could be turned into stories, and those stories could touch a wider audience.

For example, one section of the IPCC Climate Change 2023 report calmly stated: "If climate goals are to be achieved, both adaptation and mitigation financing would need to increase many-fold. There is sufficient global capital to close the global investment gaps but there are barriers to redirect capital to climate action."[7] The report provided more detail under this statement, but the language remains technocratic. Yet it's one of the vital stories that more people need to understand. We have the money to solve the climate crisis, but it's currently going elsewhere. Where is it going, and why? Where does it need to go, and why? What are the barriers to it being redirected? What needs to change to lift them? What do governments need to mandate or incentivize? What practices do our banks and investors need to adopt? And with a clearer understanding of the mechanisms involved, could voters, workers, individual investors, and account holders be a stronger lever for change?

I'd say yes—and I'd go further and say that wider awareness could lead to greater change right across the realm of climate science.

In the end, this is a communications exercise. Who needs to understand what to do in order to enable real change? The IPCC and other climate scientists have picked their audiences and chosen their language. If other communicators in the climate movement—for example journalists, storytellers, illustrators, filmmakers, designers, and data designers—were equally intentional in how they applied their imaginations, the climate movement could be so powerful.

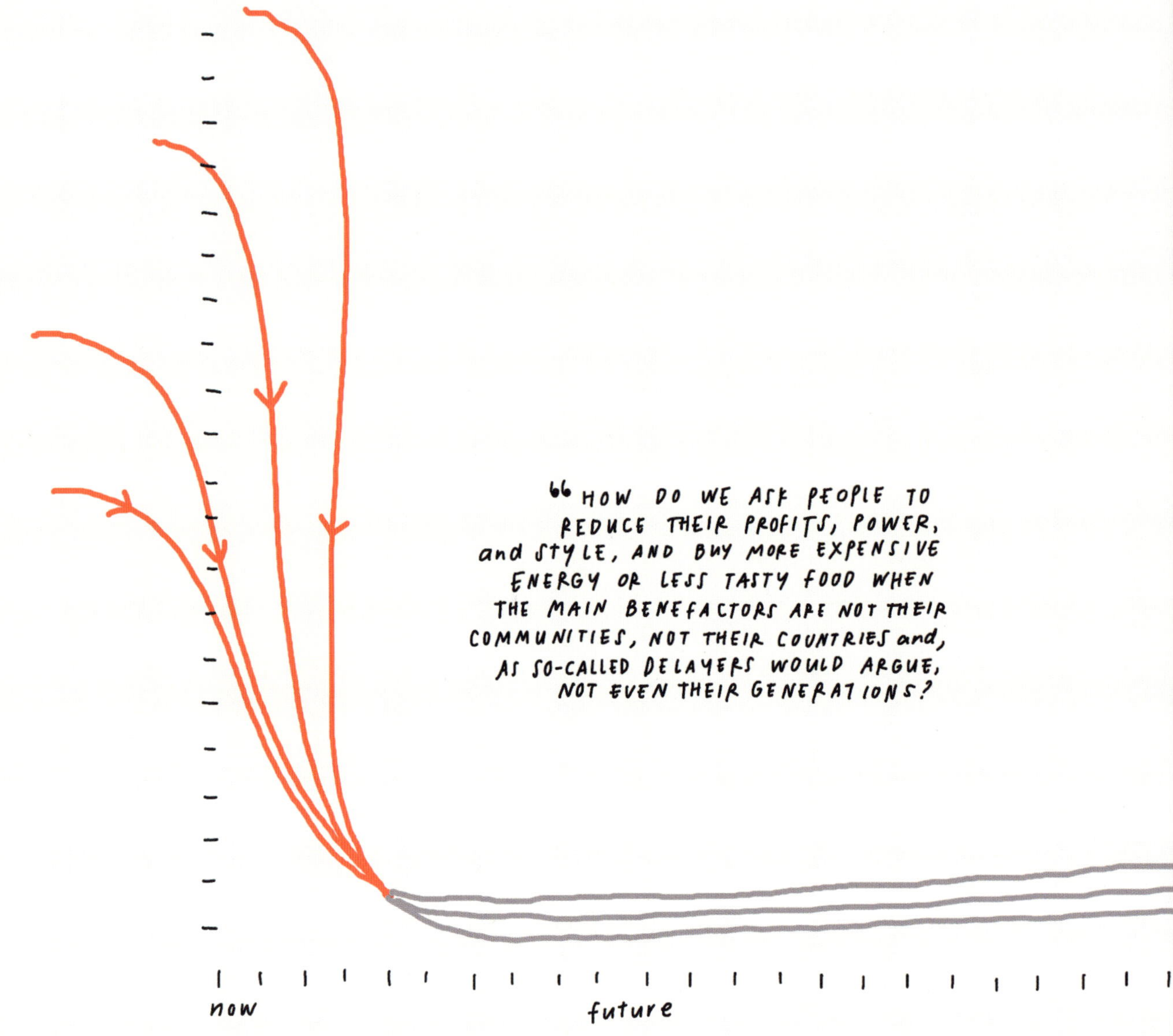
"HOW DO WE ASK PEOPLE TO REDUCE THEIR PROFITS, POWER, and STYLE, AND BUY MORE EXPENSIVE ENERGY OR LESS TASTY FOOD WHEN THE MAIN BENEFACTORS ARE NOT THEIR COMMUNITIES, NOT THEIR COUNTRIES and, AS SO-CALLED DELAYERS WOULD ARGUE, NOT EVEN THEIR GENERATIONS?
now
future

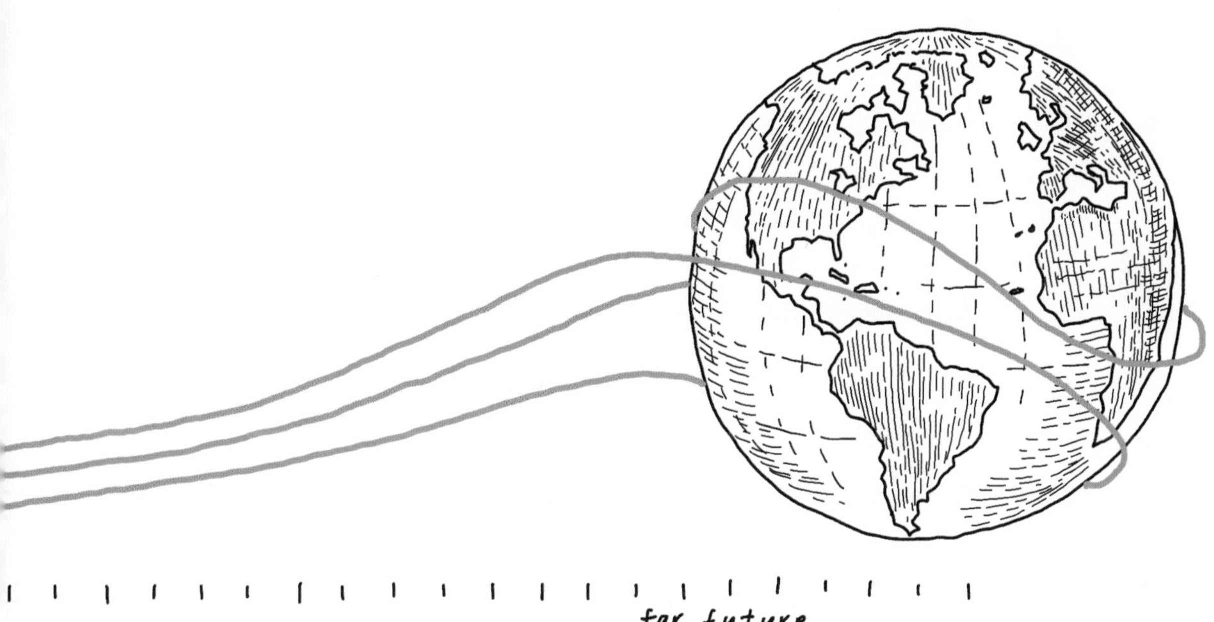

—NARESH RAMCHANDANI

A good story takes words and images. The verbal and the visual need to work together seamlessly to become something greater than the sum of their parts.

It's great when we're all aware of what one another's crafts are capable of and then bring them together in the most purposeful way possible. Graphic design presents an idea or organization compellingly and distinctively. Writing articulates an idea or organization's core purpose, offer, and arguments. Data design evidences the change that the idea or organization is here to make. They each do different but related things, and together they do powerful things.

Whether at Pentagram or Do the Green Thing or elsewhere, the most exciting projects I've been part of are the genuinely multidisciplinary ones, where each discipline is pointed not toward individual input but toward shared outputs and outcomes. Where the skill in the room is matched by the modesty in the room. Where the real craft is to work out how each craft can defer to the others, support the others, dance with the others.

What makes a good story for you? The content? The structure? The actors involved?

A compelling story involves the characters, stakes, conflict, sacrifice, and resolution all working together. It needs to start with jeopardy: A person, a community, or an idea we care about is at risk, or has already been put at risk. This is the hook, the reason to pay attention. After that, it needs to develop through its people: the people at risk, the people who are presenting the risk, the people who are stepping in to prevent or overcome the risk. And they shouldn't be presented simplistically as victims, villains, and heroes. The more rich and convincing their motivations and characteristics, the more compelling the story will be.

Conventionally, it helps a story if the people tackling the risk find they need increasingly more time or resources or strategies to overcome the risk. In other words, the people presenting the risk have more strategies and resources than was first apparent. That way, the story escalates. In a story where a lot is at stake, there are casualties of the risk—often human lives. Finally, the risk is overcome, but not in the way that was first imagined, and everyone involved in the story has gone through a process of learning.

In this context, how would you define data?

Plot points. Points at which a story turns. Something gets worse. Something gets a *lot* worse. Something gets better. Irrefutable points of drama in a real story.

Do you think normal people even care about data today?

Stories make us care. They get us to think, feel things, do things. And while it's possible to extract a story from data alone, you need to be extremely data literate to do that. That's where data by itself falls short as communication. But when data is embedded in a story, it can do wonderful things.

It can make a story more dramatic. For instance, "The drought caused 85 percent of the district's crops to die in one month. The families who have stayed are fighting a losing battle with the land. The families who left are refugees struggling to find a new home." Or it can make a story more authentic: "Black communities in London are disproportionately more likely to breathe illegal levels of air pollution. In 2020, nine-year-old Ella Adoo-Kissi-Debrah became the first person in the UK to have air pollution listed as a cause of death." Or it can make a story archetypal: "Nine out of ten children in sub-Saharan Africa are like Abeo, heading toward fewer jobs, less agency, more poverty, and poorer health."

When I think about it that way, I care about what the people or communities are going through, and I care or fear for what they'll do next. In other words, I'm invested in their stories, in no small part thanks to the data. Alongside characters, stakes, conflict, sacrifice, and resolution, I'd say that data is a core tool to make a real story vivid.

NOTES

1 Natasha Berting, "'Climate Change Is the Most Challenging Brief I've Worked On': Naresh Ramchandani on Creativity, Sustainability and Designing Out Waste," *What Design Can Do*, March 16, 2021, https://www.whatdesigncando.com/stories/naresh-ramchandani-interview-2021/.

2 Timothy Morton, *Hyperobjects: Philosophy and Ecology after the End of the World* (University of Minnesota Press, 2013).

3 A lightning rod for conversation and controversy, the so-called hockey-stick graph was originally published in 1999 and visualized temperature anomalies from the years 1000 to 2000. See Michael E. Mann, *The Hockey Stick and the Climate Wars: Dispatches from the Front Lines* (Columbia University Press, 2013).

4 "The Climate Issue," *The Economist*, September 21, 2019. The "climate stripes" graphic was created by Ed Hawkins, a climate scientist at the University of Reading, based on an initial motif by Ellie Highwood.

5 The reference is to the iconic cover of Joy Division's 1979 album *Unknown Pleasures*, designed by Peter Saville based on a visualization of pulsar radio waves. See Jen Christiansen and Harold D. Craft Jr., "The Pulsar Chart That Became a Pop Icon Turns 50: Joy Division's *Unknown Pleasures*," *Scientific American*, September 1, 2020, https://www.scientificamerican.com/article/the-pulsar-chart-that-became-a-pop-icon-turns-50-joy-division-rsquo-s-unknown-pleasures/.

6 Roman Krznaric, "Empathy and Climate Change: Proposals for a Revolution of Human Relationships," in *Future Ethics: Climate Change and Apocalyptic Imagination*, ed. Stefan Skrimshire (Bloomsbury Academic, 2010), 154.

7 "Climate Change 2023 Synthesis Report," Intergovernmental Panel on Climate Change, https://www.ipcc.ch/report/ar6/syr/downloads/report/IPCC_AR6_SYR_LongerReport.pdf.

Data is

IRREFUTABLE POINTS of DRAMA IN A REAL STORY

—NARESH RAMCHANDANI—

Bernadette Woods Placky

Al Roker. Jim Cantore. Dallas Raines. Janice Huff. If one or more of these names sound familiar to you, it's because you've likely seen them on TV. But they're not actors or professional athletes; they are television meteorologists, reporting rain or shine for the day's weather. Bernadette Woods Placky is a meteorologist too—she cut her teeth at WJZ-TV in Baltimore—but she's also the vice president for engagement at Climate Central, a scientific nonprofit using the power of mass communication to fight climate change. Every week, Climate Central produces free climate reporting materials, customized for more than 245 US cities and media markets. Local media partners, like your favorite TV meteorologist, then use Bernadette's insights to report science-based stories on climate change's impact on local communities. In this conversation, Bernadette talks about meteorologists as trusted messengers; the shifting public sentiment around climate change; and why she's (cautiously) optimistic for our climate future.

We think you have one of the world's most interesting jobs.

I'm a meteorologist. I see the world through weather. It's how I've always been. Weather isn't just an impact of climate change; it's also a solution. With climate change being one of our biggest challenges as a society, weather is one of the most obvious ways to move forward. People are interested in weather. We have really robust technology already in place around wind and solar energy—the technologies, the implementation, the building workforces. We also have new laws that have been passed that are helping to accelerate the transition to wind and solar. And experiences with weather prompt conversations where you can make the climate connection. There are so many reasons to focus on weather. I can keep going if you want!

When you think about it, the local TV meteorologist might be the only scientist that the average person actually knows. It seems so obvious, but also profound. For communities today, what does the weatherperson represent, and how are they a conduit for data?

TV meteorologists are trusted in their communities. They are a part of their communities. Most of them are scientists, but if they're not, they're at least skilled science communicators. And they are on the front lines of our changing climate. One of the primary ways we experience climate change is through our changing weather. TV meteorologists have access to a wide audience, and weather is nonpolitical—for the most part. If a big storm is coming your way, life stops. Life changes. People are interested. They tune in locally to see how it's going to affect them.

Now, the weather app on your phone has come a long way and today provides a range of data, but it's still just an icon, limited numbers, and maybe a warning. But a TV meteorologist can give the context of what's happening, and guide and even teach you. They are like a local celebrity with knowledge that people keep coming back to.

It's funny on some levels. When I was on TV, it was amazing how much people connected with me. I'd see them after a storm and they'd tell me their personal story of that storm: where they were or how they got through it or what else happened in their life that day. There's something about weather that drives interest. People love weather. They love talking about it.

It's interesting to think about these big, catastrophic events as triggers for turning to trusted messengers and information sources. We imagine the same phenomenon happened with the pandemic.

There have been some very interesting studies comparing climate change and COVID-19, from communication to societal response. That said, the pandemic was so immediate, whereas for some people, climate change is not so immediate. Nonetheless, the pandemic showed us that when we put our minds to it, we can accomplish big things through science-informed decisions and actions. We just have to commit. And that's the thing with climate change: we need to get people to commit to changes.

What, from your perspective, is the ideal role of data in this? Whether it's the TV meteorologist or the president of the United States, how should trusted messengers use data to communicate to the public?

To me, data is the foundation for the conversations we're having. We know our climate is changing because of data. We understand the growing climate threats because of data. And data also guides our solutions. There are stories within our data that help us learn. For example, when our data team is working on our weekly reporting package, they see the trends and patterns that translate into longer, stronger allergy seasons; mosquitoes moving into new geographies; or risks to beer and coffee.

What is your definition of data?

I think first of numbers, but it's so much more than that. To me, data is the grounding of fact with truth.

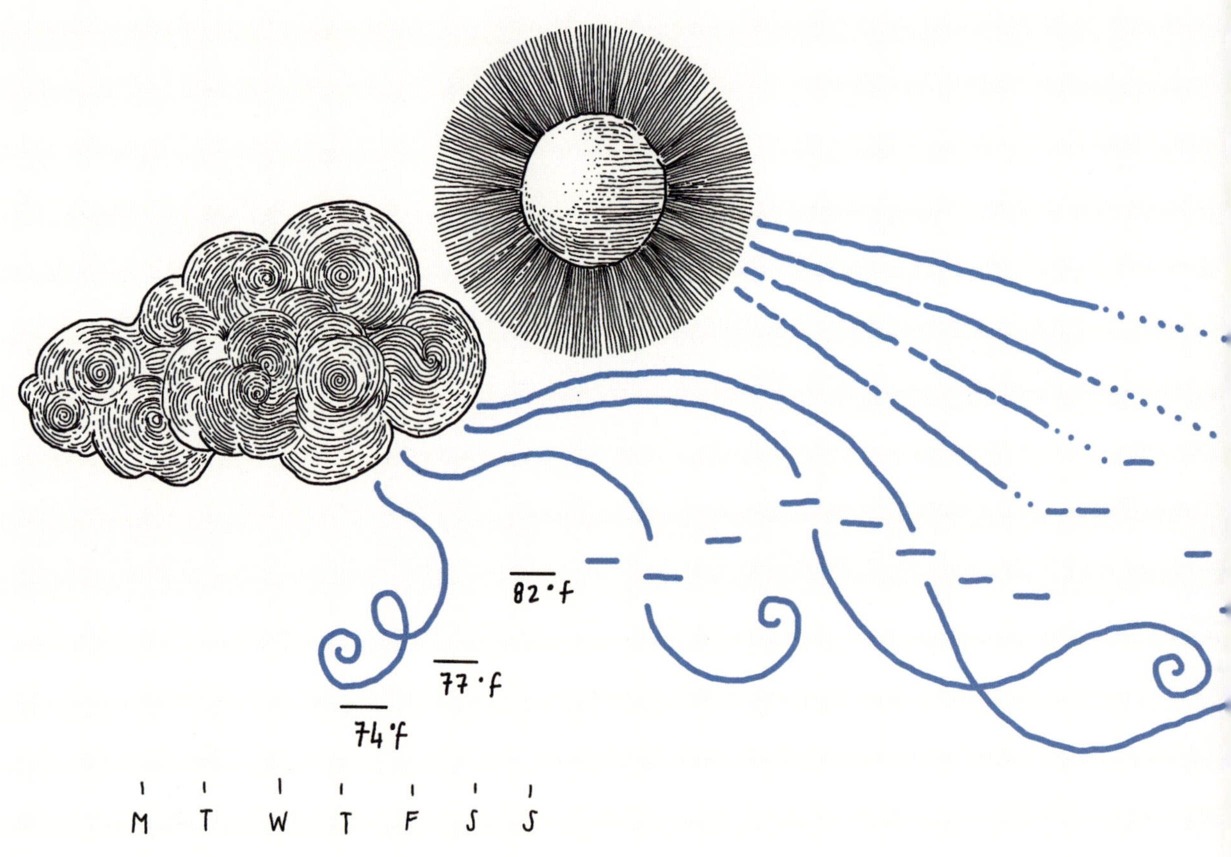
82°f
77°f
74°f
M
T
W
T
F
S
S

"WE UNDERSTAND THE GROWING CLIMATE THREATS BECAUSE OF DATA. AND DATA ALSO GUIDES OUR SOLUTIONS. (...) WHEN OUR DATA TEAM IS WORKING ON OUR WEEKLY REPORTING PACKAGE, THEY SEE THE TRENDS and PATTERNS THAT TRANSLATE INTO LONGER, STRONGER ALLERGY SEASONS, MOSQUITOES MOVING INTO NEW GEOGRAPHIES, OR RISKS TO BEER AND COFFEE.

— BERNADETTE WOODS PLACKY

Are there generational differences in how people perceive the science of climate change as based in truth?

Generally speaking, we know that 70 percent of society is convinced that climate change is happening. Of course they have other questions: What does climate change mean for me? What can I do about it? Is it human caused? How much do scientists really understand? But at the end of the day, 70 percent of people understand it's happening. And for the younger generation, there's no convincing needed. There's no need to show that climate change is happening. They are leading the charge for climate action. Whereas some of the older generations still have questions about the fundamentals. Different types of data will move generations differently because their interests and concerns diverge.

When did that shift toward public acceptance of climate change happen?

In my eleven years at Climate Central, public acceptance of climate change has transitioned dramatically. The "Global Warming's Six Americas" research by the Yale Program on Climate Change Communication and George Mason University's Center for Climate Change Communication has shown us this in their survey data. On the political right, there are of course those we're never going to reach. They're really anchored in conspiracy theories and have an outsized voice. But about 60 percent of the population is either alarmed or concerned.

So there's been a dramatic shift in that understanding. Still, what can we do about it?

There's a lot that we can do. There are a range of mature climate solutions already in place such as renewable energy, home energy efficiencies, electrifying transportation, implementing climate-friendly farming practices, and more. Plus, communication is a key climate solution, and all of us have the ability to start a climate conversation. This is where I come back to weather. Weather is a way for us to advance climate understanding and solutions. There's a huge opportunity here in visualization, communication, and data. We need to help people see a cleaner, healthier, and more sustainable future.

One of the things we've been working on at Climate Central is attribution science. This is when scientists can dissect the impact of climate change within individual weather events. The science has advanced so rapidly that we can now quantify the role of climate change within daily temperatures through our Climate Shift Index. For instance, on that random November day in New York City where it's seventy degrees, or in Kansas City in February when the temperature spikes to seventy-five degrees, with data we can answer the question: Is this normal? Not only is it abnormal, but these events have that climate fingerprint.

How optimistic are you?

I firmly believe we are on a path to change. The question comes down to speed, and that is a big conversation with climate change right now because we *are* making changes. We are doing big things. But we've waited so long, and the longer we wait, the more this becomes a cumulative problem and much harder to solve. It costs more money. It's already taking more lives. The transitions are harder. Had we done all this in the 1980s, it would be a lot easier and we could take a slower path, but we waited until the 2020s. So we need big changes quickly.

Data is

THE GROUNDING OF FACT WITH TRUTH

—BERNADETTE WOODS PLACKY—

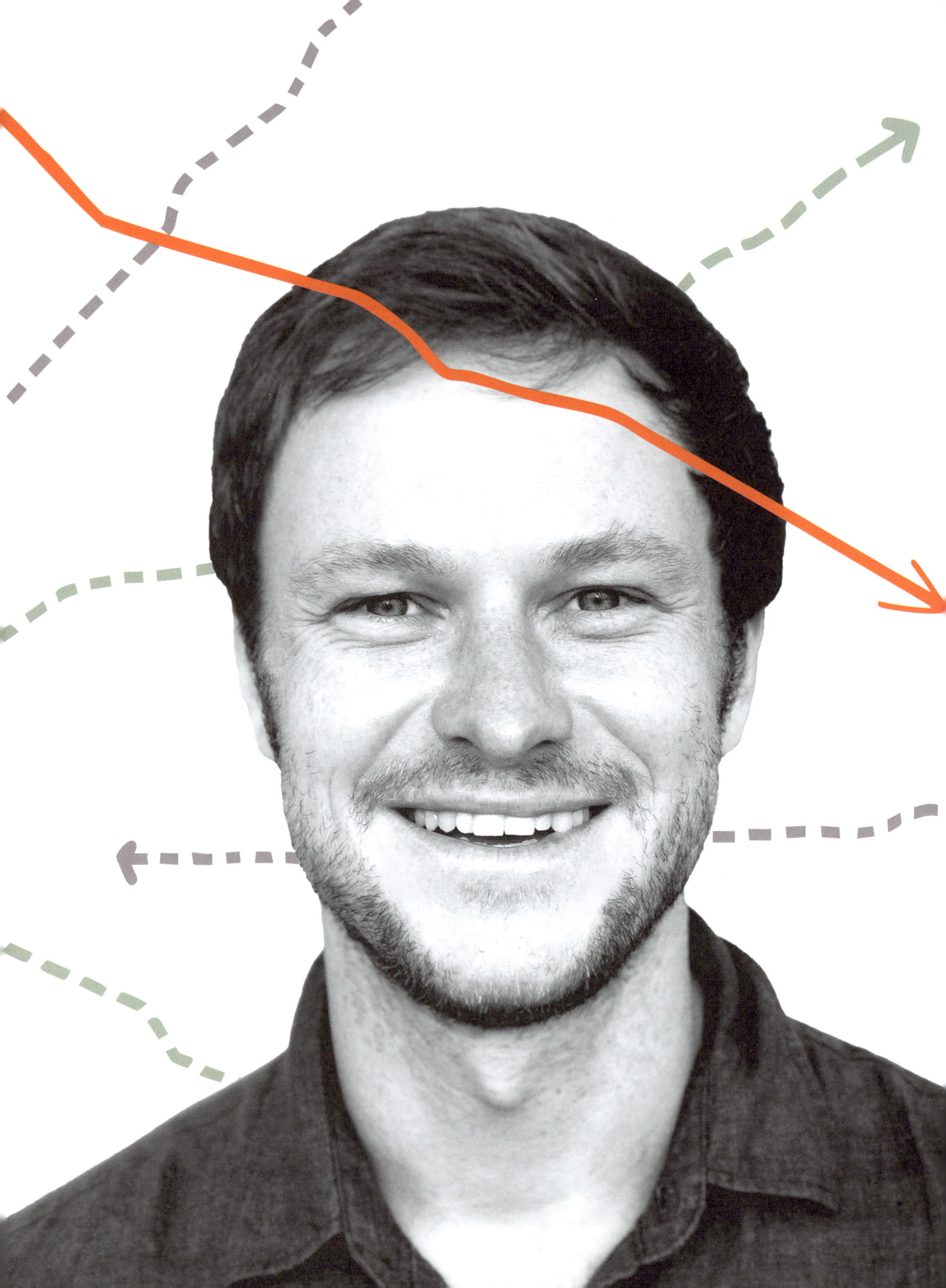

Max Roser

Max Roser is an unlikely public figure. An economist by training, Max was working as an academic researcher at the University of Oxford when, in 2011, he founded an unassuming website called Our World in Data—a place, as he put it, to collect data on "where the world stands today and what we know about how to change it." Since then, Our World in Data has flourished into a powerhouse media initiative and an indispensable resource for understanding the world's most pressing topics, from global development to human health, gender equality, population growth, and technological innovation. In addition to leading the Our World in Data team (now thirty strong), Max has written trenchantly about the course of human progress and the necessity for truly accessible data. In this conversation, he speaks about the origins of Our World in Data, pandemic misinformation, and how words can sometimes better explain data than numbers themselves.

We're huge fans of yours. What are you currently working on?

How do I put this? The news is full of all of these tragic stories, but at the same time it's missing what I've started to call the "everyday tragedies." They are the things that are so common, so normal, so part of what's happening every day, that our usual ways of learning about the world don't capture them. I think you need data to capture those everyday tragedies. Does that make sense?

It does. And it's fascinating. We're also interested in the mundane, the tiny details, the contexts and stories that are behind the data. Why do you think these so-called everyday tragedies get ignored?

Consider a topic like child mortality. The scale of it is so massive that I'm not quite blaming the news for not reporting on it. I think we just don't have the space in society to report on it. Globally, five and a half million children die every year. On average, sixteen thousand children die a day. If anything of that scale, of that magnitude, happened on one particular day, it wouldn't just be the news of the day—it would be the news of the year, right? If today there was some kind of event in which sixteen thousand children died, you would remember the day and year when that happened. Yet somehow, because these deaths are so common and so normal, they're in the background of everything else that we think about in the world. I don't know quite how the news could be different there. *The New York Times* can't open every paper with the headline, "Another sixteen thousand children are dead."

The pandemic is a good example of this. In the beginning, we had counters everywhere totaling how many people were infected, or how many people died. We don't have those anymore, but those deaths are still happening.

Exactly. I think we are very sensitive to things worsening, but we're neither sensitive to things improving nor sensitive to things that are just plain bad. Both of these aspects you can only really see through the data. I think improvements are, in a way, perhaps the hardest to see because you need to monitor something that's bad to notice the absence of it. Data is the way to make the absence of something bad visible, to see the declining trends. But I think a similar thing is also true about things that are just bad, like how COVID-19 is still bad.

But it's not all bad, right? You have talked about how looking at data over a longer time span helps us see a lot of improvements. You once observed, "I used to be a pessimist, but the data shows the world improving."[1] Yet despite your work and the work of many other practitioners showing quantitative proof of things getting better, I think the overall perception is still that the world is falling apart. Why do you think that those positive numbers, the ones that show things improving, are not convincing?

One reason is that when we point out that something is improving, we always feel this tension of wanting to also acknowledge that we are still facing problems. Pointing out that we see improvements can feel like we don't care about the problems that still exist. I think that's a very understandable struggle.

Another factor is that often the data is lacking or not available to most people. With many of the things where we see big improvements, the data is not there, or it's in the hands of researchers who bury it in the appendix of some PDF. That's very much the angle that we are taking at Our World in Data—we're trying to bring data out of spreadsheets and visualize it, make it accessible for everyone.

Overall, it's also true that the media isn't exactly helping. We know that we have all of these cognitive biases that put a lot of emphasis and attention on what's worsening, as we just said. If we want an accurate understanding of how the world is changing, we need to actively take this into account and work against it to some extent. And I think the news media isn't doing the best job in countering our biases.

This feels like a good place to ask how Our World in Data started. What problem did you want to solve?

It started when I realized how wrong I was about very fundamental developments in the world. I studied philosophy and geoscience. Geoscience is a lot about the environment and the climate, so people there have a reason to be pessimistic. Philosophy, especially in Germany, where I am from, has always been quite pessimistic, viewing the world as in decline since the ancient Greeks. Then I went to an economic history lecture and saw data on the decline in global poverty, and I just didn't believe it. I just didn't believe that this could be true. That was probably the biggest moment.

Over the following years, I tried to read more economic history, more social history, and get a more quantitative understanding of how the world has developed over the last centuries. I realized how negative—and just wrong—my view had been. I collected a lot of data for a book that I never ended up writing, and instead made all the data accessible so that others could build on it.

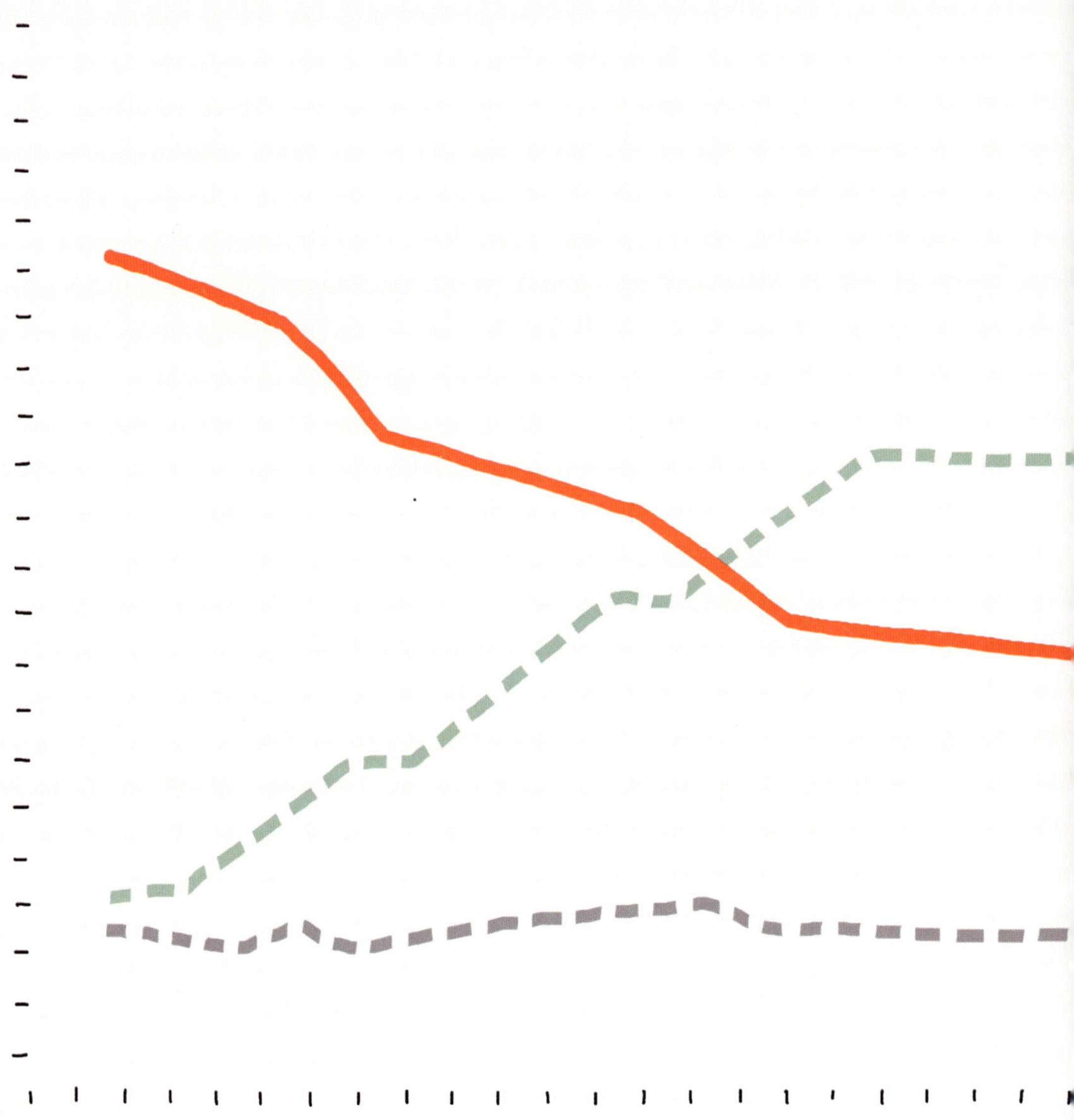

“WE ARE VERY SENSITIVE TO THINGS WORSENING, BUT WE'RE NEITHER SENSITIVE TO THINGS IMPROVING, NOR SENSITIVE TO THINGS THAT ARE JUST PLAIN BAD. BOTH OF THESE ASPECTS YOU CAN ONLY REALLY SEE THROUGH THE DATA.

— MAX ROSER

Our World in Data is very much a source of quantitative information. It's like an encyclopedia for it. But there's also lots of explanation of the data for readers. How did that approach evolve?

Overall, there's this separation between a quantitative look at the world and a qualitative look, and that comes down to the tools people are using to do their work. In a lot of quantitative work, you get stuck in spreadsheets very quickly, and you only make use of the data that is right there in the spreadsheet. But good quantitative work means trying to understand what the data in that spreadsheet is about, what exactly it measures, what caveats the reader needs to be aware of regarding how it was collected or for what purpose it was collected. But because our tools are so separate, whether you're in a spreadsheet or using pen and paper or a text editor, it's hard to bring them together.

So a lot of effort in recent years at Our World in Data is to tie writing to data. We internally call it technical text. It's basically the textual information that the reader needs to make sense of the data in the spreadsheets. In the future, Our World in Data should work in a way that whenever you see some data displayed, all of this textual information about how this data came to be and what you need to be aware of is displayed right there as well. So the separation between writing and spreadsheet is torn down.

During the pandemic, Our World in Data became such an important resource. You were publishing explanations about what COVID-19 data meant and how to interpret it in a moment when we sorely needed clarity. How did the pandemic shift your strategy?

I have lots to say about this. During the pandemic, we often had this situation where an original publisher of some data was making a huge effort to explain what kinds of shortcomings accompanied it. Yet once that data ended up in a newspaper, in some pie chart or bar chart or web graphic, all of that crucial context was stripped away and readers were potentially left with a really wrong idea. Even now: I just went to *The Guardian*'s website, and they have a COVID-19 tracker that's still active. It starts with the question, "Which countries are currently being hit the hardest?" And then it shows a world map of the highest case rates. And that's just wrong! It's awful misinformation. I've written to them, but they haven't changed it.

It's wrong because they are suggesting that the countries that report the highest number of cases are the countries that are being hit the hardest. And that's obviously not true because it's not the rate of cases—it's the rate of *confirmed* cases, and since rich countries do more tests than poor countries, this map falsely suggests that rich countries are being hit the hardest.

Such mistakes have been really harmful, especially in the conversation around vaccines. You had all of these maps floating around in which Africa was green or some light-shaded color, and the dark red was reserved for the rich countries of the world. For someone who looks at these maps, it's understandable that they might come away with the idea that it's not a problem for poor countries to not have access to vaccines. This situation has been common, and really tragic.

Data is power, and the service you provided during the pandemic was a public help. One could say that this is what the government should have been doing, at least in the United States. At the same time, no one asked you to do this. It's just something that you just decided to do. In a perfect world, do you think Our World in Data should even exist?

No, it shouldn't be us who do this work. During the pandemic, it was always my expectation that, at some point, we wouldn't be responsible for this work anymore. When we began tracking COVID-19 data, we started a bit reluctantly, thinking that surely the relevant health organizations were going to take over. And then we found ourselves in this position where suddenly everyone was relying on us. We fully expected that some institution with the mandate to do this work would come and pick it up from us and then we could end it. But that didn't happen. So, no, I really don't think it should be us.

You were talking about how missing data and uncertainty is not rendered in datasets. We've been struggling with this a lot. There are some countries that still test and have free PCRs, or there's different mechanisms to report positive cases, or different restrictions, or COVID-19 is treated differently. Yet, all that being true, we still plot data on a map as if that context didn't exist, and as if missing data is not part of the picture. We think that missing data is as important as a data point. And rendering the uncertainty of a chart is as important as rendering what's certain. It's hard for the public, though, to trust data if we admit to how much we don't know. It's an ever-present tension, right?

For sure. It's the key tension to navigate. And it's difficult because the audiences are so different. Sometimes you have people who believe everything that is printed in a chart and take any chart as a perspective from God. That it's just the pure truth. Then you have people who don't believe any data, ever. The challenge is to find that middle ground where, even in the best cases, the data is imperfect and wrong in some sense but still more helpful than anything else we've got to understand the world.

What's your personal definition of data?

Wow. I've never thought about the definition of data. I think it's something like—structured information about something that matters?

That's a good one.

I'll probably regret this after we hang up.

It should be said that the data visualizations you produce at Our World in Data are marvels of simplicity and intuitiveness. You're also always very clear about where you're getting your source material and how you're analyzing it. I wish other media outlets would take a similar approach.

A big guiding principle of ours is to keep it simple. If a line chart does it, then it's a line chart. If a bar chart does it, then it's a bar chart.

Social media has helped, I think, improve the design. You can quickly share your work online, for instance, and see what people understand or don't understand, what kinds of questions they come back with, what kinds of wrong conclusions they're taking from a chart. It's fast to iterate. That was a big change.

Most importantly, and I try to get this across to everyone on the team: We're standing on the shoulders of others. We're a platform for others to present the data that's out there. We shouldn't understand our work as beginning with us and ending with us. We're always trying to see our work as a place to build on and from. So we make it easy for people to pull our data into their tools, or to explore the data on our site and visualize it in the ways they want to.

NOTES

1 "Max Roser," University of Oxford, https://www.ox.ac.uk/research/research-in-conversation/our-place-world/max-roser.

Data is

STRUCTURED
INFORMATION ABOUT
SOMETHING THAT
MATTERS

—MAX ROSER—

3

Vital Signs: Data and Health

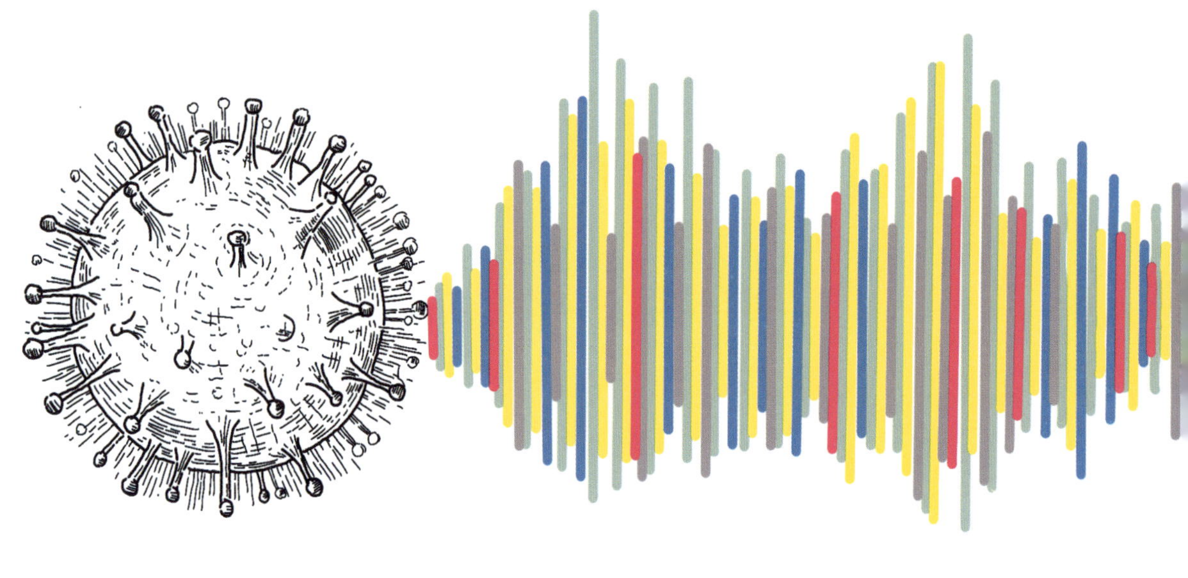

2020 2021 2022 2023 2024

Vital Signs

As data obsessives, we would be the first to admit that we have an unusually intimate relationship with quantification. For us, data is both a professional pursuit and a personal passion—the frame, filter, and language through which we understand the world. It's a creative material with which we express ourselves. And when life is confusing, or scary, we tend to turn to data for answers. It never let us down.

That is, until the COVID-19 pandemic. Until I, Giorgia, got long COVID.

In total, long COVID robbed me of more than three years of happy, healthy life. While today my health is much improved, my diagnosis continues to affect me in profound ways. And it has fundamentally changed my relationship with data. When I think back to a few years ago, my mind fills with memories of fear and agony. Sensations of dizziness and nausea were my almost daily reality. Pain constantly pulsed through my body, and my limbs felt simultaneously as heavy as concrete and weak as jelly. It was as if a machine were squeezing my skull, and extreme exhaustion often overtook me.

In no way were these symptoms just a lingering cough, or a few weeks of fatigue after an acute infection. They were so serious that at times I was completely bedbound, an unwilling prisoner in my own unruly body.

Long COVID is a chronic illness that, as of this writing, has affected an estimated seventeen million people in the United States.[1] Despite its deceptive name, this mysterious condition is not just one disease, but multiple afflictions that attack various parts of the body, including the respiratory, circulatory, and nervous systems. This makes the illness particularly difficult to identify and treat. For reasons not yet understood, long COVID affects women and Latinx people disproportionately, as well as those with underlying health conditions.

I, Giorgia, first got COVID-19 in March 2020, just as New York was going into lockdown. My case was mild, and I was not hospitalized. Like many who got sick in those early days, I experienced what felt like a bad flu. But a few weeks after I seemed to recover, strange symptoms emerged: extreme fatigue, frequent low-grade fevers, general temperature dysregulation, chills, heart palpitations, brain fog, burning sensations all over my body, and more. And my symptoms persisted.

In December 2021, I got COVID-19 again. Excruciating nerve pain began to radiate up and down my side. I visited more doctors and took more tests without getting any answers. I was awash in data, but meaning was elusive. I tried more than a dozen medications, injections, and physical therapies, but this new pain never went away. My doctors were confused when I wanted them to be alarmed. After more inconclusive results, they told me that I was probably just stressed and should take a break from work. Or I should try to push through and exercise. Or maybe I should start antianxiety meds.

Then, after a third infection, my symptoms became entirely debilitating. Unrelenting chest tightness and tachycardia, dizziness while being upright, frequent nausea and headaches, systemic reactions to most foods, tinnitus, severe insomnia, a persistent feeling of being poisoned, blurry and double vision, and exhaustion relegated me to bed with the lights off for days at a time.

I'm not a medical expert, but I had to become one to try to figure out what was happening to me. And as I've done so many times before, I turned to data: the tool I've always had to help me cope with life when I am afraid, confused, and looking for answers. I started logging all of my symptoms. I tracked everything in an enormous spreadsheet: my symptoms' intensity, whether they came on suddenly or gradually, when new symptoms appeared, the medications and supplements I was taking, the treatments I was trying, what I did that day, if I felt stressed, what I ate and drank, and scores of biometrics from my newly purchased smartwatch. Days on my data canvas became thick with color: red for bad, green for good. Most months, there was far more red than green.

No matter how much data I collected or how many correlations I tried to draw, answers eluded me. At the same time, the act of tracking my data brought its own perverse pleasure. I assiduously kept the spreadsheet updated, noting with as much precision as possible every twinge of pain, every haze of brain fog. My spreadsheet was the only thing I could control in a life I no longer recognized. I thought that if I collected enough data, I would eventually figure out what was wrong with me. In a sea of uncertainty, it was the life raft I clung to in hopes of finally returning to my predictable, knowable life.

But still, I was sinking. And dry land was nowhere in sight.

In a moment of extreme desperation, I started to question whether the data I was collecting was still serving me. Was something that had given me a semblance of control in these years of uncertainty actually becoming my enemy? In that moment of extreme desperation, I decided to shift focus. I started a new data collection, this time populated with qualitative and quantitative information focused not on the bad, but on the good. Instead of tracking my pain and symptoms, I started to track my progress: when I was able to climb stairs, take a walk around the block, or sleep through the night. As I got better, my logs became longer and more specific. I noted when I was able to go out to dinner with my boyfriend without feeling adverse effects the morning after, or hang out with my friends and feel at home in my body. Finally, I also retired my smartwatch—a device that, truthfully, was giving me more alarming than encouraging news. I stopped logging symptoms, and therefore no longer gave them constant attention.

At first, this new approach felt scary. Monitoring my body every day had given me a semblance of control. Now I felt naked and unprotected by the statistical biometrics that had for so long described and defined me as a living, breathing human being. Yet through it all, I've realized that changing how I look at things also changes how things look. I'm no longer paying constant attention to my symptoms. It doesn't mean that the symptoms have gone away; far from it. I just refuse to give them the same priority in the mental picture I paint of myself.

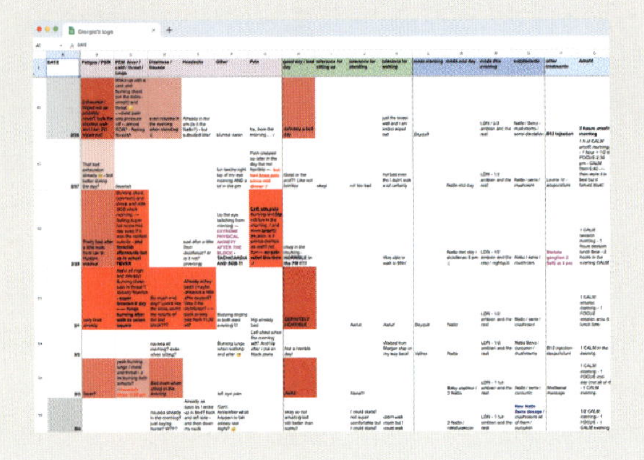

↑
In 2024, Giorgia's story of long COVID was published in *The New York Times* as a print and digital guest op-ed titled "1,374 Days: My Life with Long COVID"

↑
The spreadsheet Giorgia used to track her symptoms

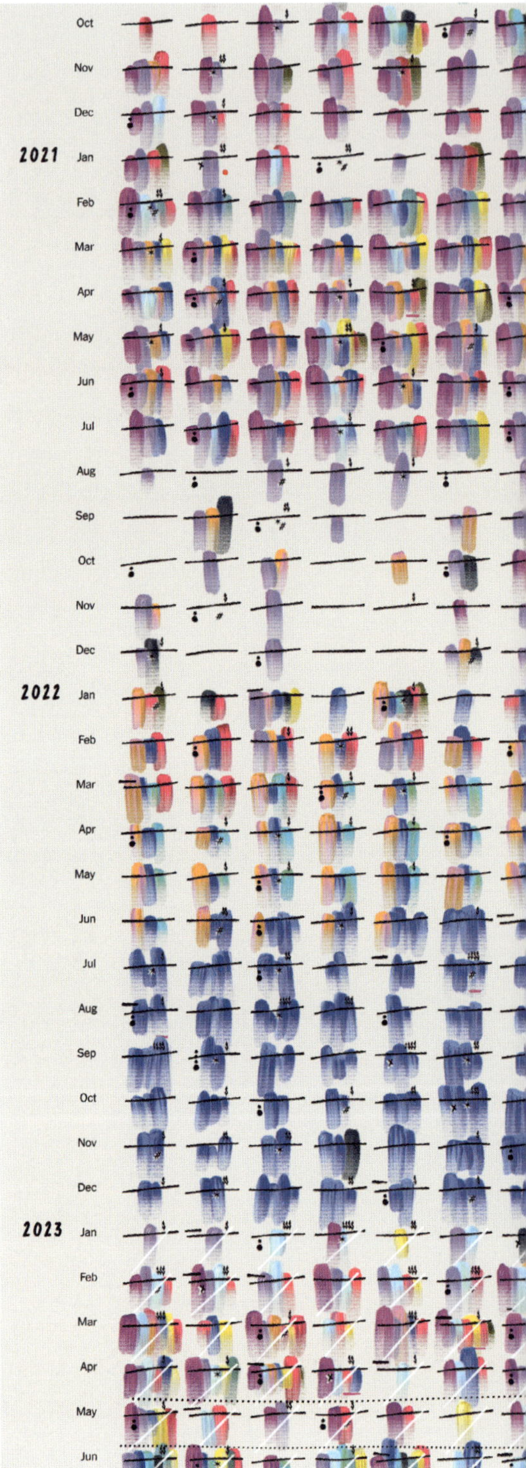

↑
A visual representation of Giorgia's long COVID symptom tracking

To be clear: We're not suggesting this approach can "cure" long COVID, or even worse, that these illnesses are just "in people's heads." Positive thinking cannot cure chronic illness. Today Giorgia is doing much better thanks to a combination of medical treatments and alternative therapies undertaken in close consultation with her doctors. But this new dataset, the one *she* decided to give attention to every day, reshaped the way she saw her personal health journey. It's also taught us both something fundamental about life and data. The world is made of data—not just the data we produce with our phones or our credit cards, but the data we decide to direct our attention to at any given moment. It's important to acknowledge that we do have a choice regarding which data to collect, which data to store, which data to present, and how.

As Giorgia's journey takes her further into the complex landscape of health care, it's clear to both of us that data can be both a tool of clarity and a source of confusion. How we choose to measure our health—and which metrics we prioritize—can significantly influence not only the treatment we receive, but also our perception of well-being. The decisions we make about data collection and interpretation hold profound consequences for patients, practitioners, and policymakers alike.

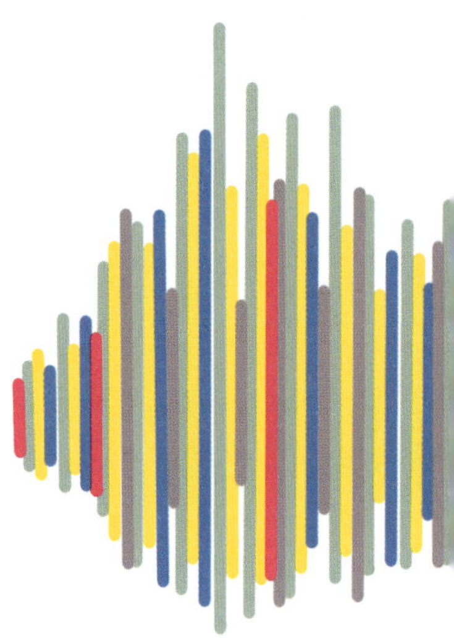

NOTES

1 Alice Burns, "As Recommendations for Isolation End, How Common Is Long COVID?," *KFF*, https://www.kff.org/coronavirus-covid-19/issue-brief/as-recommendations-for-isolation-end-how-common-is-long-covid/.

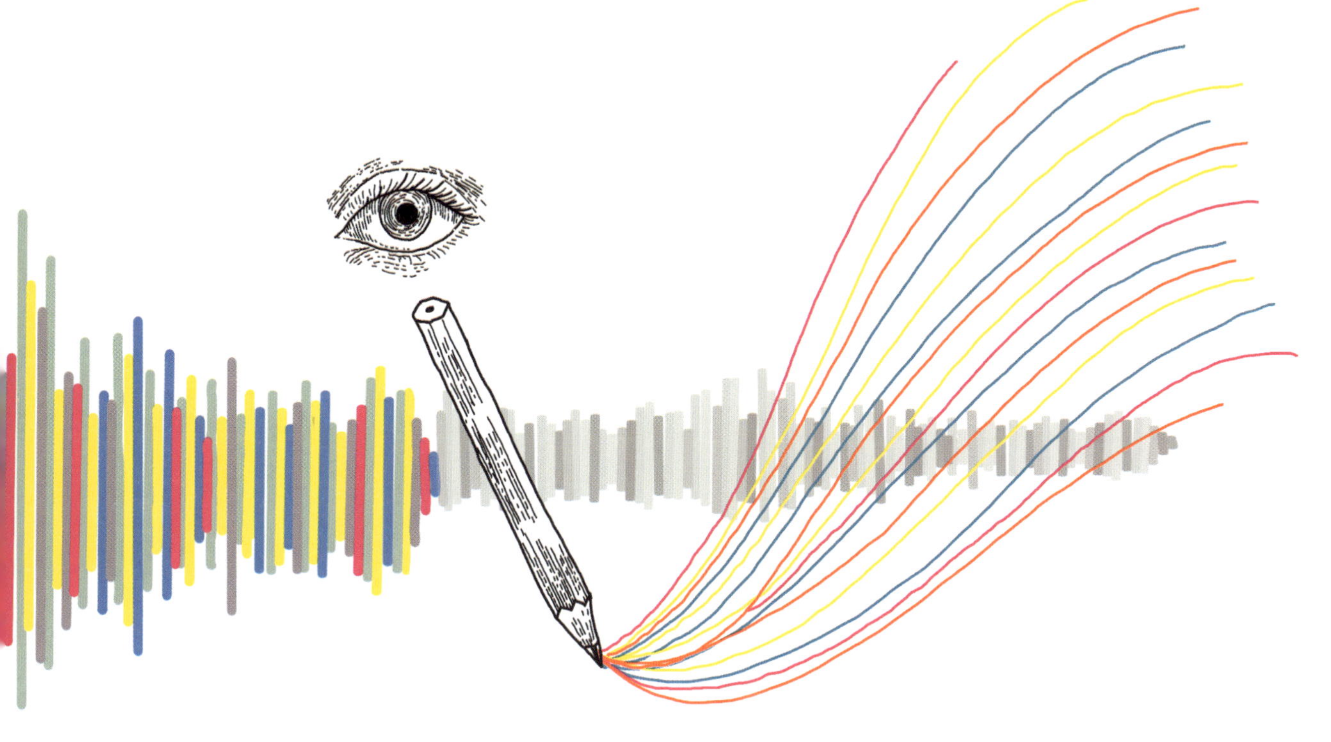
2022
2023
2024
2025

PhD
Innovation

David Putrino

David Putrino is a decorated academic with a PhD in neuroscience who marshals interdisciplinary research to tackle some of the big medical mysteries of our time, from depression to Parkinson's disease. His mission is simple: "Use technology to save lives." That usually means using data too, and lots of it. More recently, David and his lab have also turned to investigating mysterious but debilitating chronic diseases, including long COVID. In this conversation, David explains how he came to this work; how he thinks about patient data versus patient experience; and getting comfortable with the uncomfortable.

Your background is unique. You're not a typical physician or researcher. How did you get into this work?

My title at Mount Sinai is director of rehabilitation innovation. My clinical training is as a physiotherapist. Initially, I was interested in helping people recover from neurological injuries. I worked a lot with stroke and spinal cord injuries. I also—interestingly, weirdly—got pulled into sports performance. I was training the adult nervous system to change, which is actually very hard. Whether you're dealing with a stroke victim or an elite performer, training that nervous-system change requires similar strategies and similar uses of technology. I did my PhD in experimental neuroscience, trying to understand how the brain controls movement.

I'm interested in disruptive innovation. When I started at Mount Sinai, my pitch to my new employers was that I was going to partner with industry, partner with people who have ideas that I think deserve the main stage right now. I'm going to run rapid, pragmatic clinical trials for them, and then we're going to adopt the technologies that we prove work. To take an idea from bench to bedside in the medical world takes, in the United States, an average of seventeen years. And I think that number is just ridiculous. It should be much smaller. So I've created a division within our department that does nothing other than try to get new treatments to patients as quickly as possible.

We've grown from one small center to five centers across three different hospitals in the Mount Sinai Health System. We've brought in more than $30 million in funding. And we continue to grow. If we see a good idea, we get that good idea into the hands of patients as quickly as we can. We don't want patients to be told that there's nothing more that we can do. Even if we have a patient who is not responding to an array of therapies, we're never out of ideas. We've always got two or three more things that we can try.

On the clinical side, we've always got an answer for them: This is what we'll try next, or this is the next thing we're going to test for. On the research side, we collect data in a large registry. We rarely run highly controlled RCTs [random clinical trials] because for the most part, even though we're told that RCTs are the gold standard for doing things, they rarely provide actionable information. What they usually do is say, hey, when you control for every element that makes something useful, yes, you might get a little bit of signal here and things might improve. But what I want to know is: For the three hundred stroke patients who come through my clinic in a year, if I give this to everyone, what percentage are going to respond? I believe a lot of mono-therapeutic approaches are designed by people who want to sell you one drug to solve your one problem. Unfortunately, biology is more complicated than that.

How did you get interested in long COVID?

Our interest in long COVID arose out of necessity. Our lab was well poised in March 2020 when things hit the fan here in New York. We had a lot of technology that we knew could help patients, so we immediately put it to use. For instance, we had an app called Precision Recovery. We were using it specifically for stroke survivors: After they were discharged from the hospital, we would check their blood pressure, make sure they were doing okay. So when COVID hit, we quickly made the decision to reprogram our app to start asking questions about respiratory symptoms and risk of respiratory failure. We started deploying it to thousands of people in New York who were symptomatic with COVID and concerned that they might end up dying of their symptoms. We onboarded our first patient on March 15, 2020. Soon we had about seven thousand people on the platform.

Those numbers just kept growing. By about late April, we started to notice that 10 to 15 percent of the acute people we were monitoring weren't getting better. They kept reporting symptoms, but the symptoms started to change. Now they were talking about fatigue. Cognitive impairment. Many other symptoms. All that stuff now seems commonplace, but these people were reporting it before we had a name for it. It wasn't an identifiable disease, it was just a collection of symptoms—but a collection of symptoms that were highly consistent across hundreds of individuals. And they weren't going away. So as we started seeing them, we started listening. As we listened to symptom presentation, we built this structure. Fatigue: What questionnaire can we use to measure fatigue? What can we use to measure post-exertional malaise, or PEM? So that was initially how we started measuring long COVID and its severity. We listened.

I get suspicious whenever I hear someone say that they've "cured" long COVID because we know that long COVID is not just one thing. It's many things. We know that in all complex chronic illness is this big mess of things going wrong with the body all at once. So we've started this very multidisciplinary approach. We collect a lot of data because we need to be systematic in coming up with the highest-priority treatments. And then as treatments either succeed or fail, we go down the line of what needs to change.

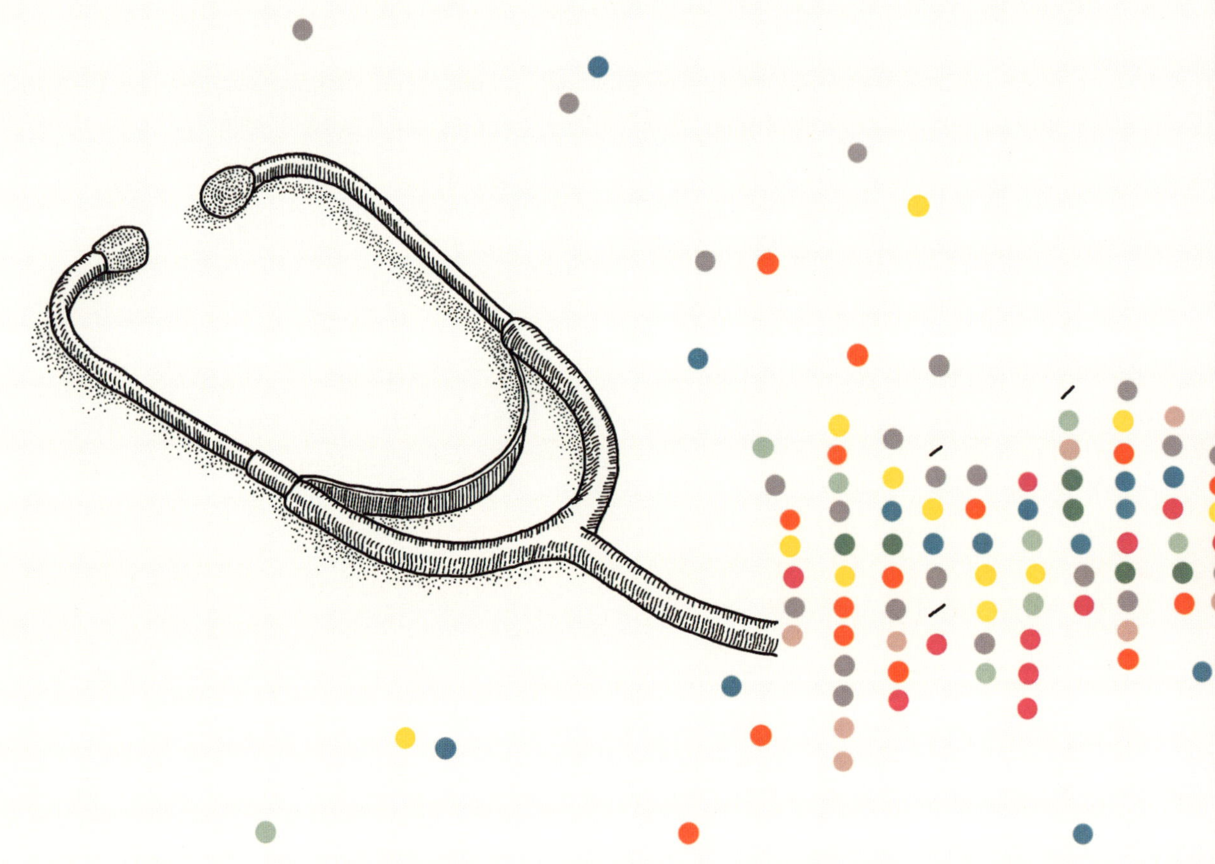

“If you don't listen, you harm. Listening to our patients and deriving as much structured qualitative data as we can is super important.

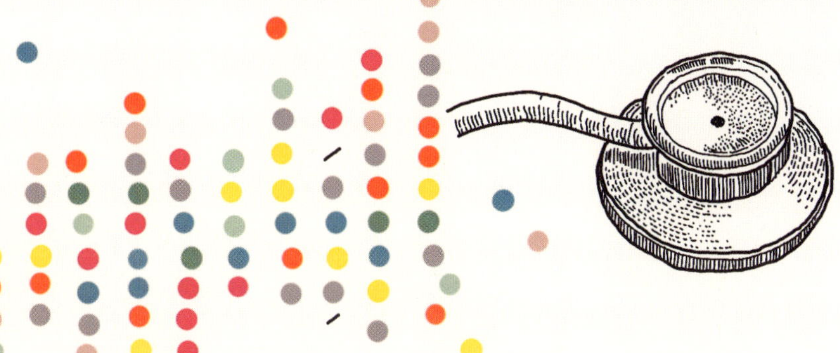

— David Putrino

There are always measurable aspects of human health, but also more subjective and personal perceptions. How do you balance the data from tests you perform on a patient with the more anecdotal data that a patient shares with you?

It's an important question. A large portion of the data we collect is objective biological data. But another large portion comes from formally designed patient-reported outcomes. And we definitely need both. But right now in our clinic, we often rely more on the patient-reported outcomes than we do on biological data because many of the complex conditions we're seeing are poorly characterized. Meaning, we don't know what the "right" biology should look like.

For instance, look at human performance in athletes. When I'm working with an elite female athlete and I look at the existing literature on how to optimize female athlete performance, the textbooks look like they were written in the Dark Ages. They literally say things like, "When a woman is on her period, she shouldn't run because she's going to be irrational and her performance will dip." And it's just like—oh my god! So some of the work that we're doing is daily hormone monitoring to understand how hormones of menstruation and ovulation affect performance output or muscle strength, because work of this nature is rare, and we have few guidelines. In the short term, if you're a responsive performance professional, you listen to what your athlete is saying. And if an athlete says, "I'm not lifting my best today," we can say, "Yes, that's because your progesterone is peaking and you're going to have issues with resistance training." But right now, we can only really listen to what they're telling us and guide appropriately. If you don't listen, you harm. Listening to our patients and deriving as much structured qualitative data as we can is super important.

What is your definition of data, if you have one? Or how would you explain what data is?

I would explain data as any piece of information—whether it comes from personal communications, questionnaires, or biological testing—that you can use to form or reinforce an opinion or guide an act.

It makes me think: We had a conversation just the other day with the US Food and Drug Administration for our brain-computer interface trial. We're studying whether people with severe paralysis can receive a minimally invasive implant to allow them to communicate and perform computer-based tasks at home. The majority of the patients who are enrolled in the trial have end-stage ALS. They're completely locked in with their illness. They're ventilated. They have minimal eye movement. And yet the majority of them actually have pretty good quality of life on the quality-of-life scale because they've got their family around them. They've got their needs met. They've cognitively and psychologically adjusted to their illness. And so they're kind of just living their lives and they still have joy. One of the guys loves tasting scotch. They put a little bit of scotch on a sponge and sponge it around his mouth and he loves that. His quality of life is sky-high.

The main questionnaire that the FDA was interested in to show patient benefit was a quality-of-life scale. We advised the FDA that we felt it would be an ableist approach to just assume that these folks currently have terrible quality of life. If you implant them, yes, their quality of life is going to soar—but that doesn't mean they don't have a good quality of life now. So the FDA listened, and is looking to develop a new questionnaire that will evaluate these things more holistically. We always need to be recalibrating the ways in which we collect data from patients as we learn about how we have marginalized and biased ourselves against the patient population. We need to update the questions we're asking and our understanding of what's important.

Is it a catch-22, though? You keep collecting data to be able to then collect better data, but then those new data are not always comparable to the data you collected before. So you don't have long-term, solid, comparable data. But maybe that's just part of the process of innovating? We'd never do anything disruptive if we only did incremental little things. This applies for all types of data collection, right?

Absolutely. I'm not against incremental discovery or incremental innovation. I just don't think it's the only thing we should be funding, because while we're waiting on that incremental discovery, we're missing disruptive discoveries that could really improve quality of life for patients.

In my lab, you need to be comfortable with discomfort, because we're never doing the same thing for too long. We're always changing. It maybe sounds silly, but it's something we need to tell people in the academic and clinical worlds, because most academics and most clinicians want the algorithm, the protocol, the step-by-step. We're always churning over, working out what works and what doesn't, and collecting new data.

Data is

ANY PIECE OF INFORMATION THAT YOU CAN USE TO FORM OR REINFORCE AN OPINION

—DAVID PUTRINO—

Bon Ku

Bon Ku is a physician, public health researcher, and design strategist working to reimagine what health and health care can be. The coauthor, with Ellen Lupton, of Health Design Thinking: Creating Products and Services for Better Health, *Bon is a leading proponent of a more humane, patient-centered health care system. Today a program manager for Resilient Systems at the Advanced Research Projects Agency for Health, he previously led Thomas Jefferson University's Health Design Lab, a uniquely interdisciplinary think tank exploring newly inclusive paradigms for the patient experience. In this conversation, Bon discusses the role of empathy in medicine; what doctors can learn from architects; and whether data is truly destiny.*

You recently made a career change. How's it going?

Yes, I left a career in academia. I previously ran something called the Health Design Lab at Thomas Jefferson University, but I've just joined a new government agency called the Advanced Research Projects Agency for Health, or ARPA-H. It's modeled after DARPA, the Defense Advanced Research Projects Agency, which developed everything from stealth technology to Siri on your iPhone. DARPA makes investments in new technologies, and because they're willing to fail on some of them, it's an effective model to explore innovation. We at ARPA-H are applying that same methodology to health care. We're guided by the principle of prototyping quickly, and thinking of future solutions that don't currently exist but could really expand our imaginations. I think my background in design suits me well for the work we're doing.

It sounds very, very exciting. It's hard for people to think about health and design together, but you've used this as a prototype for how hospitals can work better, for instance.

I'm interested in the intersection of design and health care. As a physician, I'm trained in the scientific method. But humans are messy, and sometimes the scientific method alone cannot provide the best solutions. I was attracted to design for its ability to apply a creative mindset, and to couple that with a scientific method when thinking about human health. I argue to physicians and other clinicians that the skill set of creativity is fundamentally important to healing people. But many physicians don't think that way. We think of those with a "creative mindset" as designers or maybe architects or musicians. But applying design principles can open up our imaginations to explore future possibilities that otherwise would not have been available to us.

What would be an example?

One of my favorite research collaborations was with an architecture firm called KieranTimberlake. They're based in Philadelphia, and they have a research division. I was interested in them because we have this problem with overcrowding in emergency departments. As you can imagine, emergency rooms are chaotic environments. They're open 24-7. Overcrowding is rampant. Patients might wait three, six, nine, twelve hours to see a doctor. There are constant interruptions. Even violence can occur.

I wondered what we could do to design a better emergency department. So I reached out to KieranTimberlake to see if we could apply their mapping methods to a hospital setting to understand how patients, clinicians, and nurses interact in time and space. I have no training in this at all! But they do.

We started off with a research prototype. We had research assistants use pen and paper to track a physician's movements in time and space over an eight-hour shift throughout the emergency department floor plan. Eventually that led us to publish research exploring questions like: Does the specific layout of the emergency department impact the volume of interactions among staff? We would never have gotten there if it weren't for this new type of research and collaboration that is normally not done in health care. It was a fascinating exploration into a whole new research area, and it happened because of our willingness to go beyond our domain expertise.

You also have a major focus on the patient experience.

What I appreciate about seeing patients in the emergency department and taking care of them is that they're like health data personified in a human. When I look at public health studies and especially mortality statistics, it's abstracted. You know, just numbers and tables. But when I practice in the emergency department and see a Philadelphian who was shot and have to take care of them, that data becomes real. It's manifested in humans. So even though I'm dealing with a sample size of one, my interaction with a human at bedside gives me a lot more empathy than when I look at datasets.

I think if I were just a data scientist without interacting with humans, I would not have as much passion to scale interventions to help underserved populations in our country. A lot of the work I have done over my career is with underserved populations because I see them every time I work a clinical shift. When I treat a person with unstable housing, someone with substance use disorder, someone who is a victim of gun violence—if I were just a researcher working with those datasets, I don't think I would be as motivated to spend a lifetime working with these populations and dedicate my career to them. Some people are a lot more empathetic. But I'm not that empathetic of a guy. But if I see the human who is represented in that dataset, that to me is motivating.

Is data destiny? Or, said another way: How much can you predict about a patient by their data—their biometrics, their presenting symptoms, even the zip code they live in?

It depends. For instance, one thing I'm working on now is improving access to high-quality care for rural Americans. There are about sixty million people living in rural areas, and in almost every disease category, they have worse health outcomes. They die at an earlier age. They have to travel long distances to get care. There's many disparities there. My work as a clinician and, you know, seeing inequities show up in the emergency department has shown me that certain populations have worse outcomes just because of their zip code. Generally, if you live in a poor zip code, you're going to have worse health outcomes.

That has inspired me to do stuff at scale through ARPA-H because we have the ability to impact millions of lives. Again, I don't geek out about datasets. When you just look at numbers and read about statistics, it's easy to be very detached from them, right? But because I see the end results of inequities in our system manifested in patients showing up in the emergency room, that motivates me to design interventions at scale.

As you said before, humans are messy and nuanced. Where have you seen "traditional" medicine overlook something important because of a purely quantitative, purely analytical, approach to data?

I've done some research on super-utilizers, which are patients who use hospitals excessively, like more than ten ER visits a year. In particular, there was one patient who had made almost a hundred ER visits in a year. This patient was an outlier. He had end-stage renal disease. If you just look at his emergency department utilization stats, you would label him as an abuser of the system. Based on the data, it's easy to make that conclusion because no one should be going to the emergency department that much.

Well, I got to know this patient. I actually made a home visit, which is a little bit weird to do as an emergency room doctor. But it allowed me to understand his environment and dig into the reasons why he showed up in the emergency department so much. He had an unstable housing situation. He had children, which was surprising to me. I'd assumed that he wasn't a father. But he actually had people who cared for him. He lived with his aunt at that time. And he had a lot of fear and anxiety. I think that's what drove him to go to the hospital—he felt that the hospital was the safest place for him. That helped remove some of my bias against this patient. It helped to humanize him.

I try to do that with every patient encounter because it's so easy, working in a stressful environment, to dehumanize patients. Being able to understand who he was as a human, to understand his fears and anxieties, gave me more empathy for him.

It doesn't help that the field of data visualization, in our opinion, is still very focused on communicating quantitative information. What you're talking about, the stuff that might be better at building empathy, is often left out. This is particularly true in the medical field.

In terms of data visualization, I think we're at version 1.0, and we've been stuck in a very outdated form. The data visualizations that I have seen in medical journals have not changed in over a hundred years. It's tables, bar charts, pie charts. That's why I am fascinated by ways that we might get to a version 2.0 of this and start to humanize the data.

I think one powerful example was when *The New York Times* published data visualizations of numbers of deaths during the pandemic. In fact, I have on my wall right here a clipping of one of those front-page articles as a reminder of the deaths caused by COVID-19. Those representations of the data triggered emotions for me in a way that what I read in a medical journal cannot. So I think there are ways. I think the work that you do is a powerful example of that—meaning, how we can represent data visually to trigger an emotion. Often, data is very scientific, and it's easy to divorce yourself from these sometimes terrible statistics we see.

COVID-19 changed our understanding of data. How did it affect your thinking?

I have a lot of thoughts on this. One is that we saw the rampant misrepresentation and misinterpretation of data. Yes, it was great that the general public got familiar with public health data, but most of the general public has not taken a class in epidemiology. I appreciated that it's very easy to misrepresent data. But when we think about new ways to represent data, we also need to think about how important it is to do so in a rigorous, scientific way and to educate the public about it. It's so easy to put wrong information out there on the internet and people think it's true. If we're putting more data out there, how do we also give people the tools to validate that data? We also need to think about how we collect the data, which can have its own bias. Which data do we collect? Many people assume that data is neutral, but it's not. We all bring our biases into which data we collect, and especially thinking about machine learning and AI algorithms and generative AI, I think this is going to be the greatest challenge of our time. How can we design an equitable and fair algorithm? That's going to be determined by the ethics of how we collect data.

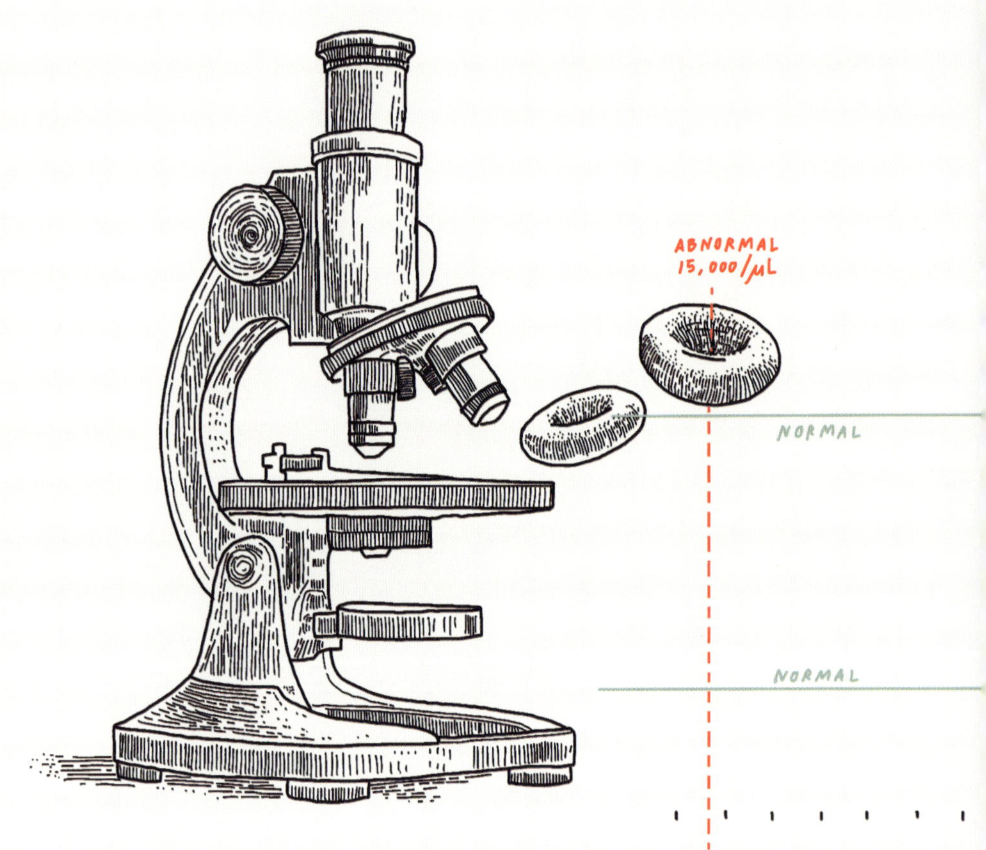
ABNORMAL
15,000/μL
NORMAL
NORMAL

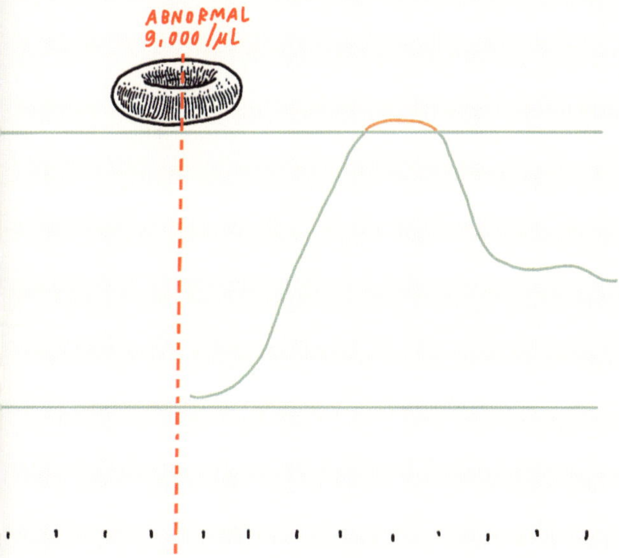

“IN MEDICINE, WE LABEL DATA AS NORMAL OR ABNORMAL. IT'S VERY BINARY. BUT AS YOU KNOW, DATA IS CONTINUOUS. ALSO, IN MEDICINE, WE OFTEN ONLY GET SPOT CHECKS OF DATA. SO INSTEAD OF MEASURING YOUR WHITE BLOOD CELL COUNT ONLY ONCE, WHAT IF WE WERE TO MEASURE IT OVER A WEEK, OVER A MONTH? THAT WOULD GIVE A FAR MORE ACCURATE REPRESENTATION THAN A SPOT CHECK.

— BON KU

Moving forward, how should we define data?

Oh my gosh, this is a hard question. I don't know! I'm going to riff here as a physician and a researcher. Data are a representation of patients—but not a complete representation. It allows us to quickly make generalizations about larger populations. I guess that's one of the benefits of being able to abstract information from patients in an incomplete way. There are benefits to that, to generate therapies and treat patients at a population level.

When a patient receives their lab test results and looks at those numbers, something strange can happen. For example, maybe a patient has always been on the very low end of a certain range of white blood cell count. They take a new test, and the result says their cell count is elevated, but still within the acceptable range. And the doctor says, "Well, you're still within the range. There's nothing to worry about." But the patient knows that this is an outlier for them! They are a unique individual with a journey and a history that is not being taken into account. It can be a very stiff and rigid way of measuring.

One hundred percent. In medicine, we label data as normal or abnormal. It's very binary. But as you know, data is continuous. Also, in medicine, we often only get spot checks of data. So instead of measuring your white blood cell count once, what if we were to measure it over a week, over a month? That would give a far more accurate representation than a spot check. Blood pressure is the same way. Patients will take their blood pressure at home and say, "Oh, it's so high. It was like 160." Then they show up in the ER, and it's 120. That's why you shouldn't base anything on "normal" or "abnormal," or on one measurement. Checking blood pressure every day for a month, recording the data, will lead to a better assessment.

It happens every day. I'm not blaming the patient. I'm blaming American medicine because that's how we have operated in the past. The tools we have for collecting data are very rudimentary, right? We have a blood pressure cuff. We check it. Thankfully, as technology advances, we'll be able to take continuous measurements of vital signs, and continuous measurements about other diseases.

But to play devil's advocate: Is there such a thing as too much data?

This is also something I think about all the time. I don't think we could label too much data as bad or good. That's too simplistic. Before we start collecting data, we have to ask ourselves, what are the repercussions? And is that data going to be actionable for that patient? We see over diagnosis and overtreatment all the time. Almost every patient with a chronic disease has been through something like that. We're going to be seeing a lot more of that as we are able to extract ever more data from our human bodies through advanced technologies.

That's a whole other conversation.

Yes, but I think one of the most important questions we have to address now is: Who owns the data? Does a patient own their health data? Because right now, data are not owned by patients. Data are not easily portable. Data are owned by hospitals, by insurers, by pharmaceutical and device companies. That data is powerful. How can we enable patients to have more control of their data—decide where it goes, and who takes a look at it?

Again, I'm not saying that the current situation is bad. All these other entities need access to our data because we need data to come up with therapies. A patient with a rare disease is often willing to open-source their data, to share it, in order to help develop a life-saving therapy. But most of us have so little control of how our health data gets used, who owns it, how long they can have it. I think we need to figure out ways for patients to safely have autonomy over their data and control who accesses it, how it gets shared, how it gets stored, especially as we're able to collect more data from humans.

Data ~~is~~ ARE

A REPRESENTATION OF PATIENTS... BUT NOT A COMPLETE REPRESENTATION

-BON KU-

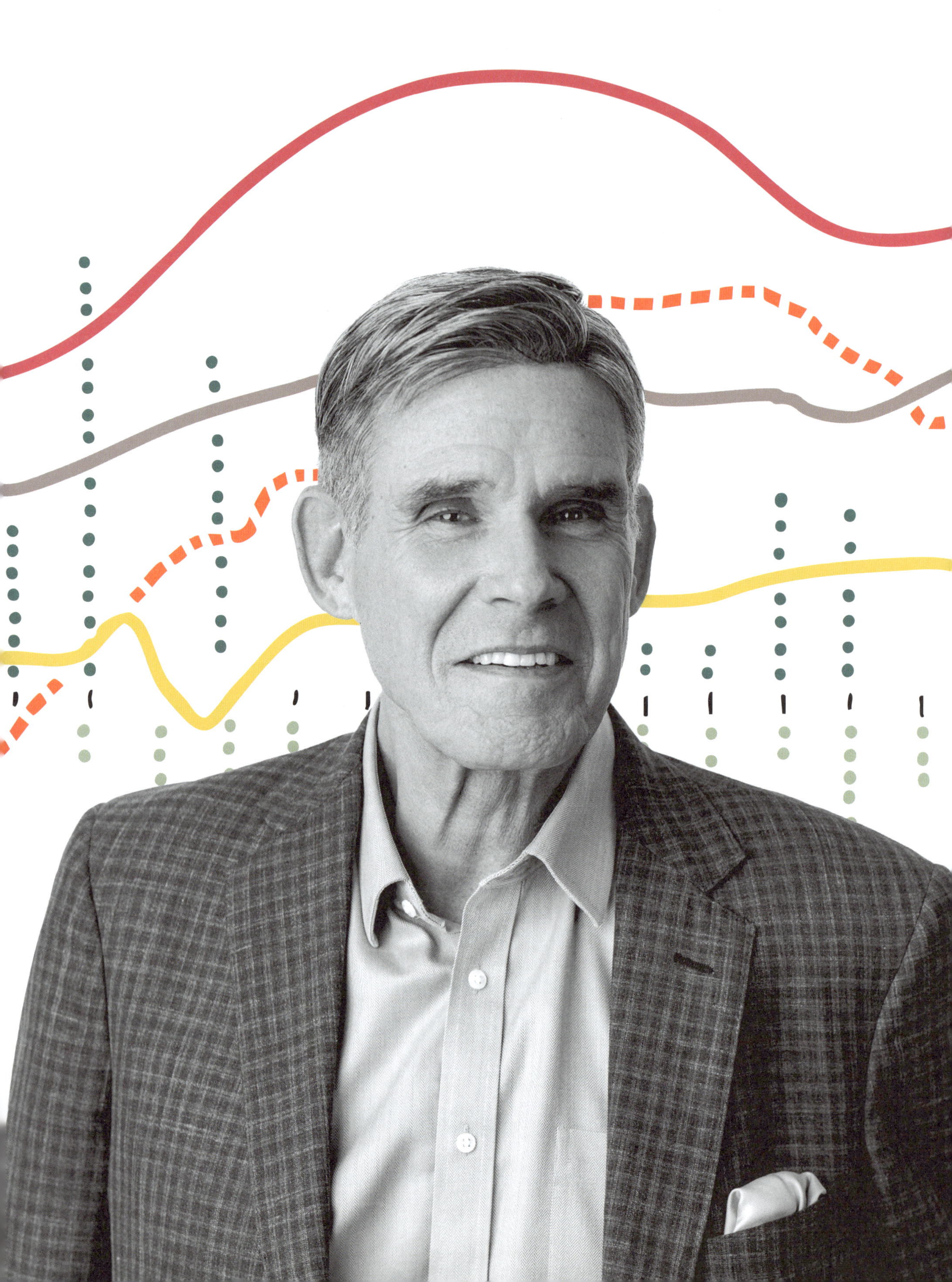

Eric Topol

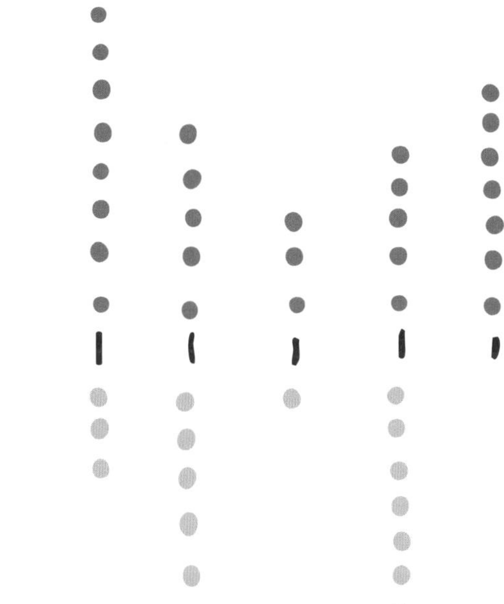

Eric Topol is a physician-scientist at Scripps Research, where he leads the Scripps Research Translational Institute. He is also a prolific author, public speaker, and advocate for individualized medicine using genomic, digital, and AI tools. The author or coauthor of more than 1,200 peer-reviewed articles, Eric is one of the top ten most cited researchers in medicine, and his weekly newsletter is read by tens of thousands of subscribers. In this conversation, he talks about empowering patients with their data; the future of AI in medicine; and communicating scientific research to a larger public.

You were one of the most incisive voices in the medical community during the COVID-19 pandemic, advocating for science and treatments in a very patient-focused way. What's exciting to you these days?

There's a convergence of many things, from genome editing to vaccine drugs. Never in the history of modern medicine has there been a time where all these incredible, cutting-edge advances were occurring at once. That's what gets me excited. We can improve human health more than ever before.

Why are you focused on the patient?

People talk about breakthrough drugs, but the patient is and can be a breakthrough driver of their own health. They are a missed opportunity. Right now, electronic health records exist in multiple provider and health systems. Nobody essentially has all their data. There's genome data sequences or the microbiome. There are sensors that people commonly wear and use, and more to come. There's the environment, you know, whether it's pollution or carcinogens, micro- or nanoplastics. There are layers of data that are not brought together. Ultimately, the patient should be able to aggregate their own data.

But now, with AI, we have the capability to do all that analysis in real time and be a virtual coach to patients. This isn't going to happen in the medical system; it has to be done at the individual level. It's waiting to happen, and when it does, it will give patients more agency. Patients can interact with their results and the analysis of their results with their physicians. It will be a very powerful tool in the future, but it relies on multimodal AI.

Do you imagine a near future where one can go to the doctor with all this aggregated data, and the doctor will be able to make sense of it? It's a lot about educating physicians too, isn't it?

Yes. One of the layers I didn't mention is the corpus of medical literature, which no doctor can fully digest. As much as I aspire to know the medical literature, no human being could keep up with the massive knowledge-base expansion that's occurring every day. So, to get to your question: Progressive physicians will realize that we're past the point of human beings as the experts. Doctors, who were historically the purveyors of information, will now provide guidance and wisdom and experience and oversight. We want patients to have all their data and have help from AI to validate it. Of course, this has to be done carefully. But as long as it's accurate in helping patients and promoting health, it's a big win, because it decompresses the doctors' work.

What you're bringing up, though, is this tension. Since Hippocrates, doctors have ruled the roost. They ran the show and had total control. Now they're being undermined. They're no longer the supreme being of sorts. Because the truth is that the patient knows best. Younger physicians and progressive physicians of all ages will realize that that's where this is inevitably headed because data is eminently portable, and AI tools to analyze people's data are building quickly and gathering tremendous momentum.

I think this is a vital step. When a doctor sees a patient, it might be once a year. It's not in the real world. Whereas we now have tools to track, if need be, every five minutes, or even more continuously, certain metrics like glucose or heart rhythm or you name it. This is medicine that's continuous. It's far more insightful than the artificial white coat syndrome where you go in and you're scared of what the doctor is gonna do to you. This is an upgrade, a profound upgrade, of medicine's capability. But you're right that it's both data dependent and physician dependent.

This entire conversation is obviously inflected by what we learned from COVID-19. As a medical professional, as a researcher, as a physician, what did COVID-19 teach you? We're always wondering, if we could zoom back to March 2020, what we would do differently.

There's a lot in that question. I mean, a lot. We had one of the greatest triumphs of biomedicine history with the march from the sequencing of the virus to the vaccine. That was unparalleled in history. But so far, it's just been a one-off. What if we had a similar success with long COVID? What if we had it for nasal or oral vaccines, and many other things that are desperately needed?

Then at the same time, there are these anti-science, anti-vax people. How can you question the need for a mask to protect against respiratory illness? Unfortunately, there hasn't been any aggressive response to them, and they've just grown, gotten more organized, more financially backed. We've been really hurt by this. They're the same people who are saying that there's no such thing as long COVID. It's just despicable.

12/7/24
marie cranford
DOCTOR yuri
212-082-9973
Rx
12/7/24
3x day
DR.

"Progressive physicians will realize that we are past the point of human beings being the experts. Doctors (...) will now provide guidance and wisdom and experience and oversight. We want patients to have all their data and have help from AI to validate it.

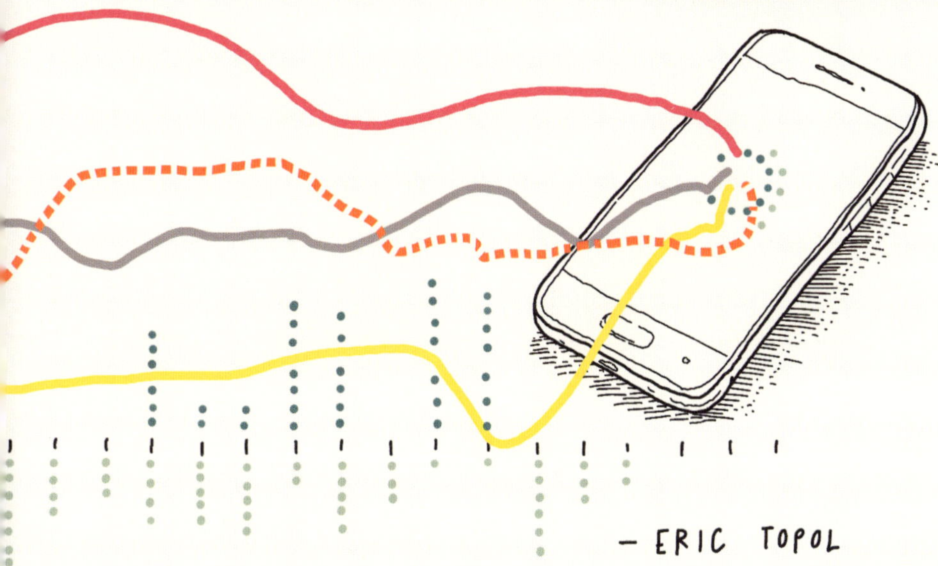

— Eric Topol

You were a coauthor on one of the first and most formative long-COVID studies, which was published in January 2022.[1] Notably, your coauthors weren't fellow academic researchers, but members of a patient advocacy group. They're researchers, but they are also dealing with long COVID themselves in a personal way. Historically, it's an unusual thing to share credit and expertise in that manner. Did you get pushback?

Actually, I didn't. There may have been some pushback, but I didn't see it because I block those people online! But I actually can't imagine how you could write a paper about long COVID without a coauthor who is experiencing long COVID. In fact, that's been part of the problem from the get-go. We have tens of millions of people around the world affected by long COVID, and we have the pseudo-experts who have never experienced it themselves. I've been a proponent of citizen science for a long time—long before the term ever came alive. And this was a perfect example of why we need such collaborations. Even though my three coauthors on that paper have long COVID and I don't, I could still be an external questioner, trying to get the right balance on the topic. We had, I think, an exceptionally important collaboration in putting it together.

I was actually the one the journal invited to write the piece. I told the editor, "I can't write it myself. I don't have long COVID, thank goodness. But I do know some people who have it who are exceptionally sharp." That was the formula. We need more of that.

The paper was also incredibly accessible. Even a nonexpert could understand it.

That's a great point. I mean, these days you can take a paper and put it through AI and make it understandable at any level of education. We didn't have that at the time. But yes, it's important to write in a language that everyone can understand. If you're only trying to impress your peers, you're in a microcosm, and the work is never going to have the impact it should.

How do you do that? How do you reach more people? It's surely more than just dumbing down the language.

Stories are big. You need to tell a good story. But graphs, to me, are also so powerful. When you do that well, you're also telling a story. It may not have the emotional charge, but it can quickly reveal that something big is happening. I rely a lot on simple graphs. I think they're extraordinary. Qualitative data can be powerful. But hard data—now that's compelling. It's the tool I favor most.

How do you define hard data, or just data itself?

I don't know if I can get more atomic-level than that. Data is data.

It just is.

Of course, there's good data and bad data. But to me it's the equivalent of an atom.

We like that.

NOTES

1 Hannah E. Davis, Lisa McCorkell, Julia Moore Vogel, and Eric J. Topol, "Long COVID: Major Findings, Mechanisms and Recommendations," *Nature Reviews Microbiology* 21 (2023): 133–46, available at https://www.nature.com/articles/s41579-022-00846-2.

Data is

DATA. I DON'T KNOW IF I CAN GET MORE ATOMIC-LEVEL THAN THAT

– ERIC TOPOL –

4

Machine Thinking: Data and Technology

Machine Thinking

We're typing these words in late autumn of 2024. As we write, we're thinking about data and technology—what they are, and what they do for us. Why they matter now, and how they will evolve in the future. Data and technology are so intertwined, and together so completely enmeshed in daily life, that it's difficult to apply criticality to our thoughts. We reach for metaphors in hopes of making sense of it all: Data is like a power source, the computational jet fuel that animates technology's potential. It's the informational lubricant for digital processing. It's the instructional code, telling the machine what to do. If technology is the frame, data is the art within it.

That sounds pretty good. We type it up.

On second thought, maybe we've gotten it all wrong. Data doesn't tell the machine what to do—in fact, it's the opposite. The machine tells *data* what to do. By providing the frame, technology shapes the data to fit inside it, sculpting binary code into a form that can be read, understood, and acted upon by machines (and the humans who operate them). Technology is a tool—increasingly, a dizzyingly omnipotent one—for manipulating data, for organizing it and slicing it open to see what's really inside it. How we use this tool, and do so with an eye toward ethics and sustainability, seems to be the most pressing question.

That sounds good too.

But then we stop ourselves again. Because by the time these words make their way from our computer, to the printed page, and into your hands, they may well be obsolete. When it comes to data and technology, bankable descriptions—much less predictions—have always been a futile proposition. Over the past century the world has witnessed exponential growth in technological innovation, an annual doubling in computational power famously known as Moore's law. Moore's law was first theorized in 1965, when the full promise of personal computing and digital transformation was imminent, but still beyond the horizon. Today we stand on a new horizon line of a fourth Industrial Revolution, and many believe that Moore's law no longer applies as originally conceived.[1] Artificial intelligence represents an entirely new paradigm for computational reasoning. Big data, on humanly incomprehensible scales, operationalizes warehouses of knowledge with ease. Quantum computing bends the rules of physics to outdo the performance of classical computers one hundred million to one.

What does this all mean for us? As society hurtles headfirst into this new reality, we believe it will be essential to return to first principles. Let's remind ourselves *what* technology really is, *why* it matters in the first place, and *how* it can improve our lives and the lives of others. This doesn't mean being afraid of technological innovations, but instead embracing their possibilities with a necessary level of criticality and discernment.

Across our careers, we've used technology in many ways, engaging with new forms of hardware and software to create data-driven experiences for many types of users. Yet ironically, at the core of our practice has always been an emphasis on the least technologically advanced tool we have: the human hand. For Giorgia in particular, the creative process usually starts with drawing, sketching, and working ideas out on paper. One can draw with data in the mind, but with no data in the pen, to understand what is contained in numbers and in their structure, and how to define and organize those quantities for greater insight.

Today the word *digital* means any machine-readable code constructed in a binary language of ones and zeros, but its etymological origin actually refers to digits, as in fingers—our most human, individualized way of counting and communicating information. A foundation of analog knowledge and human agency helps us to remember that technology, no matter how powerful or awe-inspiring, is ultimately just a tool—a means to an end rather than an end unto itself. Just as we use data visualization to communicate meaning, we can use technology to bring the user into closer proximity to that meaning, to amplify its emotional resonance or underscore its real-world impact.

Back in 2018, this was Giorgia's goal for a collaboration with Google News Lab, in which she and her team utilized augmented reality and an unusually poetic form of information design to connect the user with a shared sense of optimism for the future. In a world increasingly consumed by polarization and despair, the project was an attempt to tap into more positive ideas around progress and possibility, and use data from Google searches—the world's great barometer of human interests—as a doorway into these ideals. This very nontraditional AR experience was named Building Hopes, and it allowed users to build "data sculptures" in virtual space based on what they believed mattered most to humanity's future. Each sculpture's size and color was specified by the user to indicate thematic focus (immigration, sustainable development, technology, et cetera) and intensity of interest.

These colorful, floating sculptures functioned as personal totems of belief, metaphorically embodying the desires and dreams of each user. Users could arrange their sculptures next to those of others to see how their values "stacked up" to the rest of the world. Do we share the same dreams? How much optimism is there for the things that matter to me? In its unique way, augmented reality allowed these questions to take physical form, to have real shape and presence, and manifested as human-scaled structures in our spatial environment. Technology was the tool, but hope was the ultimate reaction.

Sometimes the solution isn't more technology, but less. This was the lesson when Giorgia and her team collaborated with Samantha Cristoforetti, the European Space Agency astronaut who made history in 2014 by becoming the first Italian woman to venture into space. In the lead-up to the mission, a chance conversation between Samantha and Giorgia on Twitter led to an interesting project: an "extraterrestrial" social network that would connect us earthlings to Samantha, and Samantha to us, as she orbited the globe in the International Space Station (ISS) for 199 days. Giorgia called it Friends in Space, and it served as an unlikely interface for very human conversations.

The project developed after a key realization about how technology, at least in this situation, might best facilitate connection between Samantha and those back on Earth. After all, a mission to the ISS is a feat of technological accomplishment. Each flight also generates terabytes of data—more quantitative material than we know what to do with. But the data and technology that would power the space shuttle's ascent was in fact far less profound than the simple miracle of launching a living person into the cold depths of outer space. Samantha would be up there: a human

↑ →
Building Hopes, 2019

↑
Friends in Space, 2014

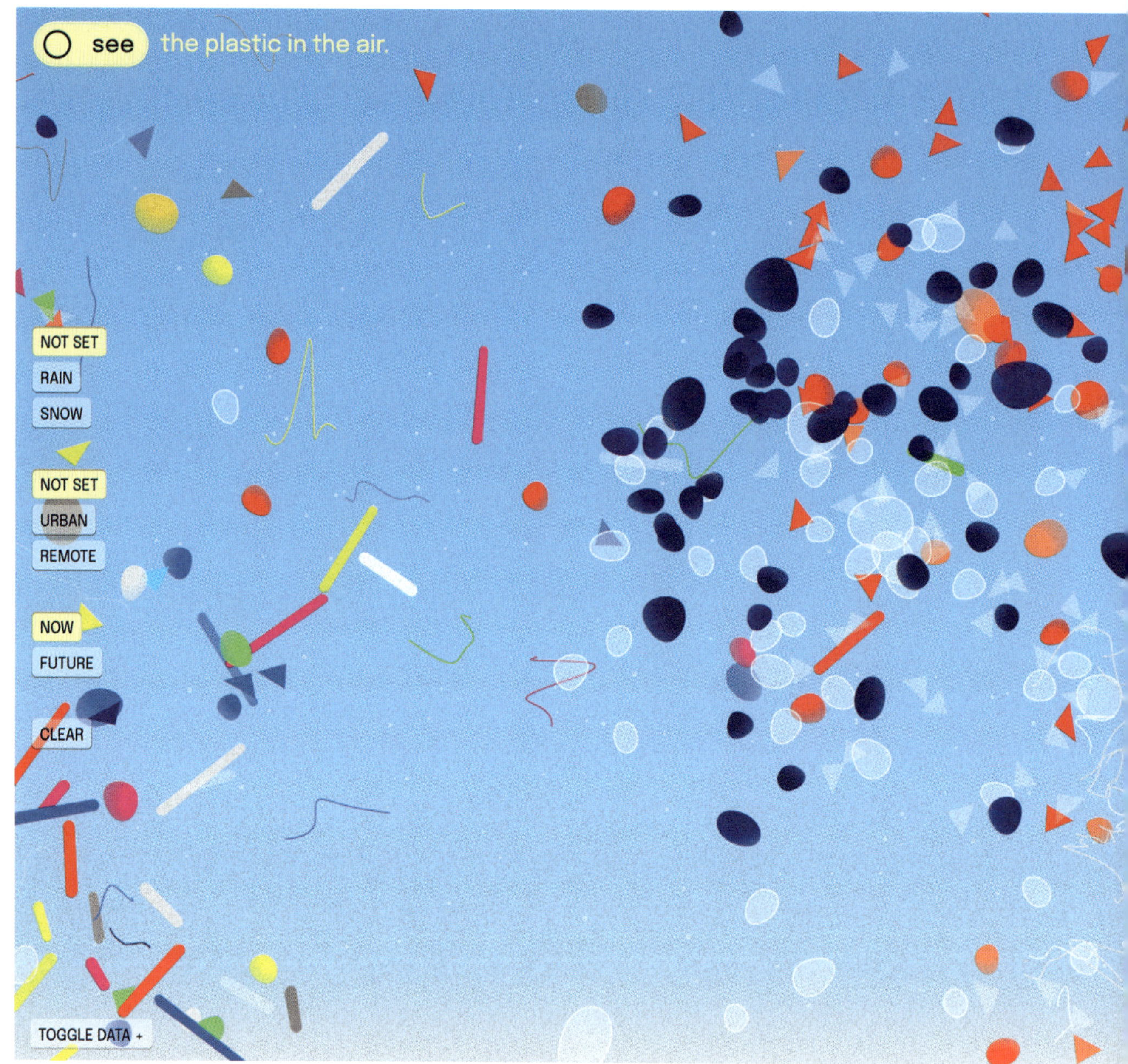

↑
Particle view,
Plastic Air, 2020

↑
Trash view,
Plastic Air, 2020

being in a flying metal box. On a clear night, one could see her with the naked eye, and although she was just a tiny flash of light in the dark sky, that instantaneous connection would prove to be more moving than any statistical readout could ever hope to be.

This form of interstellar poetry became the inspiration for the design. With a simple digital gesture within the interface, a person could say "hello" to Samantha when she was in orbit overhead, and "hello" to all the other people around the world who were online at the same time. These greetings were rendered as yellow bursts of light, pinpointed to the user's exact location on a map. Naturally, Sam could say "hello" back to the world via Twitter from the ISS, which also allowed users to see her own position along the ISS's flight path. During its first three weeks online, Friends in Space hosted more than two million interactions, merging the physical, the digital, and the emotional in moments of joy and connection.

Friends in Space used technology to bring people together, but we can also use technology to shine a light out onto the world and reflect our place in it. In 2019, our team at Pentagram worked with Google Arts & Culture to create a digital data visualization experience intended to raise awareness about microplastics, the tiny particles of plastic waste that are expelled by everyday household items like clothing, furniture, packaging, and appliances. Microplastics are a pressing environmental issue, but they also can be a somewhat obscure concept. Most are smaller than the width of a human hair, and thus invisible to the human eye—literally out of sight and, thus, out of mind. As we learned more about microplastics, we became shocked and alarmed by their pervasiveness. While most concentrated in and around cities, microplastics have been found in remote locations around the world far away from human settlements, indicating their ability to travel long distances in air or water.

Using a simple web app and real data of microplastic incidence culled from scientific studies and conversations with researchers, our solution bridged the gap between the visible and the invisible, the tangible and the abstract. Called Plastic Air, the experience consisted of a speculative window onto a data-driven approximation of the plastic particles that float around us all the time. Users could drop identifiable objects like a lawn chair, a T-shirt, a cigarette butt, or a couch cushion—all containing plastic polymers—to "pollute" the sky, and then witness those items breaking down into millions of microplastics, like colorful confetti scattered to the wind. The result was, by design, both beautiful and horrifying. Here, technology gave us the power of sight. Plastic Air let us peer into a world that is normally opaque but nevertheless real, revealing the hidden impact that we as plastic consumers are having on the planet that we all share.

These experiments show what's possible when we use technology as a tool; when we view data through a humanistic lens; and when we wield both to ask, and sometimes answer, big questions about topics greater than ourselves. We can't predict the future, except to know that digital innovation will continue to reshape our lives in dramatic and unexpected ways. New possibilities are always just beyond the horizon. As new technologies bubble and burst, it is our duty to remain critical of their promises.

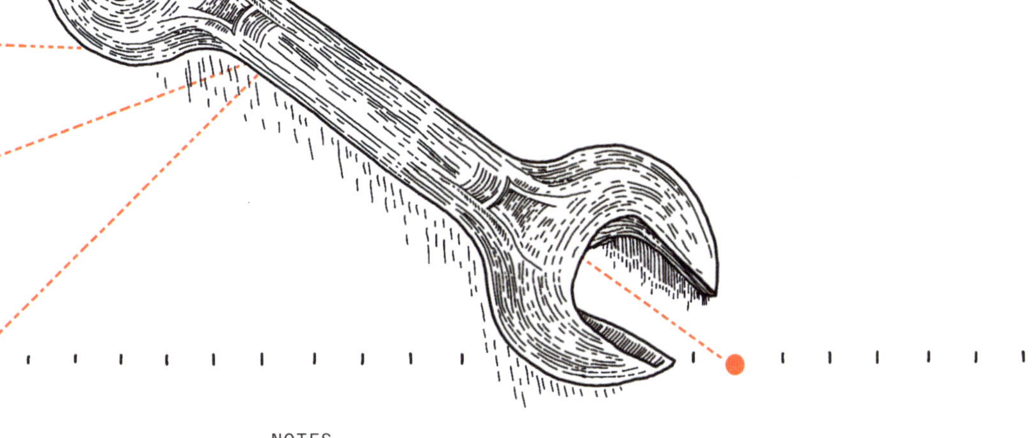

NOTES

1 Tom Simonite, "Moore's Law Is Dead. Now What?," *MIT Technology Review*, May 13, 2016, https://www.technologyreview.com/2016/05/13/245938/moores-law-is-dead-now-what/.

Kate Crawford

Kate Crawford is an internationally known scholar who studies the social and economic systems of artificial intelligence. Her 2021 book Atlas of AI: Power, Politics, and the Planetary Costs of Artificial Intelligence *made headlines for spotlighting the hidden implications of AI for the environment, the economy, and human laborers. In addition to being a writer, Kate is a globe-trotting public intellectual, often found on panels or collaborating with artists to create new pathways for understanding technology's deeper meaning. She is one of our most sage voices on the ethics of AI, and her vast knowledge of what lies behind the proverbial curtain of this new technology is often eye-opening. In this conversation, Kate unpacks what every person needs to know about AI; how we arrived at what feels like a perilous moment, and where we're going next; and why the future of AI is a conversation everyone has a stake in.*

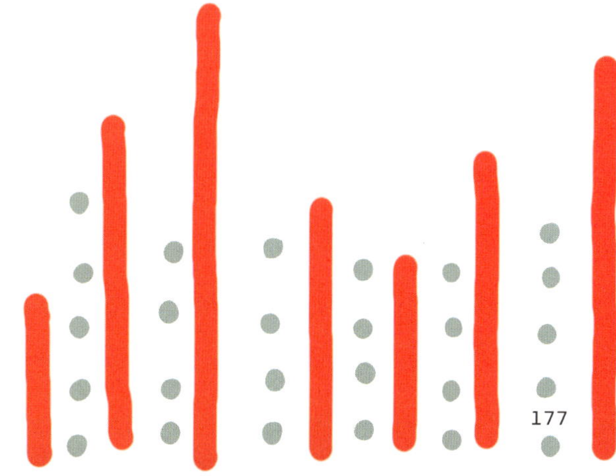

It seems like today everyone is talking about AI, but you've been thinking about this topic for some time. You've also been very worried about, and focused on, the ethics of AI. Can you help contextualize where we are right now in the longer history of this technology?

Right now we are undergoing an enormous transformation in AI. I think it's no exaggeration to call it an inflection point—a moment of transition to a way of using artificial intelligence that will profoundly influence all cognitive professions. What is significant about this shift is that compared to the last stage of AI, which was about more specific domains like autonomous vehicles, facial recognition, worker surveillance, we now have a set of tools that profoundly interrupt the kinds of core practices that we saw as somehow quintessentially human.

This shift is extraordinary. ChatGPT is the fastest-growing consumer application in history. That shows how significant the scale is. We're used to technology slowly rolling out, having an adoption that might take a decade, like an iPhone. But instead, what we're seeing is like a global switch being flipped. The large tech companies are essentially turning on the tap and putting AI in everything. It's instantaneous, and it's across existing infrastructures. It's an experience of everything, everywhere, all at once. That produces a type of culture shock.

If you had to explain AI to someone who doesn't know anything about it, what would you say?

It's important that we demystify AI. All of the marketing hype says that AI is a set of magical algorithms in the cloud that can produce profoundly accurate predictions and extraordinary original content. Yet in actual fact, as I've shown in my work, AI is neither artificial nor intelligent. It isn't this mathematical, neutral, objective set of functions. It is a profoundly resource-heavy industry that relies on vast amounts of data, huge amounts of natural resources, and a lot of hidden human labor. The material footprint of AI is extraordinarily large, but often made invisible, and it's crucial that we put that absolutely at the forefront of the discussion.

It's also assumed that AI is magically intelligent, able to do things that humans can do, except better. But again, the intelligence of these systems is not like human intelligence at all. It's large-scale statistical pattern recognition that has considerable flaws, biases, and skews within it.

Okay, so that's what AI is. But why should we care?

This is a public issue. This is fundamentally a democratic question. If we can't have a say in how and where these systems are used, then we're losing so much of the traditional agency and voice and participatory ethic that the societies that I grew up in were founded on. This is the most important public conversation to be having right now. These systems are affecting every single core social institution. They're cutting right to the heart of things: What is a shared reality? What is truth? What is a fulfilling job? If AI is going to be playing such a profound role in influencing these questions, we all need to have a say in it.

We're also seeing the biggest experiment in copyright-free production in human history. A crisis in copyright law is already playing out around generative AI. All of the work that's being produced through a generative system has no copyright. That's a profound question mark over the space.

So we have these moments of almost really profound, radical uncertainty. And that to me is also a space for potential. We have to think more creatively about how these systems can be redesigned to give credit to the people whose artistic creations are forming the basis of training data. What is exciting about this moment of uncertainty is that we can say we want creative producers to be part of this shift, have their work acknowledged, and be recompensed. That to me is part of not just how we collect data, but how we design AI from the very beginning.

Speak to those flaws, biases, and skews a bit more. Is there such a thing as an ethical dataset?

It's such a good question. These are truly gargantuan structures. You're looking at multiple lifetimes to really understand this data. The scale of data behind AI has risen exponentially, and with that comes a whole lot of new questions, because that data is us. It's everything we've ever put on the internet, and also everything that exists in human culture that has ever been digitized. It's all now moving into these training datasets. That is an enormous cultural shift. We can think about these gigantic datasets as like a capture of the commons, a capture of this resource that we thought was collectively owned. That is to say, all of the data on the internet is now being harvested by a very small number of tech companies for profit.

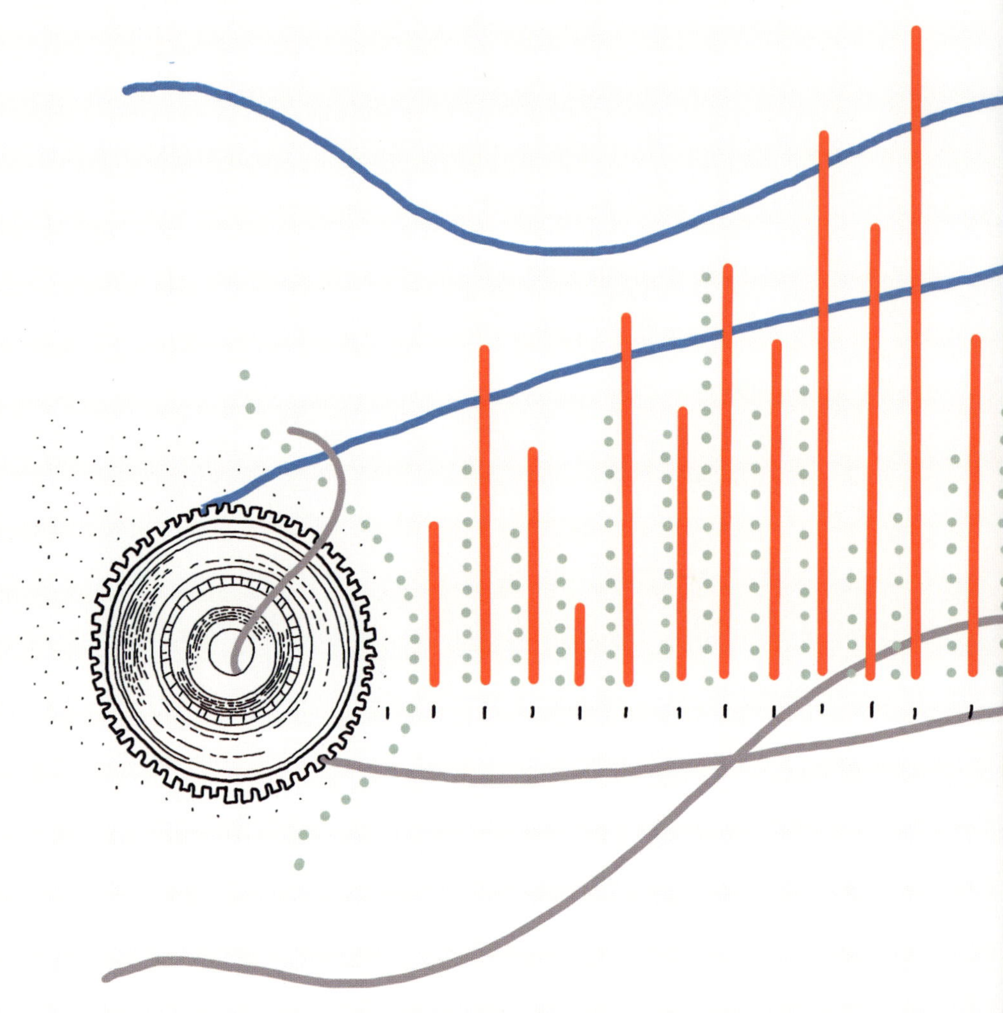

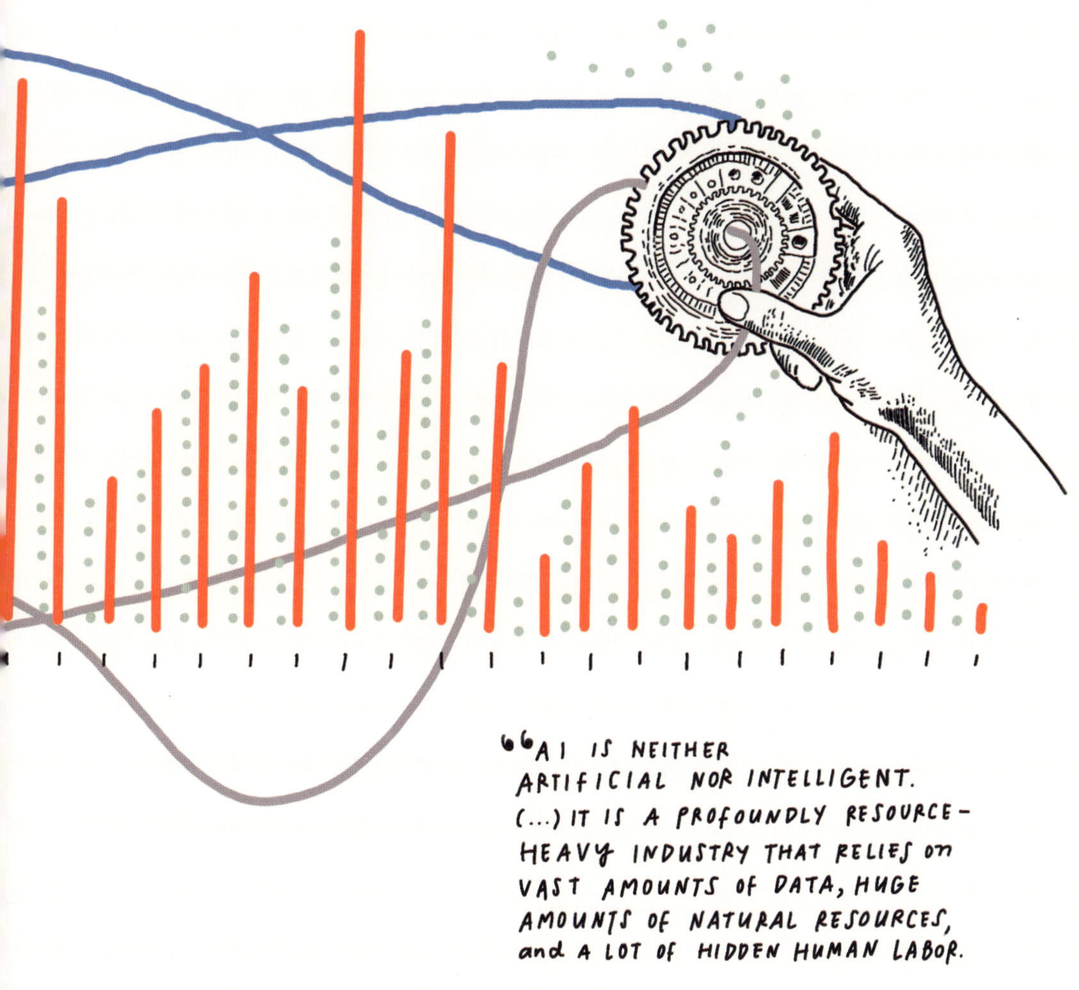

"AI IS NEITHER ARTIFICIAL NOR INTELLIGENT. (...) IT IS A PROFOUNDLY RESOURCE-HEAVY INDUSTRY THAT RELIES ON VAST AMOUNTS OF DATA, HUGE AMOUNTS OF NATURAL RESOURCES, and A LOT OF HIDDEN HUMAN LABOR.

—KATE CRAWFORD

There's this widely held belief that training data is this kind of inert substance, that it's this amorphous mass of stuff and only the scale matters, not what it represents or who is represented or who isn't represented. This is completely wrong. Training datasets matter more than ever. They literally encode worldviews and determine the boundaries of what is known and what is unknown. It's critical that we understand how they're representing the world, and what might be left out. If we gave an almost "craft" level of care to data, and if we emphasized data stewardship, we wouldn't have systems producing such toxic results. We could be training AI systems from the very beginning to be much more nuanced, responsive, equipped with that sort of thinking around how they will represent the world.

Are there any examples of that being done right now?

A classic example that the data artist Jer Thorp and I have worked on and find really interesting is NABirds, a biodiversity website, sponsored by the Cornell Lab of Ornithology, which was designed to allow bird-watchers to annotate examples of a bird dataset. When you look at the dataset, it's so careful. It's so precise. It's so accurate. The dataset is then used to train bird recognition systems. Let's be clear: It still has issues. It's not perfect by any means. But the level of care that's given to the data curation is exceptional because it's done by people who are deeply invested in the end result. They care about this domain, namely of bird-watching and bird recognition, so they're going to have a different relationship to the data.

What are you most excited about regarding the future of AI?

Let me approach that question from a different perspective. One of the really interesting capacities of generative AI is to use these tools creatively, to use them to produce anything from a sonnet to a book or novella, from an illustration to a film storyboard. But the only way this is possible is because all of these systems have been trained on the work of creative laborers over centuries, and that has all been captured and used for training material without any consent, credit, or compensation. So we can think of the three C's here that have been ignored in order to create these systems.

For creative producers of all kinds, we face a big question right now, which is: In using these tools, are we not only contributing to the exploitation of creative producers, but also potentially putting them out of work by making their work easier to automate? We've already heard stories of programmers no longer getting jobs because you can do basic programming with ChatGPT, and of illustrators losing work. This is often in the case of people doing creative work for hire. It's not impacting the high-end art world in the same way, but it's impacting someone who might take a contract to produce some code, to build a website, to draw a storyboard for an upcoming film. If you can do this in generative AI, we have a very serious set of questions to address.

And so when you ask what's exciting, I think one of the big problems to solve is how to think about ways in which we can design these systems at the very least with opt-out capabilities so that creative producers can choose not to be in datasets. Here I'll point to the amazing work of Holly Herndon and Matt Dryhurst's Spawning AI, which created one of the first large-scale opt-out systems called haveibeentrained.com. I think it's the beginning of a very important set of conversations about how artists or anyone can start to say, "I don't want my face being used to train this system" and to actually have the data removed.

But then we also have to think more creatively about how these systems are going to be redesigned to actually give credit. So you can say, "Oh, this work I'm producing owes so much to the style of this particular writer, of this illustrator, of this painter." These are things we can do. They're not impossible. Similarly, but much more radically, we need to think about how to share the gains of generative AI with the people whose work has been used as its foundation. How people can be paid for the work they have done is now creating extraordinary new capacities. That, to me, is part of not just how we collect data, but how we design AI from the very beginning. Until we answer these questions, we continue to face a type of crisis.

Data is

A CAPTURE OF THE COMMONS

—KATE CRAWFORD—

John Maeda

As an artist, designer, technologist, writer, educator, and more, John Maeda has a uniquely interdisciplinary perspective on data. He began his career as a professor at the MIT Media Lab, where he pioneered experiments using data and technology as artistic media. At MIT he created Design by Numbers, a revolutionary new programming language intended to demystify code for artists and designers. Maeda went on to work in academia as president of the Rhode Island School of Design; in venture capital as a design partner at Kleiner Perkins; and in advertising as chief experience officer of Publicis Sapient. At the time of this interview, he was chief technology officer at Everbridge, an emergency readiness company. In this conversation John talks about the purpose of data visualization during a crisis; how "thick" data is different from big data; and what AI means for the future of human-computer interaction.

What are you obsessed with right now?

I just finished up a role as the main nerd of a company that manages emergency communications, meaning first responders and public safety. In the corporate world, that means physical security, like intruders, hurricanes, shooters, and every other possible bad thing. I covered wildfires to terrorists to bomb removal. It was really interesting. I took the job because of the pandemic. I was working at an advertising agency, and I got a message from the CEO of this company that really works on saving lives. I thought, "Maybe I should work on saving lives too. I should do that instead of how to make people more creative," which is what I was focused on previously.

What is the role of data in your work now? Are you thinking about data in a different way than you have in the past?

By working in the crisis space, I have learned some things that are so obvious but that I'd never thought of before. Think of Maslow's hierarchy of needs. Most of design is at the top of Maslow's pyramid. It's where you find self-actualization. Who am I? What's my identity? Design takes that stuff extremely seriously. But at the very bottom of the pyramid you have: Am I going to live or die today? Or: Did someone die around me? That doesn't live at the top of the pyramid. It's at the bottom. Lately I've been living at the bottom of the pyramid.

Visual design is about form and content. If the content is my calendar, the form is how expressive the numbers and text are. But if the content is, "If you don't move out of the way, an asteroid will destroy your house in ten minutes," that's really important content! You need that content immediately. Now that there's so much information at the top of the pyramid that's so hedonistic, so positive or negative, or so delicious, when someone says to you, "Something bad is going to happen," it's sort of like, "Huh?"

At the bottom of Maslow's pyramid, you have to communicate well. Language matters. For instance, if you're a family living in New York that speaks only Spanish, and my company blasts an emergency message to you in English, you're not going to be able to do anything with that message. At the most basic level, for basic safety, you have to communicate simply. Cleverness is not going to matter. It's all pragmatic communication.

It's made me change how I think about design. I've met designers who work in disaster preparedness. They make maps, which fascinates me. You never hear about these people in the mainstream graphic design community, but they make these earthquake, flood, or wildfire maps and are doing really important work. In their case, design is a tool for communication. This type of design would never win awards per se. But I think from a data perspective, that would be good to change in the future.

In our opinion we're in a golden age of visual communication and data visualization. Look at the many charts designed during the pandemic that conveyed important information to the public about the spread of COVID-19. We've also, however, seen research that shows how people really prefer language over data visualization to learn things. Many people just aren't comfortable with graphs and charts.

Sure. "Am I gonna die? Does this chart say I'm gonna die? No? Okay, I don't have to look at it!" But something like a wildfire evacuation map is the greatest graphic design anybody needs right now. Where will I be safe? The data is where I'll be safe versus where I will die. You cannot summarize a fire evacuation map in a pithy sentence.

Data is evidence. But there are other types of evidence. Think about how Venice is sinking. Show me a picture of Venice sinking, and it becomes very real. That's also great data. Photographs are a secondary cousin to that pithy sentence.

How much do you think people care about data right now?

Everyone cares about data now. Today, anyone can pull data and make a spreadsheet. That war has been won. I think more people appreciate and understand the nuances around it and the craft around it because more people have data. Yet most of it is spectacle rather than comprehension. It's a branch between spectacle and utility. Maybe craft is relevant to the bottom of Maslow's pyramid over time. Maybe that's what you're showing with your work.

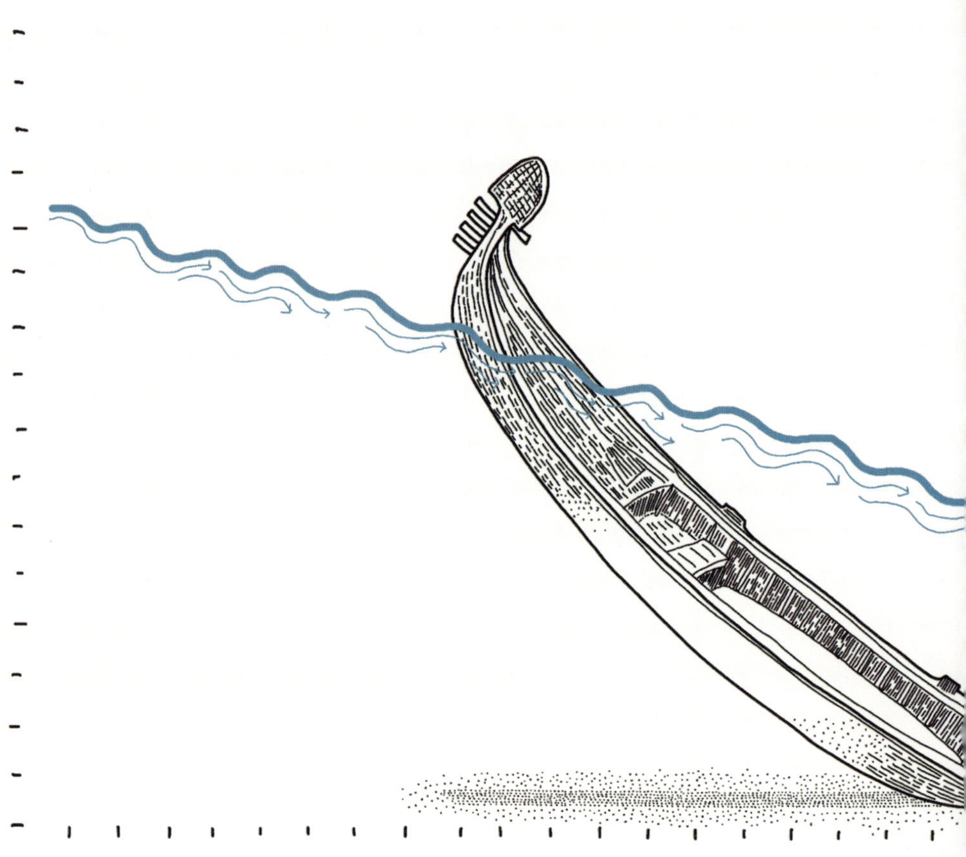

“DATA IS EVIDENCE. BUT THERE ARE OTHER TYPES OF EVIDENCE. THINK ABOUT HOW VENICE IS SINKING. SHOW ME A PICTURE OF VENICE SINKING AND IT BECOMES VERY REAL. THAT'S ALSO GREAT DATA.

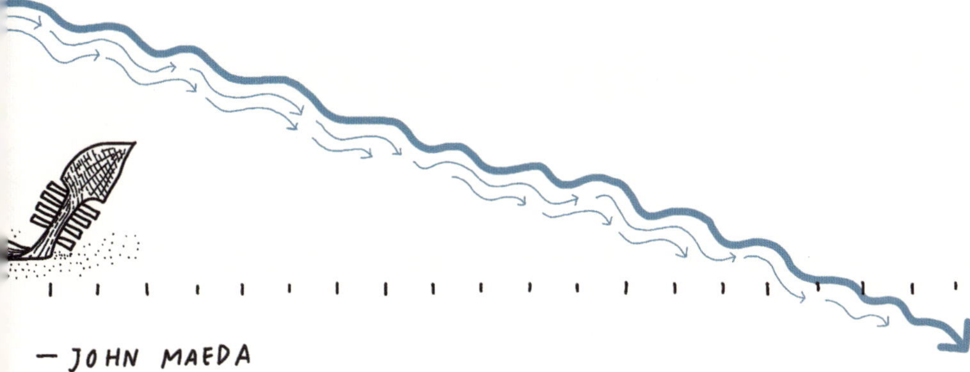

—JOHN MAEDA

You wrote the book *The Laws of Simplicity* in 2006. But simplifying data is not necessarily always a good thing, since you don't want to remove too much context. In this paradigm of design as a tool for immediate communication, is there a greater emphasis on simplicity?

The Laws of Simplicity was written when there wasn't yet social media. I could see that technology was having a greater impact, but I didn't understand. I wanted to write the book to try to understand it. At the time, engineers were in charge of all the communication. Engineers love complexity. Why? Engineers love optionality, whereas designers like to reduce. Maybe they're more strategic in that way. I think simplicity is being strategic, whereas technology strategy is to make technology more powerful. This usually amounts to more capabilities and more features.

We always struggle with definitions. Often people don't understand what data is. What is data to you?

Data is life. It's my lifeblood. Data lets me do computation. It makes me relevant.

Giorgia, you made me think about data differently. It's more real and in this world. It's the best way to understand what's been called thick data. That said, I think you have a challenge right now. In the era of large language model AI and machine learning, data lives at the scale of millions of components. The methods that you use may no longer apply. At those magnitudes, our notions of the world go away. Our physics go away. Gravity effects no longer apply. Think about Ray and Charles Eames's film *Powers of Ten* (1977). That film assumes that things get bigger as things get smaller, but that's actually not correct. In an era of AI, physicists need to invent a whole new theoretical physics to account for what happens across a whole different scale. It's a completely different realm. We're in an era right now where a quantum leap is occurring, and the ways in which design may have formerly understood data no longer apply. When you hit hundreds of thousands of gigabytes of data, it isn't about us understanding it. It's more about how machines can metabolize it.

I think that the craft you represent is super important. I'm not putting it down. I think understanding those small data stories or thicker data stories is always going to be valuable. But I just don't think it's applicable to this new era. This new phase change has the potential to do something I don't know if I understand yet. Does that make sense?

It does. But isn't it all about communication in the end? Isn't it all about making people understand those concepts and relate to them?

No, it's not. The whole idea of Newtonian physics is that when I drop an apple, it falls. It's logical. Design works in a zone of understanding physiological phenomena in 2D, 3D, and sometimes 4D space. When you get to a hundred thousand gigabytes, and machines are basically ingesting all this information, our notion of thinking is gone.

In generative AI, I would not pay so much attention to the fact that the computer is drawing a picture. I would pay more attention to the fact that a computer is understanding a sentence. A hundred thousand gigabytes of information were compressed in a very strange way down to a single-gigabyte file that no human being can read. It's been squeezed into this thing, this representation, that, when you combine it with machine learning, creates an image. That's disturbing and interesting. All that data became less data. And that much less data became the essence of what it originally was.

What is the role of design and the designer, then?

I have no idea. Maybe you'll tell me!

Does this feel similar to leaps that you've experienced in the past, such as the shift to personal computing?

It's as big as that. People are mistaking AI as equivalent to the invention of photography, or something like that. It's not that. Really, it's as if a new computer paradigm has been invented. It's like the switch from the PC to the graphical interface. It's like the desktop to the portable iPhone. It's a step function that has occurred.

Data is

LIFE. IT'S MY LIFEBLOOD. DATA LETS ME DO COMPUTATION

—JOHN MAEDA—

Refik Anadol

Refik Anadol is a pioneer of new media art and the creative use of data to understand our human reality. Born in Turkey, he first came to prominence in the United States (where he has lived and worked since 2012) with WDCH Dreams, *a groundbreaking "data sculpture" in which forty-five terabytes of archival data from the history of the Los Angeles Philharmonic were projected onto the facade of Walt Disney Concert Hall, Frank Gehry's iconic theater in downtown Los Angeles. Refik has been perfecting his wholly unique approach to AI and data visualization ever since, working globally on jaw-dropping artistic spectacles with leading galleries, museums, and brands. In this conversation, Refik discusses his unusually emotional understanding of machines and technology; the role of co-creation in his artistic process; and how AI can help us understand no less than the future of humanity.*

Data is so often seen as, and treated as, cold and inhumane. But you've often spoken of data as having a spiritual component, which has strongly informed your work and the way you talk about it. When did you discover that?

There were a couple of pivotal moments. As an undergraduate in 2008, I was lucky to join a master class taught by the artist Peter Weibel, who was deeply influential for me. He was visiting our school in Istanbul with his curatorial team, and he gave this master class about pure data, and primarily for musicians. Although I'm not a musician, I was captivated by how musicians could hear data rather than see it. I may have been the only visual artist—or visual mind—in that class, and I think it was the first time I encountered simple point and line geometry. I was also very inspired by the German artist Alva Noto and all the early Ars Electronica artists who were exploring a super-minimal universe of music. That's when I first envisioned the idea of "data painting."

The emotional context happened in 2012 when I was in the artist Casey Reas's class as an MFA student at UCLA. While learning the coding language Processing and early JavaScript, I experimented with plotting wind data. It was challenging for me because I lacked computing power, but as I worked through it, listening to the music of Ryuichi Sakamoto in the studio, I found the poetic dimensions of wind data.

The spiritual realization occurred in 2016. I joined an AI residency program at Google and was fortunate to be able to challenge them. I proposed a dialogue that went beyond engineering—bringing together an AI engineer, a neuroscientist, and a shaman. This multidimensional approach revealed profound connections among data, AI, spirituality, and humanity. It was unconventional at the time—I saw so many connections among data, spirituality, AI, machines, and humanity for the potential future of human consciousness.

Your work uses complex algorithms and software to study vast archives of information, and then visualize those archives in new, beautiful ways. Where did this interest in archives come from?

I think it all comes from an intrinsic curiosity about humanity's collective memories. Over the past seven years, our studio has downloaded more than four billion images. I think it's one of the largest datasets ever collected for this kind of deep research. When we train AI models, we always have this same concept of interacting with latent space—the hidden potential within these vast datasets. Interacting with this space isn't straightforward; it requires asking meaningful questions and embracing discomfort. It's a space for discovery and innovation, not certainty.

I still don't feel we know everything about this space, because every week is a new week. A traditional artist uses the same kind of brush and canvas every morning, right? But for me, every morning is a new "brush," a new "canvas." They just keep changing. And that's a beautifully uncomfortable zone.

What is data to you?

I think of data as a form of memory. And that memory can take any shape, form, color, or texture. When recontextualized artistically, data transforms from being cold and abstract into something deeply human and emotionally resonant. Without context, data risks remaining detached, purely mathematical. It becomes more inspiring if you bring context back to data. And then every single trace of life can be quantifiable in a form of data, and eventually a memory too. To me, data as memory is both archaeological and anthropological, capturing the essence of humanity. I'm fascinated by how data can represent the story of our existence in a meaningful way.

You are prolific, and you work with a recognizable style and aesthetic. Much of your work is very public. When you unveil a new piece, what types of responses do you get?

I think the first major emotional connection with our audience was the *Melting Memories* installation in Istanbul, which we worked on with the neuroscientist Adam Gazzaley in 2017. He trained our team on how to use EEG (electroencephalogram) data to represent what we called "the moment of remembering." The overwhelming audience response showed me how abstract concepts like memory could evoke deep emotional connections.

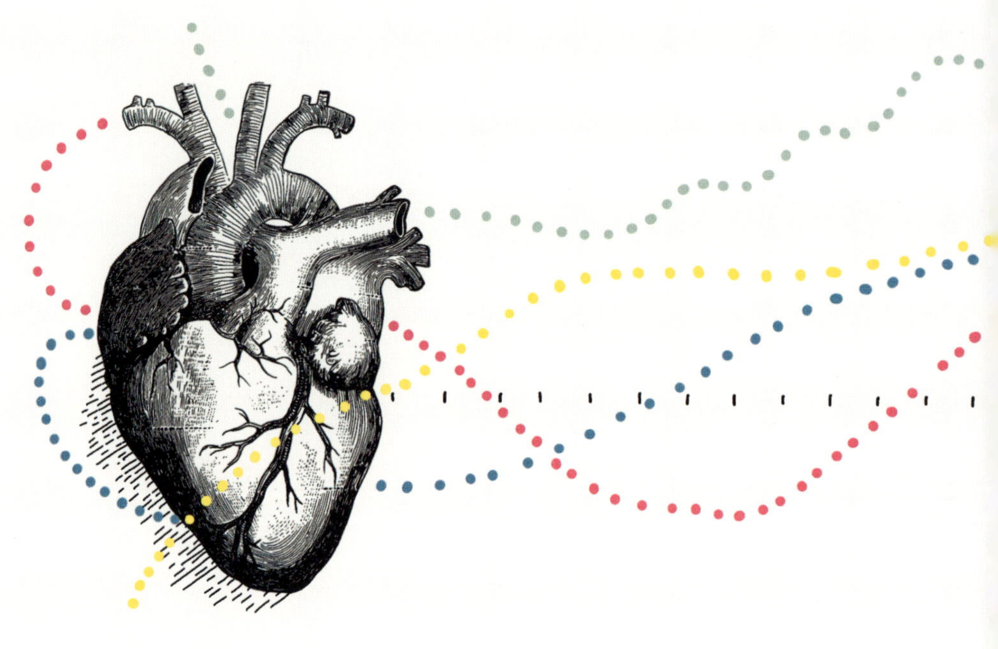

"RIGHT NOW OUR STUDIO IS DEEPLY FOCUSED ON BIOSENSING— USING THINGS LIKE HEARTBEATS AND BRAINWAVES TO CREATE ART THAT REFLECTS HUMAN EXPERIENCES. (...) I ENVISION A FUTURE WHERE EMOTIONS LIKE HOPE OR JOY CAN SHAPE ARCHITECTURAL SPACES, ALLOWING US TO "LIVE" WITH THOSE FEELINGS.

— REFIK ANADOL

Another significant moment was the *Living Architecture* piece projected on the facade of Antoni Gaudí's Casa Batlló in Barcelona. We received sixty- five thousand people in one night. We visualized Gaudí's life using an immense dataset of over one billion points. Seeing sixty-five thousand people gather in one night felt like the city itself was embracing the work.

I believe these interactions happen because we create spaces that feel safe and inclusive, allowing people to connect with the context and discourse. When that connection occurs, it's profoundly moving.

Your 2022 installation at New York's Museum of Modern Art, *Unsupervised*, was a piece of massive scale that ingested the museum's art collection, combined it with sensor data from the museum's lobby, and then visualized it in this perpetually changing work of data art. The public's reaction was astounding and generally positive. Critics also reviewed it, some positively, some negatively. What do you make of it all?

For me, *Unsupervised* wasn't about personal expression—it was about opening the door to possibilities in the field. The piece represents a collective moment for everyone working with AI and data art. MoMA's bravery in co-creating and embracing this medium was transformative. Like their early inclusion of video games in their collection, this project challenged traditional notions of art. It's not about AI making art, it's about human-machine collaboration. This installation has already sparked important dialogues with other museums and archives, a legacy I believe will endure far beyond the initial reactions.

You're very positive about the future of humanity and how data and AI will be part of our lives. Is it because of this spiritual aspect that you recognize?

I believe that AI can help us discover the language of humanity. I'm still very positive about this research. I was fortunate to witness the birth of the internet, Web1, Web2, Web3, AI, quantum computing. It's incredible to be alive, for sure. I mean, it is a very rare opportunity for humanity to witness all this. But these advancements only became meaningful to me after understanding their fundamentals. Right now, our studio is deeply focused on biosensing—using things like heartbeats and brainwaves to create art that reflects human experiences. I think the data "of us" is inspiring. It's the human context. I envision a future where emotions like hope or joy can shape architectural spaces, allowing us to "live" with those feelings.

I think what is amazing is to go beyond image, sound, and text and bring in other sensorial inputs. It's a unique take on latent space. Instead of mimicking reality, I'm drawn to exploring latent space for its serendipitous potential. I call this process "machine hallucinations." If a machine can learn, can it dream? Can it hallucinate? There is much more space there to unfold and reveal so much potential, rather than being stuck in mimicking reality and copying everyday life. So, that's the research. Many years in, and I still feel we're only just beginning to uncover what's possible.

Data is

A FORM OF MEMORY

-REFIK ANADOL-

5

Paint by Numbers: Data and Creativity

Paint by Numbers

At first blush, data may appear anathema to creativity. If the language of data is structured and defined, the language of creativity is unbound, a medium of invention shaped by expansive imagination, artistic impulse, and unpredictable inspiration. Yet perhaps it is this type of compartmentalized thinking that has limited data's potential in the past. If we tap into creativity's possibility, what else can data do?

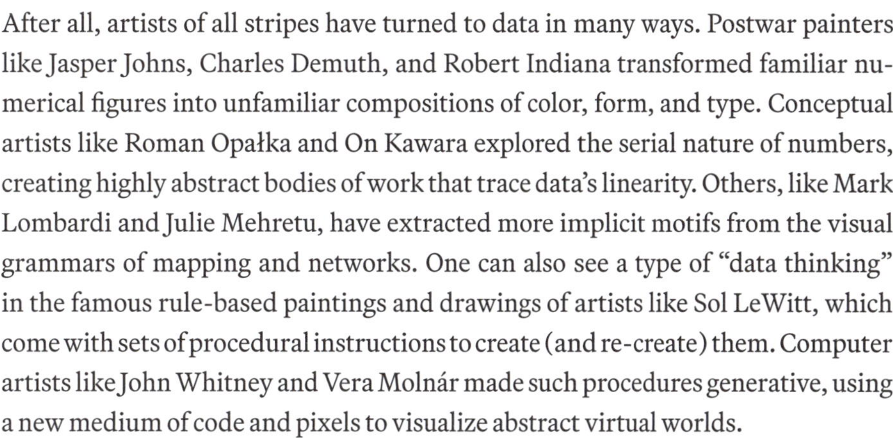

After all, artists of all stripes have turned to data in many ways. Postwar painters like Jasper Johns, Charles Demuth, and Robert Indiana transformed familiar numerical figures into unfamiliar compositions of color, form, and type. Conceptual artists like Roman Opałka and On Kawara explored the serial nature of numbers, creating highly abstract bodies of work that trace data's linearity. Others, like Mark Lombardi and Julie Mehretu, have extracted more implicit motifs from the visual grammars of mapping and networks. One can also see a type of "data thinking" in the famous rule-based paintings and drawings of artists like Sol LeWitt, which come with sets of procedural instructions to create (and re-create) them. Computer artists like John Whitney and Vera Molnár made such procedures generative, using a new medium of code and pixels to visualize abstract virtual worlds.

Data art, a category of artworks that take data (and the topics they point to) as more explicit source material, has also become prevalent in recent years. Artists like Aaron Koblin, Laurie Frick, or Rafael Lozano-Hemmer leverage data from various sources to make sculptures, installations, and websites that are both beautiful and informative. Here, aesthetics and content completely merge, but unlike traditional data visualizations one might find in a newspaper, the pieces don't always carry with them conventional legends or color-coded keys to aid the viewer's comprehension. Sometimes, their meaning is left purposefully opaque. Such is the case of Luc Tuymans's 2021 work *Polarisation* (based on a scatter plot of political partisanship developed by IBM researcher Mauro Martino) or Stefan Sagmeister's series *Beautiful Numbers*, also from 2021, which transposed Pop art–esque glyphs of mysterious colors and sizes onto Renaissance paintings. What do these shapes represent? What are they trying to say? Perhaps the questions are more important than the answers.

You might find any of the aforementioned examples hanging on the wall of your favorite museum or local gallery. That context shapes their meaning. In a way, artworks like these sequester data from the real world, cloistering them within the safety of a controlled environment so they can be examined, interrogated, and critiqued. *Incroci*, a data-based installation Giorgia made in 2022 with the artist Ehren Shorday for the Italian arts organization Fondazione Merz, took this approach to explore the so-called life lines of ninety-nine anonymous individuals. Using data crowdsourced online, *Incroci* (meaning "crossing" in Italian) abstractly visualized the path of each person's life with black lines painted on raw canvas. Seen in parallel, these timelines—some almost identical, others very different—offered a reflection on the collective and personal hallmarks of memory. There were no legends, no gridded axes or labeled tick marks. Each person's "life line" was presented as an abstract graphic shape, with the viewer left to fill in the meaning.

In a similar way, a work commissioned in 2020 by the Moleskine Foundation—the nonprofit arm of the beloved notebook company—offered another chance to meditate on how life can be understood with *and* through data. This time, the subject was Giorgia herself. Using forty years of her own personal data collection, she created a hand-stitched notebook to record all the major milestones of her life. The goal was to capture the totality of her existence in paper and thread—both key events pivotal to her trajectory, and the mundane day-to-day. Three Moleskine notebooks were deconstructed and then reassembled into one large accordion that could accommodate all the entries. She then stitched the pages with thread—14,496 stitches, to be exact, one for each day of her life up until that point. The color of the thread was white, almost the exact same color as the paper itself, to make the stitches almost imperceptible. On top of this base, a second set of stitches, this time using colored threads, marked important life moments: first words, a first boyfriend, a first promotion, first moments of grief over losing a loved one. An arduous exercise in physical and mental endurance, the final piece was titled *The Book of Life*. While the notebook was so delicate it needed to be exhibited in a glass vitrine, Giorgia liked the idea that someone flipping through its pages and touching each stitch would "know" her through her data, dimensionalized in paper and thread.

But how can art, creativity, and data come together outside the white box of the museum or gallery? We believe there is still much opportunity for us to "speak data" in far broader and more accessible ways, inviting everyone—not just the data nerds—into the stories behind the numbers. Where a classic bar chart might fail, a more artful, expressive approach might succeed.

In 2018, Giorgia was approached by the Swedish fashion brand & Other Stories, a division of H&M, to create a small capsule collection of custom-designed garments. There was no brief—a simultaneously exciting and terrifying proposition for any designer. Of course, she immediately turned to data. Clothes, like data, are inherently communicative. When we wear them, they say something about us. A little black dress says elegance, modernity, glamour. A pair of Levi's 501s says informality, youth, and American cool. In recent years, a red trucker hat signifies one political persuasion; a pink pussy hat points to another. What would it mean to *wear* data? In the same way that a fashion designer uses fabric or a tailor uses thread, Giorgia set out to see if she could use data as her own creative material.

But which data? Previous adventures in Data Humanism had revealed the power of individualized, "small data" to incite understanding and empathy, yet it wasn't immediately clear how such an approach might translate to a commercialized, mass-market product. Giorgia might have wanted a T-shirt with her own personal data emblazoned upon it, but would & Other Stories' customers feel the same? Instead, she hit upon the idea of using, as a basis for the designs, historical data from three inspiring women: Ada Lovelace, the nineteenth-century mathematician recognized as the first computer programmer; Rachel Carson, the writer and conservationist who helped pioneer the environmental movement; and Mae Jemison, the physicist and NASA astronaut who was the first Black woman in space.

Their accomplishments became the source code. A delicate embroidery of white sunbursts and multicolored rays was beautiful, but also meaningful; in this case, the length of each line corresponded to a chapter in *Silent Spring*, Carson's famous exposé about the environmental harm of chemical pesticides, and color denoted a frequently cited topic (chemicals, insecticides, water, et cetera) in the text. Silver disks stitched into a knit sweater were more than just whimsical polka dots: each

Installation view,
Incroci, 2022

↑

The Book of Life, 2021

→

& Other Stories, 2019, sweater with Mae Jemison pattern

←
& Other Stories, 2019,
dress with
Ada Lovelace pattern

↓
& Other Stories, 2019,
tunic with
Rachel Carson pattern

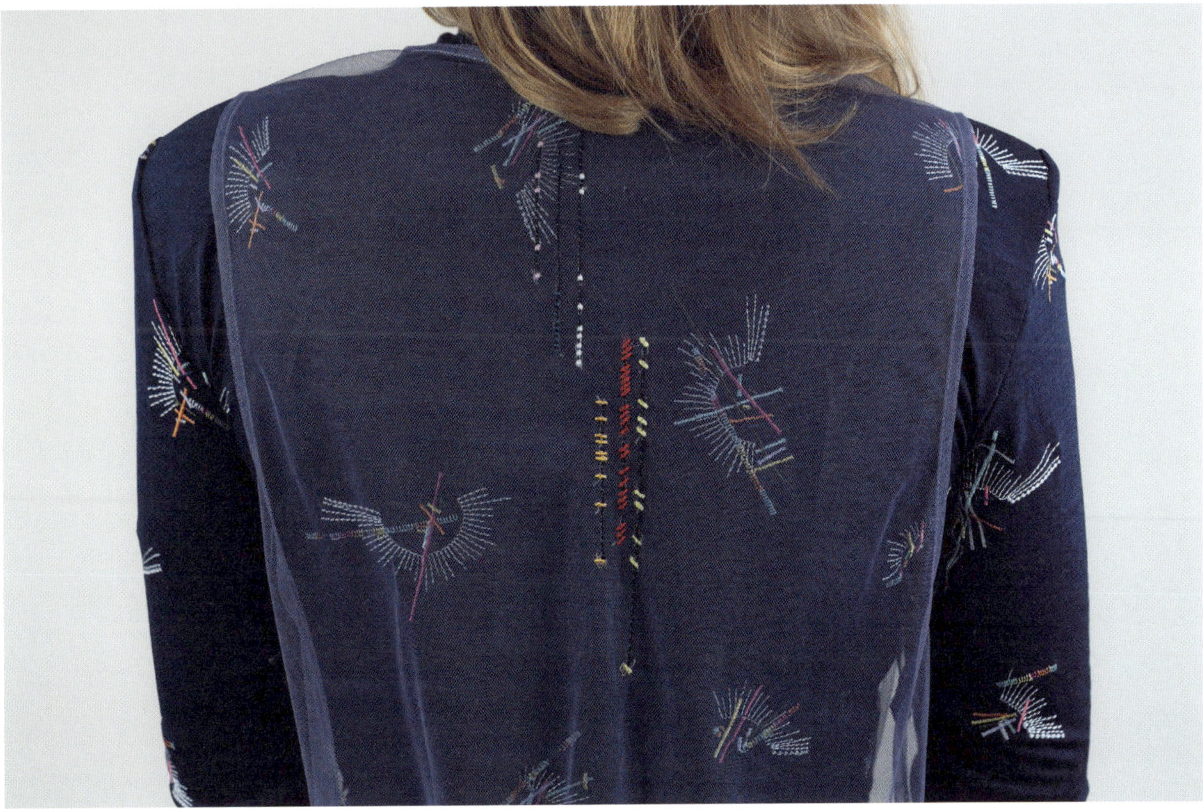

circle visualized one of Jemison's 126 orbits around the Earth, along with the time of day and the scientific experiments conducted. A distinctive striped pattern—a graphic distillation of Lovelace's first-of-their-kind computational algorithms—made for both a great dress and a provocative message about women's pioneering role in tech. There were ten garments in all, and each was sold with a specifically designed shopping bag that included a detailed legend for understanding these unique visualizations.

These clothes aren't for everyone; they were designed for a specific type of individual, and carry with them specific messages about three women and their remarkable accomplishments. But in the same way that a graphic T-shirt emblazoned with a favorite slogan can project the wearer's point of view to the world, so too can data be used to communicate histories, stories, or ideas that matter. To unlock its greatest potential, we just must liberate data from its usual containers and bring it into the real world.

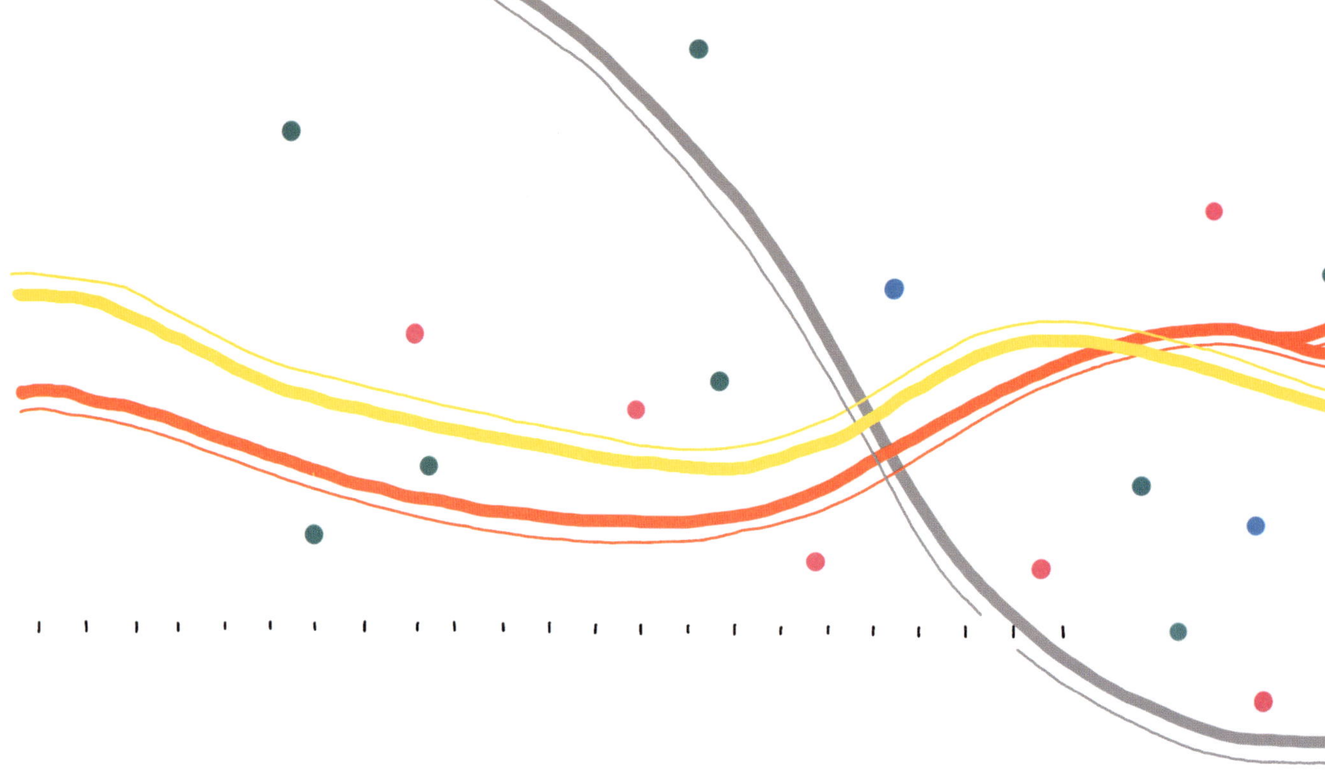

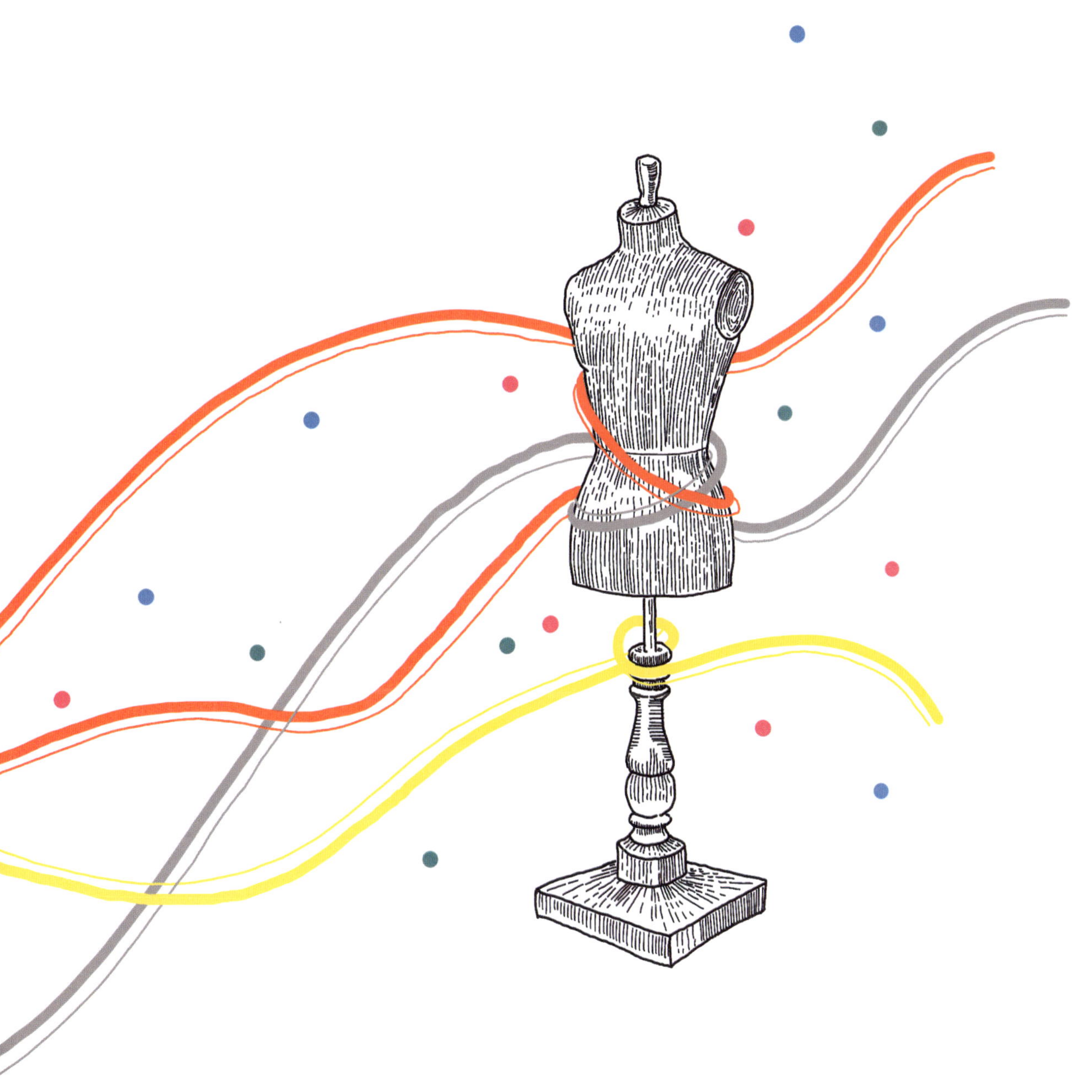

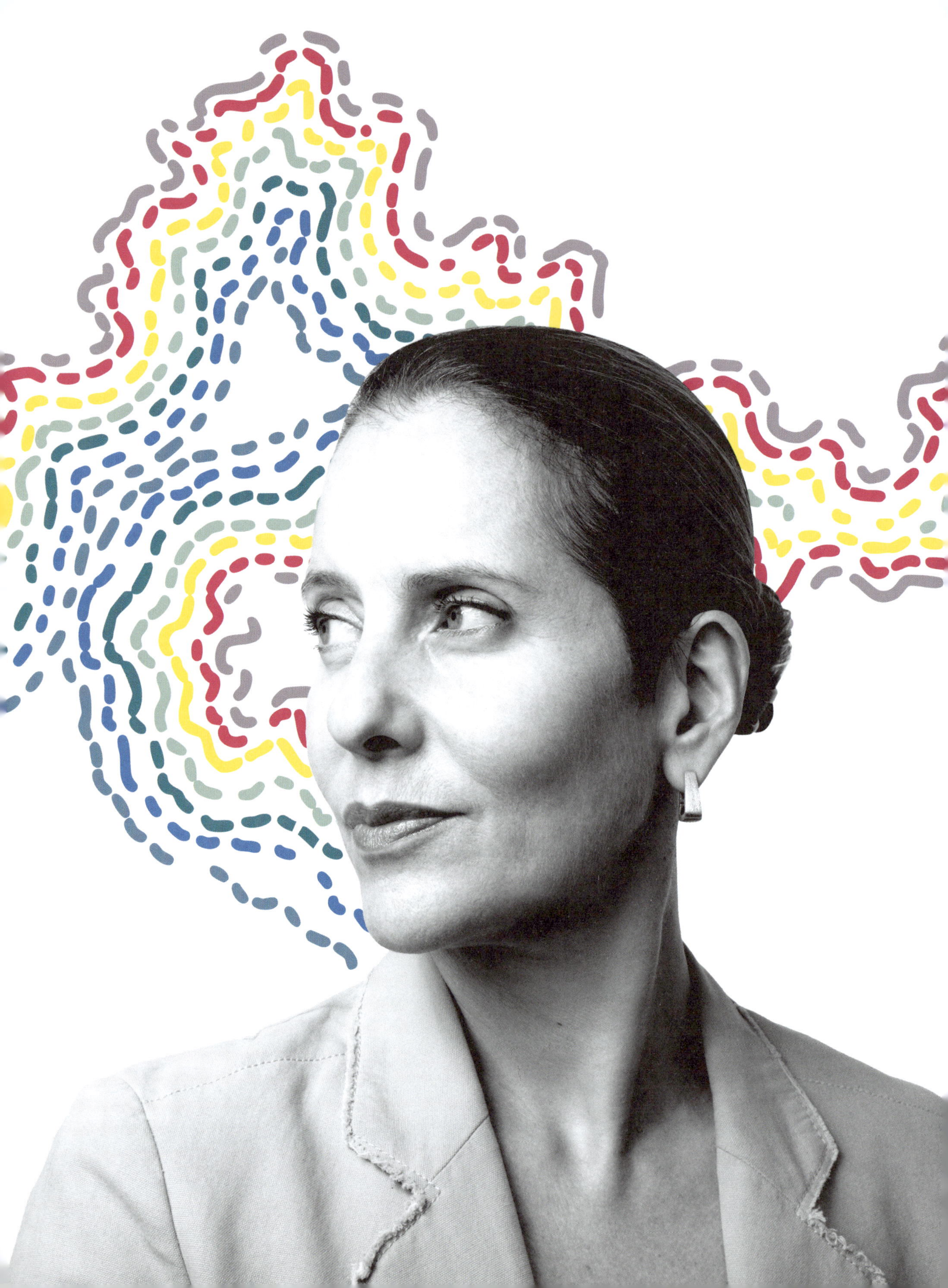

Paola Antonelli

Paola Antonelli is the senior curator of architecture and design at the Museum of Modern Art in New York. Operating at the intersection of art, design, technology, and culture, her exhibitions, writings, and public programs have consistently demonstrated design's essential role in shaping our world. At MoMA she has both exhibited data visualizations and, remarkably, acquired them for the museum's permanent collection. In this conversation, Paola discusses her unique curatorial perspective on data; whether a dataset can be considered a work of art; and how the best information design reveals truths about the world.

You began acquiring data visualizations for MoMA in 2008. Those visualizations were in your exhibition *Design and the Elastic Mind* of that same year, which reframed for many of us what design could be in the context of an art museum. What do you consider when deciding whether to bring a data visualization, as opposed to, say, a painting or a sculpture, into the museum's collection?

Collecting data visualizations is no different from acquiring chairs or video games. Form is important. I see form as a sign of respect toward other human beings. It's not prettiness. It's formal intention. We also think about function, of course. For instance, when you consider Ben Fry's *isometricblocks* (2002/2004–5), a visualization of different populations' genetic profiles, we take into account the fact that Fry is designing for an expert audience; the visualization is not meant for the general population. Therefore we consider it differently than we would a visualization that was published by *The New York Times.* We consider the goal that is declared in the beginning, and whether that goal has been achieved in an elegant way with a form that actually fits the function. That kind of balance is still there. The final litmus test is: Would the world miss out if this object did not exist? Because the opposite of elegant is not ugly—it's indifferent. It's lazy. It's wasteful. You can be superfluous and not immediately useful, but still a gift for the world.

At MoMA, we try not to tell people what's good or bad, but rather help them train their own critical sense about design. Pretty much every example of information design that we show has something in it—whether it is the *Million Dollar Blocks* (2006) project by the Spatial Information Design Lab at Columbia University, which is about unveiling uncomfortable truths about incarceration and social inequalities with incisive, unforgettable diagrams, or the *Wind Map* (2012) by Fernanda Bertini Viégas and Martin Wattenberg, which shows patterns of the winds over the United States as if they were caressing a US-shaped wheat field. As MoMA, we want to make sure that we show great examples.

Sometimes there's something very intangible about what you collect. For example, you famously acquired the @ symbol for MoMA's collection. Do you think data itself has an intrinsic artistic or design value? Can you imagine a scenario where MoMA would collect a particularly important dataset?

Data is a language. In a way, it's a language like poetry is a language. MoMA does not collect poetry. Should we? For instance, the Futurists used poetry to create dynamic images. It's possible that we would collect a dataset if the artist attributed to it a particular value or expression. I'm thinking of the work *It Began as a Military Experiment* (2017) by Trevor Paglen in our collection, which is an early AI training set composed of people in the military. That's a dataset we collected because the artist imbued it with ulterior meaning and motive.

If you had to draw a mental diagram of data, art, and design right now, are they all together?

It's funny that you put data as the third thing in that list. I think art and design are on the same plane. They converse with each other. Data is its own world. Data percolates, feeds, is kind of ogled by art and design in different ways. It's almost like a universe that you can draw from when you need it. I see data as a well that both art and design can draw from.

Fundamentally, is data a tool or a language?

To me, data is a material. You could call it a tool, but the tool is the technology you apply to it. And you perfect your tools. You know it very well because you do it all the time. You massage, you reframe, you redesign your datasets—or you design them from scratch.

What do you think about the ongoing discussion around AI-generated images being art?

I think that every time there's a new technology, there's a period of testing it. It's a sort of drunkenness. You see a lot of crap and you see a few diamonds. Then, slowly but surely, you sober up and start seeing the long aftereffects. I think it's all good. Right now might be a divertissement, but let's see what happens next.

We're thinking about how text-to-image AI tools can be like another member of our design team.

Sure. You declare what you want to the AI. You don't try to fool anyone. You declare it. Then it's like a performance.

> “You declare what you want to the AI. You don’t try to fool anyone. You declare it. Then it’s like a performance.
>
> —Paola Antonelli

In 2018 you organized a symposium at MoMA called "Artificial Imperfection." In it you said that "society is gearing up for the artificial intelligence quickening."[1] We feel that we're still in this quickening, and the pace is accelerating. What does it mean right now to think about artificial intelligence from a human perspective?

One of the biggest conversations during that salon was about the idea that AI and computers are infallible. But they are not, because they are still trained by us. For instance the whole idea of systemic racism that transpires from the training datasets is something that hasn't gone away.

Data is at the basis of AI, but data itself has a slightly different definition. How much do you think the general population knows about data right now?

Most people think of data as figures. They are trained to look at diagrams. They think immediately of percentages and indexes. That's the idea of data that statisticians, scientists, journalists, and even you and I have been feeding people for a long time. We've been telling them that data points are crystallized by figures. It's a reeducation to say that data is a form of information. But having that kind of scientific departure point, to me, is better. You start from the science, and then you discover the emotion. You discover the imperfection of data, the arbitrariness, and the fact that data are fed by humans rather than the opposite. I prefer that. That way, you have a sense of freedom and rediscovery of the human condition.

We still have so much to discover about data, so it's not about getting anything wrong or right, but rather perfecting the understanding we have and becoming more sophisticated. Right now, it's about moving beyond the quantitative aspect of data and highlighting instead their imperfection, richness, and organic nature.

People know about data through data visualizations, too.

Data visualization is about unveiling important information that might otherwise remain hidden. That's a very encompassing way to think of data visualization's role, but I think it's the truth. For instance, it was important for people to know who and how many people were dying of COVID-19, their ages, their circumstances. But it's sometimes also important to let people know about themselves in less exact terms.

It's like design. The design that I like is that which adds something to the world. And the data visualization that I like is that which reveals or unveils something about the world. Either it gives you a bird's-eye view, or it tells you more granularly what's going on. I like when it adds something to our perception of the world.

What field do you feel would benefit from a better or more thoughtful understanding of data?

What a big question! I think that economists should be reeducated to understand what data can be. They should embrace the kind of humanism that you are promoting.

Another way to use data would be in culture. I've been frustrated forever by the absence of "objective" metrics to measure the impact of culture on society. It's very frustrating because every time there's an economic crisis, the first thing that gets cut by politicians is culture because we don't have strong metrics. We don't always have a good way to tell politicians how much culture gives to the GDP every year, for example. I would like some economists to come up with indexes that are impeccable—or impeccable sounding—so that politicians could not doubt the impact of culture. Right now it's so hard because it's all intangibles.

NOTES

1 "Salon 24 AI - Artificial Imperfection," Museum of Modern Art, http://momarnd.moma.org/salons/salon-24-ai-artificial-imperfection-2/.

Data is

LIKE A UNIVERSE THAT

YOU CAN DRAW FROM

WHEN YOU NEED IT

–PAOLA ANTONELLI–

Ekene Ijeoma

Ekene Ijeoma is an interdisciplinary artist interested in the conceptual and physical form of social injustice. With a practice rooted in research and systems thinking, he uses data to create sculptures, installations, performances, and digital works that challenge preconceived notions about poverty, migration, health, and more, at both the individual and the societal levels. Ekene's work is often participatory, spanning multiple media and modes of engagement, online and off. It has been exhibited at New York's Museum of Modern Art, the MIT Museum, the Kennedy Center, and the Design Museum in London. In this conversation, Ekene talks about using geography as a cultural artifact; the problem of imagination; and why we have all the data we need.

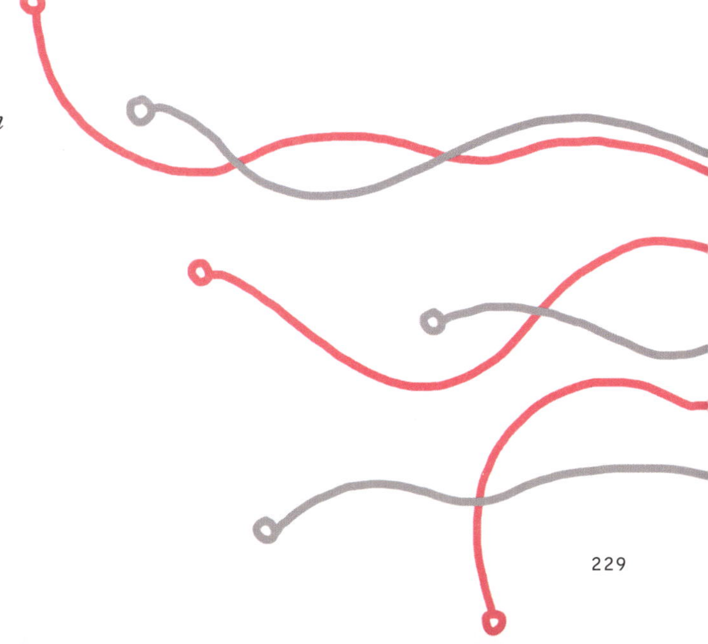

For those who aren't familiar with your practice, what are you working on right now?

I'm working on a lot of different things that are sort of related. I think of my practice as having two parts: I research the sociopolitical and environmental systems that affect us as individuals and engage communities in changing those systems. So, the first part is about representation and the second part is about intervention. In my studio, we're working on a series of sculptures. They're not data driven, but they're informed by data. If you looked at them, you would think they were data driven. However, they're not based on a dataset but rather the varied experiences that produce a dataset. It's about migration.

Fascinating.

My thinking about this started with my sculpture *Pan-African AIDS*, which was commissioned by the Museum of the City of New York for an exhibition titled *Germ City* in 2018. I started researching the disproportionate effects that HIV and AIDS had (and still have) on Black communities in the United States and found a report titled *Left Behind* that the Black AIDS Institute published in 2009. The report speaks to how Black communities in the United States were left behind in the effort to fight AIDS when, at the same time, the Bush administration was fighting AIDS in African countries through PEPFAR (the President's Emergency Plan for AIDS Relief). HIV prevalence in some Black communities in the United States was just as high, if not higher, than in some African countries. I worked with an epidemiologist to look at that data and make these comparisons.

The report also asked: If Black America were a country, how would it rank among other countries? In terms of HIV prevalence, it would be in the top twenty, alongside some of the African countries that the US government funded. So this became the idea. I kept meditating on the shape of the United States, morphing into the shape of Africa. I had that form in mind, but then I went back and tried to look at the data to see if it was telling some sort of truth based on the data. I created this chart, which showed that within a seven-year span of PEPFAR, the rates of AIDS in Africa went down while the rates in Black America went up. I used this data to determine the rate at which the morph would happen, which in 3D modeling terms is called lofting.

It's such a powerful piece.

But with this new work, I'm no longer thinking about HIV/AIDS. Now, I'm thinking about migration: Black people moving from Africa to different countries around the world. I found the countries with the highest Black populations, and then I selected ten that I had lived in or visited, including Italy, Mexico, and Brazil. I used the same lofting effect to create a series of sculptures, each with Africa morphing into each of those countries. The form it creates looks like a tree trunk or root. It also looks like a type of diagram, but I can't remember what it's called.

You could call it a Sankey diagram when a flow goes into another flow?

Yeah, a Sankey diagram, but in three dimensions. It reminds me how Black people, stemming from Africa, have rooted themselves in these countries. They're not data-driven sculptures, but there's so much information—lived experience and ancestral knowledge—embedded in their forms.

You don't necessarily define yourself as a data artist, but a lot of your work has data in it: counting, measuring, analyzing, comparing, morphing. What is your personal definition of data right now?

I'm not so interested in defining data. I'm interested in expanding vision and representation in the arts. The primary way any issue is represented, as far as social issues or crises, is through photography. Photography is one way of seeing, but data is another way of seeing. That's the way I look at it. Data becomes a way to look outside the frames of photography to see what else is happening. I'm interested in the bigger picture.

How has this thinking influenced the work you're making?

I wanted my work to be more expansive. And I felt that to do that I had to expand my use of geography as political entities to cultural artifacts. That's why I'm able to make this sculpture of Africa morphing into the United States—because people know the shapes of those entities and their various meanings. I expand these meanings, using data, to reframe how someone thinks about them. I find that to be more impactful than using geography alone. It goes from something that's more didactic to something that's more poetic. Geography becomes a metaphor, and then I reframe that metaphor to say something different about it.

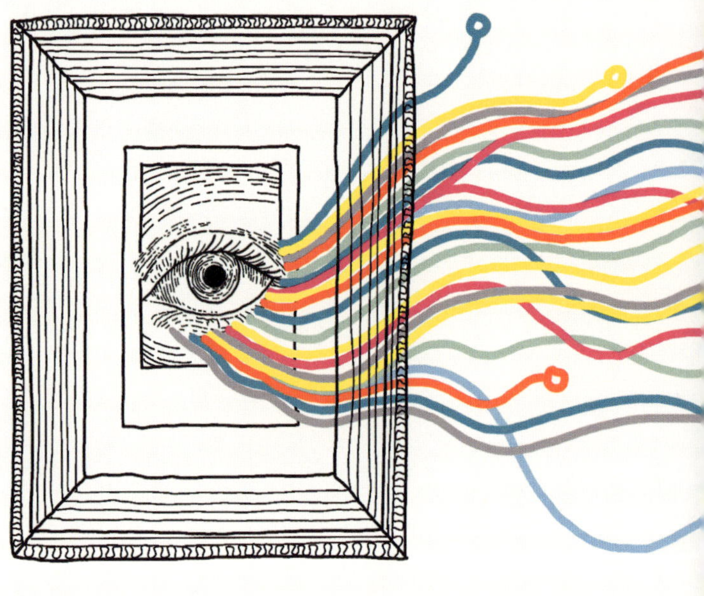

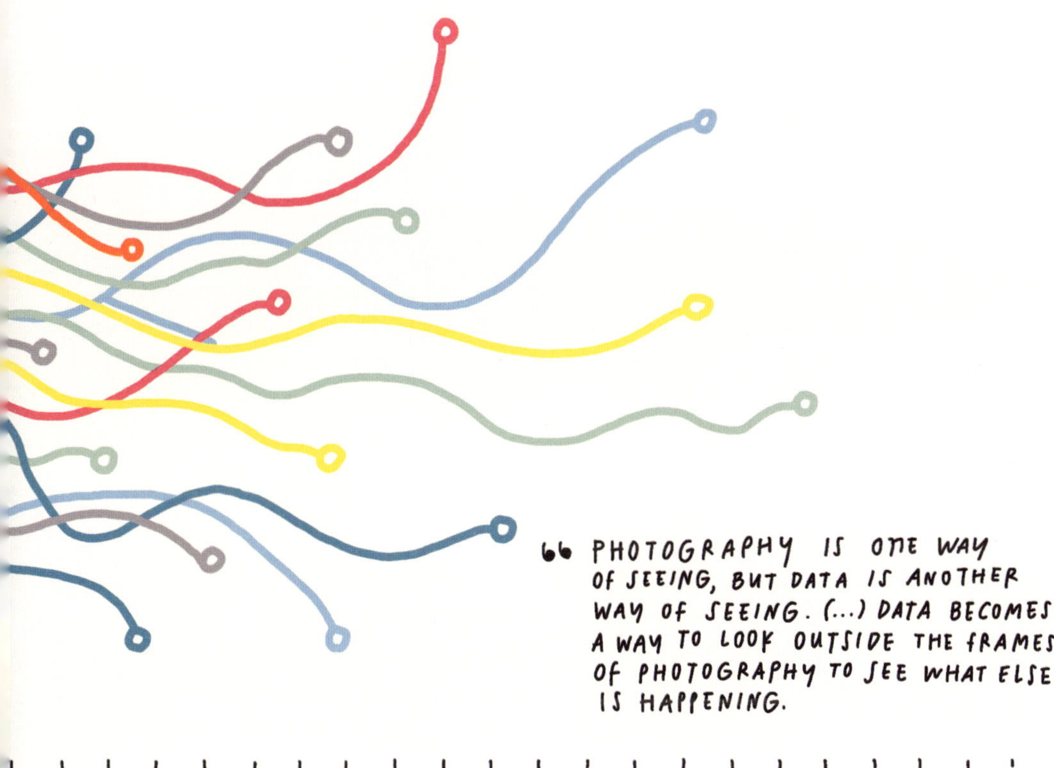

“PHOTOGRAPHY IS ONE WAY OF SEEING, BUT DATA IS ANOTHER WAY OF SEEING. (...) DATA BECOMES A WAY TO LOOK OUTSIDE THE FRAMES OF PHOTOGRAPHY TO SEE WHAT ELSE IS HAPPENING.

—EKENE IJEOMA

Do you think about the audience who will be viewing or engaging with your work?

Yes and no. There's this quote I really like from Adrienne Maree Brown. She says, "We are in an imagination battle—Claudia Rankine and Terry Marshall speak of this. Trayvon Martin and Mike Brown and Renisha McBride and all of them are dead because in some white imagination, they were dangerous. And that imagination is so respected that those who kill based on an imagined racialized fear of black people are rarely held accountable. imagination has people think they can go from poverty to millionaire as part of a shared american dream. imagination turns brown bombers into terrorists and white bombers into mentally ill victims. imagination gives us borders, gives us superiority, gives us race."[1]

Going back to why I switched from didactic to poetic use of geography, it's because of imagination. People imagine something to be something that it may not be, so I'm interested in playing with those perceptions.

Your installation work sometimes has a scale to it that confronts that imagination. For instance, your 2021 installation *Breathing Pavilion* in Brooklyn explored the idea of breathing as a shared experience in a spatial way.

Breathing Pavilion was about engaging people and communities in changing the system through breathing. It was related to how we were thinking about breath at that time as something that was not a point of connection. How can our breaths become a point of connection again, and how can we feel and understand each other in different ways? How can this become another mode of communication?

In my lab now, I'm thinking more and more about scale, specifically addressing injustice and inequality at scale. I always say we're researching how we can create art at the same scale as injustice. We're doing that by developing works that are public, participatory or community-driven, multisited, and networked. I've found that those four facets are needed for an artwork to address the scale of injustice or inequality.

Your work tackles important issues while at the same time emotionally moving people. Most people don't usually experience data in this way. Do you think that the data printed in publications and reports can move people?

I'm optimistic about a lot of things, but I'm a pessimist when it comes to thinking that we need any more data. I believe we've had all the data we've needed for a while now, and I don't think the issue of data has to do with data itself. It has to do with all the social and political aspects of what that data represents.

The communities being affected by these issues know they're happening. They've been telling people these things are happening. Still, many unaffected people don't seem to believe it when they see it. So again, it comes down to imagination. If people see something that is not aligned with their cultural beliefs and systems, then they may think it's not for them. It has to do with the imagination.

All these publications are producing the best data visualizations they can produce. But I don't think it's reaching both sides like art can. So, yes, I think we have all the data we need to make change, and at large, I think we have all the technology we need to make change. I believe that "the future is now, it's just not evenly distributed."[2] I think that's so true in so many ways, including for data, except, I'd add, it's not evenly considered and respected.

NOTES

1 Adrienne Maree Brown, *Emergent Strategy: Shaping Change, Changing Worlds* (AK Press, 2017), 14.

2 This echoes a quote often attributed to science fiction author William Gibson.

Data is

ANOTHER WAY OF SEEING

-EKENE IJEOMA-

Nico Muhly

Nico Muhly is a dynamic composer and arranger who has worked with orchestras, opera companies, and pop stars. He writes music that gleefully draws on multiple traditions—American Minimalism, Icelandic folk music, Anglican choral music, electronica—in unexpected and inspiring ways. Nico graduated from Columbia University and the Juilliard School, then worked as an assistant to the renowned composer Philip Glass. Today he is one of the most in-demand composers of modern classical music, known both in and beyond the field for his inventive, idiosyncratic scores. In this conversation, Nico discusses relationships between music, language, and data; the romanticization of handwritten notation; and how composing is like building a beehive.

There are so many parallels between music and data. Musical notation is itself a type of information design, isn't it? It transforms a melody in our head into a readable format that can be interpreted by others.

Of course, one hundred percent. This is definitely true in the Western tradition. All notation is about communication, about me giving you—and I say "you" as if you're the oboist or whoever—something that is in code. We have an agreement about how you decode it, and within that process of decoding there is X amount of room for you to bring in your own experience. Some composers are really meticulous about that. For instance, there's some cookbooks where everything is measured out to the gram, right? "One gram of xanthan gum and one gram of garlic clove." Whereas there are other cookbooks where measurement is more abstract.

As a composer, I have to figure out how much room to allow for interpretation. How much room is there for an oboist or a pianist to bring in their own history? I try to leave relatively a lot. I also try to keep things what I would call strategically vague. There's a great example in musical notation called a tenuto. It's a straight line written over a note, and it can mean one of sixty-five different things and no one agrees exactly. Some people think it means you play the full value of the note. Others think it means you put a little bit of stress on the note. Still others think that when you have five of them in a row, you put a little delineation between them. When performers ask me, "What do you mean by this?" what I usually say is a more polite version of, "If I wanted something specific, I would have told you." What I want is for you to make a decision. I don't care what that decision is because I chose not to be specific about it. If I say "play this fast" but I don't give a metronome marking, what does that really mean? When you say "play this loud," that's not a number, right? It's not like it's measured from one to one hundred, and "loud" is eighty-six and "very loud" is one hundred.

I should say that Western notation has huge limitations. Colonial limitations. A big caveat I want to put around this conversation is that one of the problems with Western supremacy is that we more or less refuse to have a working definition of what a classical technique is. You also find this in food. There's this sense that if it's not from the West, it doesn't have a classical organization. But that's simply not true. If you listen to

Southern Indian konnakol music, the rhythmic information is light years beyond what Western rhythms have come up with. And, amazingly now, there are people who listen to this music and transcribe it into Western notation, but that feels like an oversimplification, whereas it works the other way, because our system is limited in that context.

Fascinating.

The other thing that I find totally fascinating about traditional Western notation is how many languages are mixed up in it. Most notation is in Italian still, and that's amazing. It's this tradition that we've inherited. And I don't want to say it's arbitrary, because of course the delineation is clear, but if you open up fifty scores written recently by Americans or English-speaking people, you will find mostly Italian indications. For instance, you don't say "the sound dies away" at the end of a piece. You say the Italian word *smorzando*. It's no coincidence that the French word to sight-read music is *déchiffrer*, which means to decode.

When you're composing a new piece, do you ever feel limited by Western musical notations and wish you could break out of those conventions?

My music specifically doesn't require it. There's nothing that I do in my personal style that departs from the Western notational desire. However, so many of my colleagues write music that is iterative, that is both vague and specific. If you wrote out what happens in their music, it would look so complicated and illegible—with a capital *I*—in the theoretical sense.

I don't know if either of you were raised in the Anglican tradition, but in the Anglican tradition, every afternoon a psalm is chanted. The chant is written out as seven bars of music, with each bar containing one or two chords. Below it, the entire text of the psalm is printed, but not connected to the chords above. The text itself is heavily annotated with **s* and *•s* and */s*. These symbols all have different meanings, and together with the text, they determine the rhythm. They add an additional level of coding. But unless you were raised in this tradition or sing in this tradition, you wouldn't get it. If you handed a psalm like this to an orchestra player, they wouldn't know what to do. But if you gave it to me, I could easily perform it for you right now. So it's all about different traditions of interpretation and traditions of decoding.

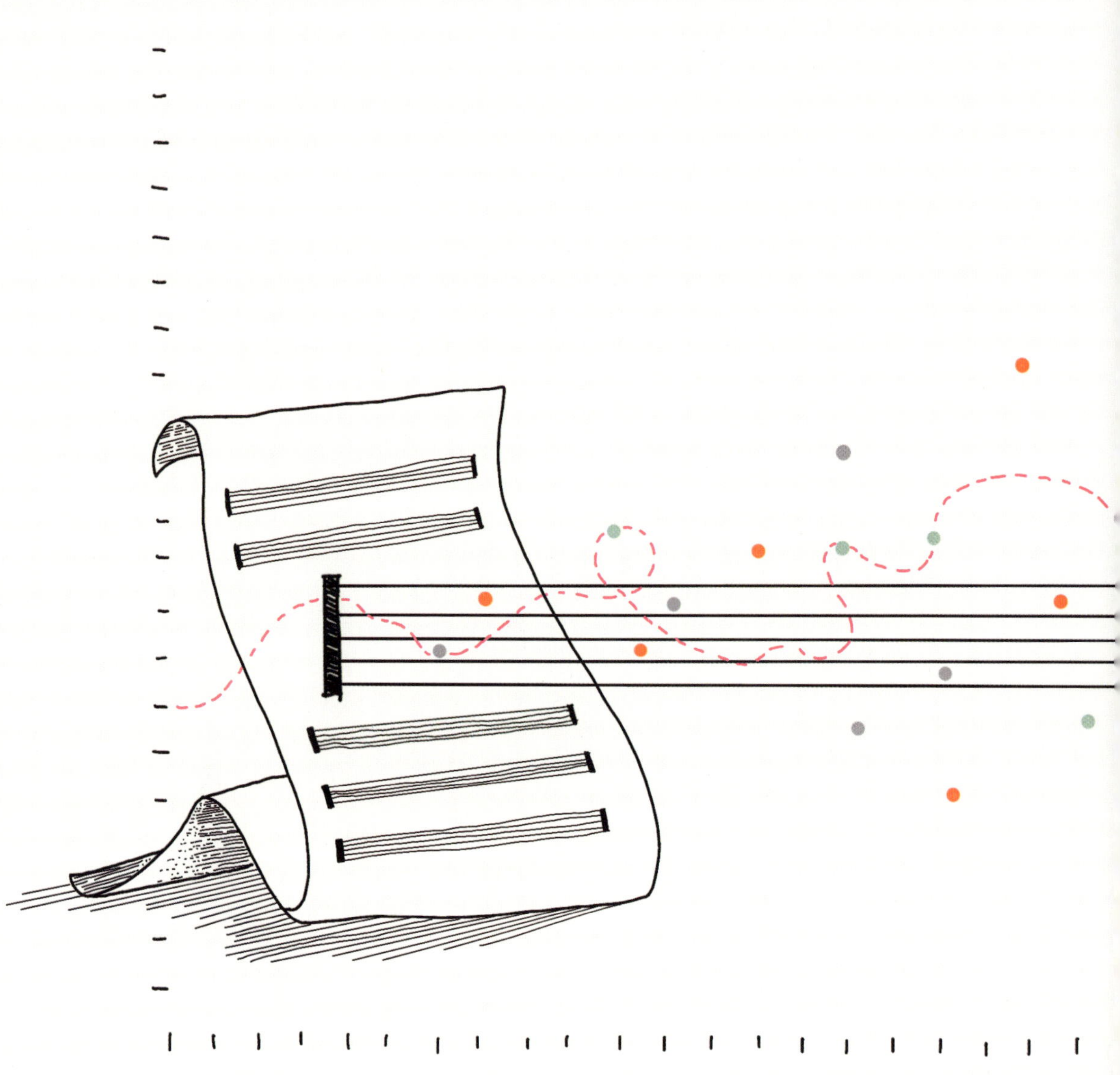

“DATA, BEFORE IT'S INTERPRETED, IS INFORMATION IN CONTEXT (...). IT'S POINTS THAT INVITE A LINE TO BE IMPOSED ON THEM. (...) THE WAY YOU DRAW CONNECTIONS—THAT'S WHERE IT GETS SORT OF ARTISTIC OR SUBJECT TO INTERPRETATION.

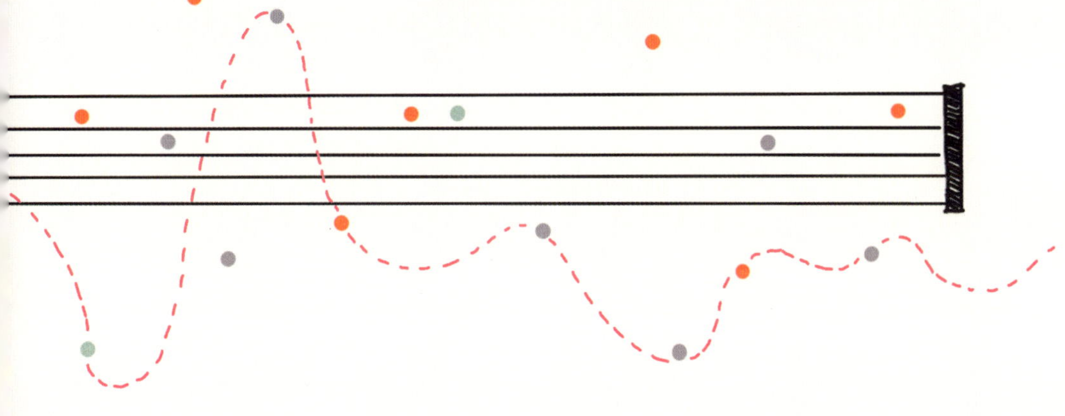

—NICO MUHLY

You can listen to five different people play the same piece by the composer Claudio Monteverdi, for instance, and it would sound completely different. You'll have people fight about this. I think the more vague the notation is, the crazier everyone is about controlling how it's done, and the more territorial people are about what they consider the "right" way to do it. That's interesting, because data is not necessarily meant to be emotional. Not even what results from it, which can be beautiful, but the interpretation of it is subject to questioning. And no one is ever casual about it. It's not different strokes for different folks!

What does your process of composing look like?

I start with visualizations. They don't contain notes. They contain shapes. I use this metaphor a lot: When you are flying from New York to San Francisco, you know where you're going. The destination is clear. But there are all these different flight paths that you can take to get there. I need to be able to see the big shape of the piece. Where are we going? What's the zoomed-out version of what's happening? And then my job is to zoom in and in and in. At a certain point, shapes turn into notation and then into actual notes.

It's all handwritten to start. To me there's a big difference between working on a screen and working with my head bent. For me, thinking can't happen by looking at a screen. When I'm at the computer, I'm in a more passive mode. There's no way to be passive when I'm looking down.

Do you think about the underlying mathematical structure of, say, a melody, when you're conceiving it? Do you think actively about triads, chord progressions, half steps—the data of it all? Or are you purely thinking about the sonic qualities?

That's a good question. Sort of both. I have a good answer to this, but I don't want to nerd out too far. One of the processes that I use to compose is I'll write out twelve chords in a row, then I will limit the notes of what the orchestra is playing to those chords. I like to think about it as a beehive, where the piece has a shape—the shape of it is not going to change—but what happens within that shape will. I can do whatever I want if I set myself this rule that the exterior shape is a single unmovable structure. The shape represents harmony. Inside that, I can make other rules—for instance the flute only plays quintuplets, or whatever. The first instinct often is the structure, or at least that's the one I plan for first, but in actuality things happen all at the same time. I hear the possibility of it even when I'm planning for it. When you walk by a beehive, you know something is happening in there. You might not know the internal structure, but you feel that energy that's perceptible without you needing to know the interior.

When we have data we have to visualize, we do something similar. We think about a legend and we test with the actual data. But it all happens in the same moment. When I describe it in words it sounds like a process, but it actually all happens together.

We've all seen bad data visualizations—it's like bad signage. You can tell they thought about what it should say but not about how it should look, or vice versa. What does a brain see when it reads a word? The at-once-ness of it, where you go between letters, a word, contextual meaning, emotional meaning, content—it all happens simultaneously.

But if I go to a country where I don't speak the language at all, I don't even have a path in. I'm faced with a wall without an articulation. I recently went to Japan, and I can't read that language at all. I was constantly in a state of wonderment. Wonderment and exhaustion. I lived in Rome when I was thirteen and went to school there. I didn't speak Italian. This was pre-internet. I just had my little Larousse dictionary, and my knowledge of church Latin. This torrent of language came at me and I had to make sense of it: Italian, but then the Latin behind it, and on top of everything was an accent. You have to start drawing lines and making connections. It's so not linear. It's code shifting, literally.

At the same time, when you become too stiff in trying to remember everything, you can't speak. You're restricted by trying to get everything right.

Right. This is why when you play music, there's stuff that you really have to practice and some things you don't. You get to a bunch of scales and you already know how to play them. I know already that that's an F major scale up. I immediately process that. I don't have to read each note individually and learn it. I know how to do this dance. If you're at the beach, it's much easier to run over rocks than to walk slowly, you know? You have to be fearless. When I'm composing, I find the best thing is to set up a structure and then play in it. Be spontaneous within the borders. It's like *SimCity*.

We also wanted to ask you about the analog versus the digital part of writing a score. It feels like everything is digital right now. But you're talking about sketching or writing with your hands, and you get a different meaning with the intentionality of the hand, how the pressure comes out. You've worked on the digitization of Philip Glass's scores. What gets lost in the transition to digital?

This comes up a lot, and I'm of two minds. I don't know if we have a choice anymore. We're past the point of romanticizing the hand. However, I still write thank you notes in my hand. I write musical thank you notes, phrases of music, in my hand, which I give to fellow musicians. They have a sentimental value. It takes forever to write by hand. It takes forever for someone to decode it.

But I think it's very generational. I was born in 1981. I'm a very specific age straddling the analog and digital. Digitization came along while I was becoming an adult. When I was in college, industry-standard software came out on normal computers, but my first two years at Juilliard, everything was done by hand. It sucked. So I don't romanticize it, even though it looks nice. Something of course is always lost, but it would be lost too if we went from the digital to the handwritten. It's not the difference between homemade mayonnaise and Hellmann's mayonnaise.

Also, these days I can access almost any musical score in fifteen seconds on my iPad. If it's in the public domain, eight seconds. That's changed everything.

We do a lot of data work by hand. Why? Because when we think about what data really is, it's fundamentally human. So designing data visualization by hand feels provocative, like a way to remind people about data's true nature. With your mindset of coding and decoding, what is data to you?

I think data, before it's interpreted, is information in context. It's not just one letter, but it's the letters next to each other that create a word. It's points that invite a line to be imposed on them. And those points, we should agree, are factual or true, and just waiting to be collated and organized in various ways. The way you draw connections—that's where it gets sort of artistic or subject to interpretation. If you scatter marbles and ask people to organize them, you'll get a lot of different systems. But data exists before that system.

Maybe that's generational, though. I remember making bar graphs and pie charts by hand, like with a protractor. I would be baffled by looking at raw data now. But still, I can do pattern recognition. I can put like with like. That's what we do in music. And that's what we do in language. And in data.

Data is

INFORMATION IN CONTEXT

—NICO MUHLY—

Sougwen Chung

Sougwen Chung is an artist and researcher who uses analog and digital methods to create works that are both conceptually rich and breathtakingly beautiful. Known for her transcendent explorations in human-machine collaboration, her pieces often feature robotics or artificial intelligence as performative "mirrors" to the physical act of drawing or painting. In 2023, she was named by Time *magazine as one of the one hundred most influential people in AI, and her piece* MEMORY (Drawing Operations Unit Generation 2) *(2017) is part of the permanent collection of London's Victoria and Albert Museum—the first AI model to be collected by a major institution. In this conversation, Sougwen unpacks the development of her practice; how drawing can behave like dance; and why* collaboration *is a loaded term.*

In your practice, there is this overlap between what could be called more traditional visual art and technology. There is also a human gesture and the human hand as a focus. Where did this interest begin?

My mother was a computer programmer, and my father was an opera singer. Growing up in that environment, exposed to performance and computer science, I saw art and technology as similar languages. As a child, I also trained in classical violin, which experience shaped my understanding of expressive gestures. I came to appreciate music and sound as an abstract form. My training in music helped me develop a sense of the interplay between precision and improvisation.

But my initial exploration of the relationship between humans and machines in art began in 2014. My time as a researcher at the MIT Media Lab was a turning point. It ignited an interest in relational computing and fluid interfaces and in collaborating with machines through custom robotic forms. The shift from screen-based interaction to embodied feedback loops with robots was a watershed moment for me—the digital leap to the physical. I became interested in alternative materialities of computational systems and hybrid authorship through mark making.

That same year, I began my *Drawing Operations* project. I create robotic units called D.O.U.G. [Drawing Operations Unit Generation] that collaborate with me to draw, and each new generation of D.O.U.G. explores a new theme or area of curiosity. *Drawing Operations* has allowed me to explore ideas of human and other-than-human subjects. It's guided the work through designing systems of blurred authorship and the dynamics between humans and complex technologies. I'm deeply interested in the human hand and its evolution in the context of technological change. I see the hand as a locus of muscle memory and physical instinct that drives the creative process, operating at multiple layers of perception and intentionality.

Do you specifically identify yourself as an artist who uses data?

Data is a rich and complex material to work with. But for me, it calls into question what is and isn't machine readable. The data is always part of a larger conversation about perspective, power, illumination, erasure. My projects involve datasets I create from my own life, like my drawings, biometric data, or data about how people move through cities. I think this personal connection makes the work more meaningful for me and helps me explore themes of identity, memory, and embodiment.

You've been deeply thinking for some time about both the theoretical meaning of AI and also its negative implications. Do you feel a little validated that some of these larger existential questions about AI are now part of the mainstream conversation?

It's been interesting to see the timeline of public understanding of AI. AI as an idea itself is constantly changing. Technically, there is no such thing as a single AI system, just as there isn't a single operating system or coding language. And conceptually, there's no such thing as a single artificial intelligence because there's no such thing as a single natural intelligence. We've all seen discussions about AI devolve into tech-theism and tech-pessimism, probably driven more by personal ideologies and faith than by a grounded understanding of the complex systems involved.

Of course, complex systems are hard to understand. I think art can play a crucial role in creating signposts of understanding for collective engagement. Art already shapes our conception of emerging technologies. I think of my work with robots and AI systems as a testing ground for examining human-machine interaction in a tangible and experiential way. And by bringing these interactions into the physical space of the gallery or the performance stage, I'm trying to demystify AI as a concept. I want to encourage critical reflection and challenge assumptions about the roles of human and machine in the creative process.

What do you think we've gotten wrong about how humans and machines can collaborate?

I think *collaboration* has always been quite a loaded term. In any collaboration, there are issues of balance, power, attribution, and agency. We've all had good collaborators, but we've all had not-so-good collaborators too, right? I always try to strike that balance with my engagement with the robotic unit.

In my work, what makes it a collaboration is this embodied mark making that happens on the page, which becomes the parallel balance. *Collaboration* is sometimes used to describe any use of technology, but to me, it's overused. With generative AI, for instance, I would question whether just writing a prompt to create an image in the style of a famous artist is "collaborating" with AI. It can be reductive at best and harmful at worst.

Do you have a definition of data for yourself?

Sometimes I think of data as a material to work with, similar to paint or clay—something to impress upon, but having its own characteristics. Sometimes I think of data as a framing. It's like a machine-readable framework to communicate with computational systems or, in my case, robotic systems. I think of it as an abstraction, but with this specific accent, depending on the format. And my engagement with datasets is personal. It's a mode of self-reflection, classification, quantification. I do relish a type of self-quantification. For other people working with open, collective data, I imagine it's different. Exploring a pond versus an ocean.

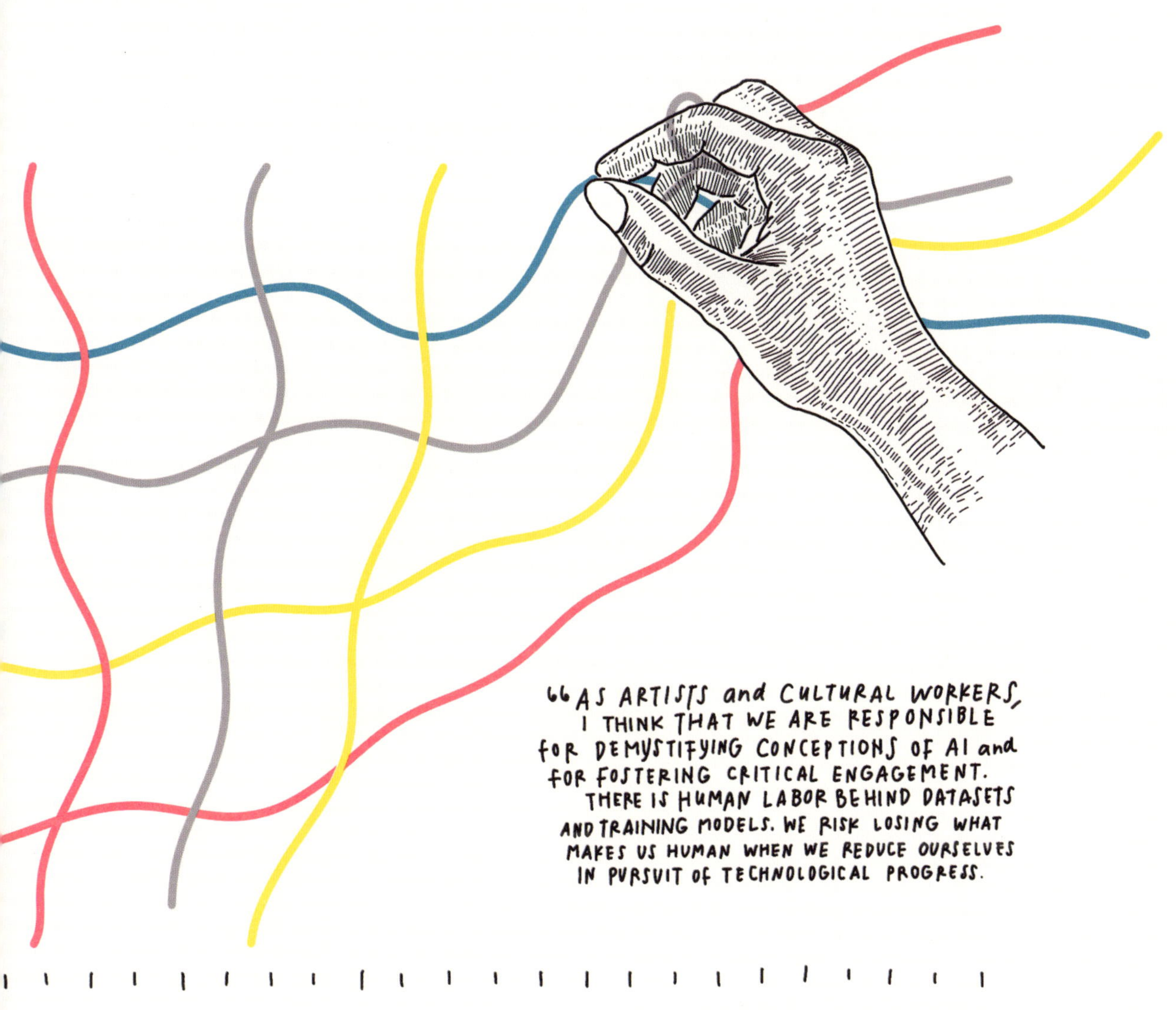

—SOUGWEN CHUNG

Of course, data is not neutral, and through the work, I've learned how datasets are collected, processed, and ultimately reinterpreted through algorithmic translation. In the case of drawing, one might say that digitization flattens and erases moments of pause and contemplation. It reduces the fluidity of human gestures to a series of data points. But by reembodying it in a robotic system, I think there's an opportunity to reintroduce those lost elements through performance and collaborative mark making. The data extends beyond the visual realm in the performances. And integrating biofeedback data from meditation into the robotic systems further complicates our understanding of how data can express internal states and explore the connections between the physical body, the mind, and technology. This is all just another way of saying that data is a means through which we can understand ourselves.

You bring up self-quantification. People who are into self-quantification often come to it in a non-artistic, non-emotional way. It's very analytical or technocratic. What does self-quantification mean for you?

Self-quantification can be a creative catalyst and a tool for exploration. While data science and measurement have their place, I'm more interested in using self-quantification to visualize internal experiences and challenge conventional ideas about the self. For me, self-quantification is not about achieving perfection or conforming to external standards. It's about embracing imperfection and the inherent unpredictability of human experience.

I use technologies like EEG headsets to capture biometric data like brain waves and then translate those internal states into external artistic expressions. For example, in my project *Mutations of Presence*, I linked the movement of my robotic collaborator to my alpha brain waves during meditation. The act of meditation was both the input and the output. The result was a much deeper meditative experience but also a unique visual record of my internal state.

I try to challenge the idea that technological perfection is a desirable or even achievable outcome. I find that there's beauty and truth in imperfection and change. It's the same with technology. The pursuit of a flawlessly functioning machine, devoid of error or unpredictability, feels limiting and unrealistic to me. Humans are flawed and capable of making mistakes, so the machines we create will inevitably reflect those imperfections. And that's okay. Robots don't always do as they're told, right? Neither should we.

Did the pandemic change your thinking about this in any way?

Sure, the pandemic significantly changed how I integrated self-quantification into my artistic practice. I think the isolation of lockdown led me to look inward. I began using my own biofeedback as source material, first with *D.O.U.G. 4: Mutations of Presence* (2021) and then in *D.O.U.G. 5: Assembly Lines* (2022). The pandemic also changed my creative process in a very practical way. Before, drawing was a way to process my thoughts and experiences, but the pandemic made me feel really unmotivated to draw. So I started meditating more frequently to find peace and stillness, which led to a deeper interest in using biofeedback as a creative tool.

I also started exploring spectrality, these invisible flows of energy within humans and machines. So in *Mutations of Presence*, I used an EEG headset to record brain waves during different kinds of meditation—Vipassana, aural meditation, qigong, and visualization. I then used those signals to control the movements of a robotic unit as it painted. Incorporating biofeedback into my artistic process became a way to cope with anxiety and uncertainty. It was a way to create a record of this moment of isolation, to establish rituals within this catastrophe happening around me.

So yes, my understanding of self-quantification expanded. It became less about tracking external data and more about translating internal experiences into art.

If we zoom out from these for a second, what do you think we as a society are losing if we keep thinking that data is perfect, or that technology is perfect?

If society continues to view data and technology as perfect, we risk losing many crucial aspects of the human experience and our capacity for growth. When we strive for perfection, we often limit ourselves to predictable outcomes and shy away from the unknown. We also risk losing our capacity to critically engage with the world when we accept technology and data without question. Blind faith overlooks biases and errors. We shouldn't forget that machines are us in another form, shaped by our values and flaws.

As artists and cultural workers, I think that we are responsible for demystifying conceptions of AI and for fostering critical engagement. There is human labor behind datasets and training models. We risk losing what makes us human when we reduce ourselves in pursuit of technological progress. I'm interested in challenging the human-versus-machine binary. Hopefully by embracing a more relational paradigm between us and our technology, we can better explore the interconnectedness of all things.

Data is

A MACHINE
READABLE FRAMEWORK
TO COMMUNICATE WITH
COMPUTATIONAL SYSTEMS

–SOUGWEN CHUNG–

Conclusion: How to Speak Data

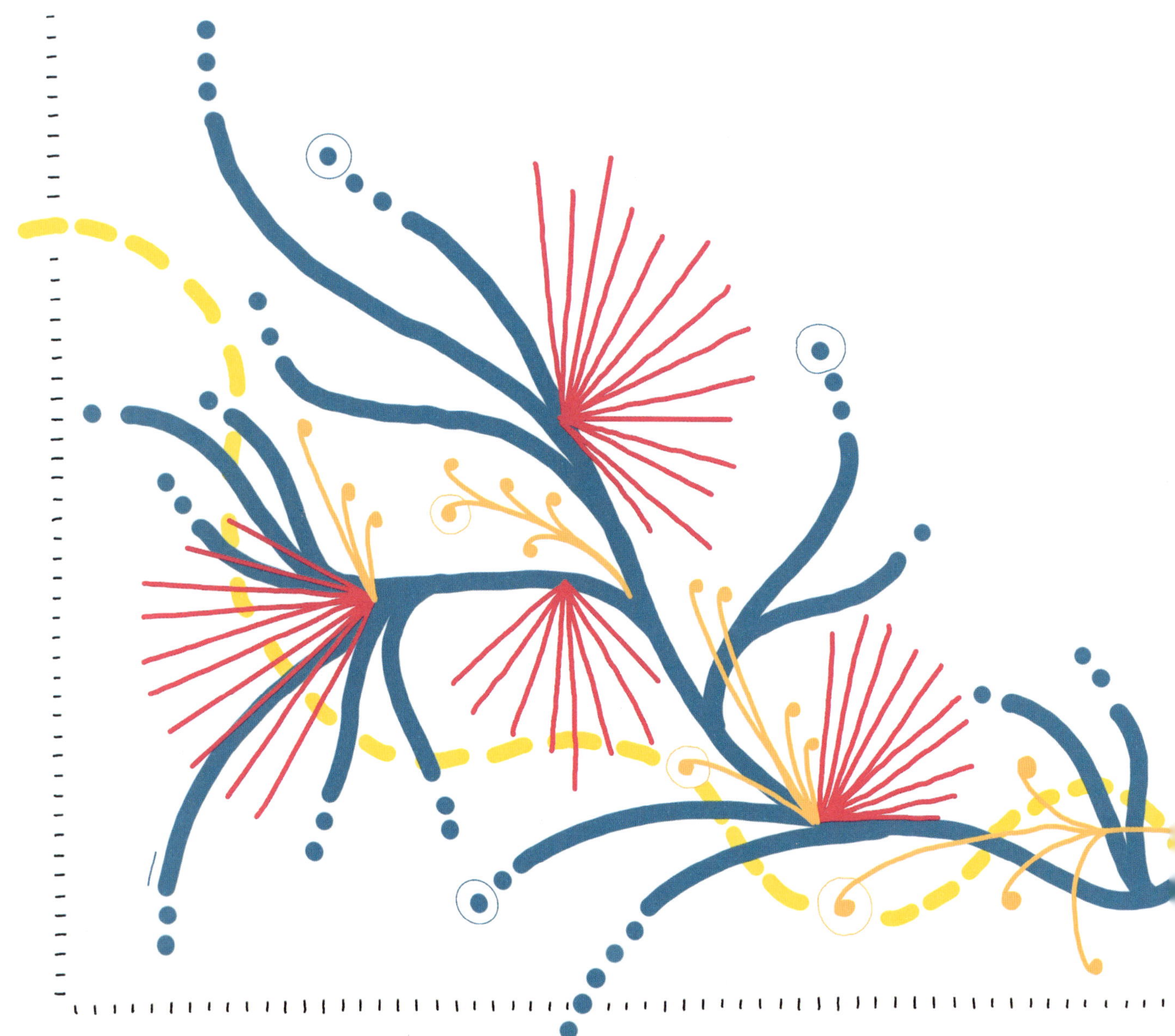

Conclusion: How to Speak Data

As the conversations in the preceding pages have demonstrated, there are no easy definitions of data. Data is exact, but also variable; tangible, but also abstract; singular, but also plural. Across questions of identity, communication, health, technology, and creativity, data serves as a filter for observation, a tool for measurement, a base map for representation, and a medium for expression. And like any language, the grammar of data is malleable. It responds to what the speaker wants to say, the accent with which they speak, and the times in which they live.

Instead of attempting to define what data is, maybe it's better—and more useful—to describe how to make sense of data in a world increasingly ruled by it. How do you speak data? Or, for those already comfortable with this language, how can you speak data better?

We hope the following points can help.

START WITH QUESTIONS

Good data starts with good questions. Think like a detective: What are you curious about? What might data help illuminate? Where is the human dimension in the numbers? Let these questions guide what data you collect, analyze, and ultimately communicate.

SEE THE FOREST, COUNT THE TREES

All big data starts small. While analysis of aggregated data helps us understand the full picture, it's the individual data points that truly capture any phenomenon. Both matter.

LOOK FOR CONTEXT

A data point is like a photograph—a finite record of a moment in time. The image may be artfully composed, but what essential information is lurking just beyond the frame? Widen your aperture to find out. Contemporary methods of data collection often edit out nuance or irregularity. To speak data with fluency, we must welcome these features back into the picture.

EMBRACE THE UNKNOWN

For many of us data implies certainty, a calcified image of truth. Yet what we don't know can be just as important as what we do. Missing data—gaps and holes in our record—is still data and should be treated as such.

VALUE ACCESSIBILITY, NOT SIMPLICITY

We live in a culture that equates simplicity with perfection, and reduction with resolution. Resist this. After all, life is complex and full of asymmetries, edge cases, and half-truths. The most powerful data gives us access to reality in all its untidy abundance.

FIND THE STORY IN THE NUMBERS, AND THE NUMBERS IN THE STORY

Data is a powerful storytelling material. Narratives elevate numbers with emotional resonance; numbers anchor narratives in concrete truth. To speak data, embrace qualitative *and* quantitative information with equal enthusiasm. Both are necessary to unlock data's fullest potential.

USE YOUR FULLEST VOCABULARY

When visualizing data, don't start with the numbers; start with their meaning. What idea do you want to communicate? Let this guide you in crafting the most effective visual solution. In doing so, you'll avoid the graphic conventions that too often deaden ingenuity. The space between logic and beauty is often where the most interesting—and memorable—solutions are found. Find the balance between pragmatism and poetry, without neglecting either.

STAY IN CONTROL

Data gives the illusion of power. Our impulse to *know* everything can quickly devolve into an impulse to *quantify* everything. But more data is not necessarily better data. Instead, treat data as a tool, and wield it with intention. First decide what matters, and then use data to capture it.

END WITH QUESTIONS

Now more than ever, we must question the impersonality of data. Whether culled from a spreadsheet or collected from a sensor, numbers are human made. "Data-driven" doesn't mean "unmistakably true"—it never did. Data literacy is not enough. Our contemporary world demands full data fluency, where all of us are empowered to speak data with confidence and clarity. Let data be the beginning of the conversation.

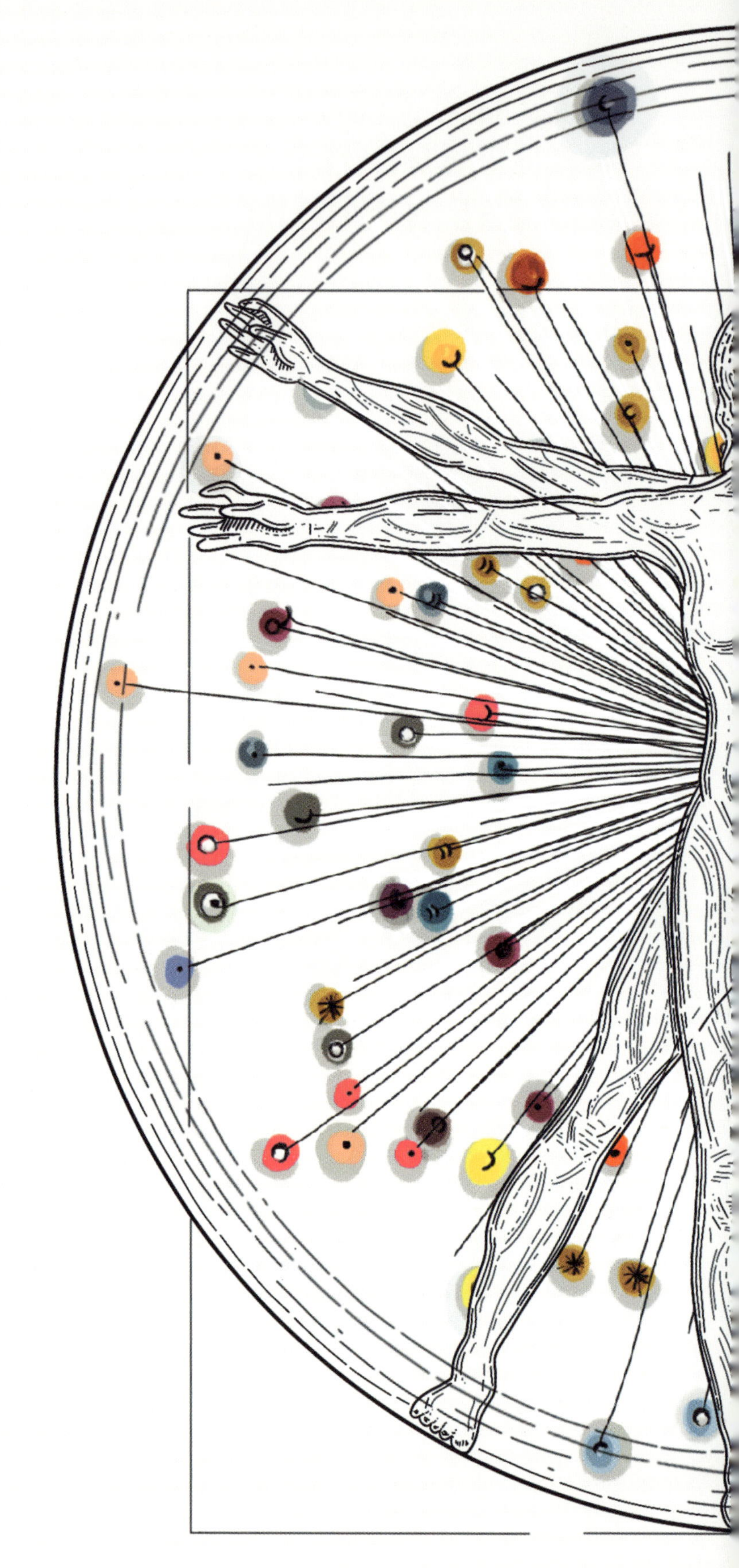

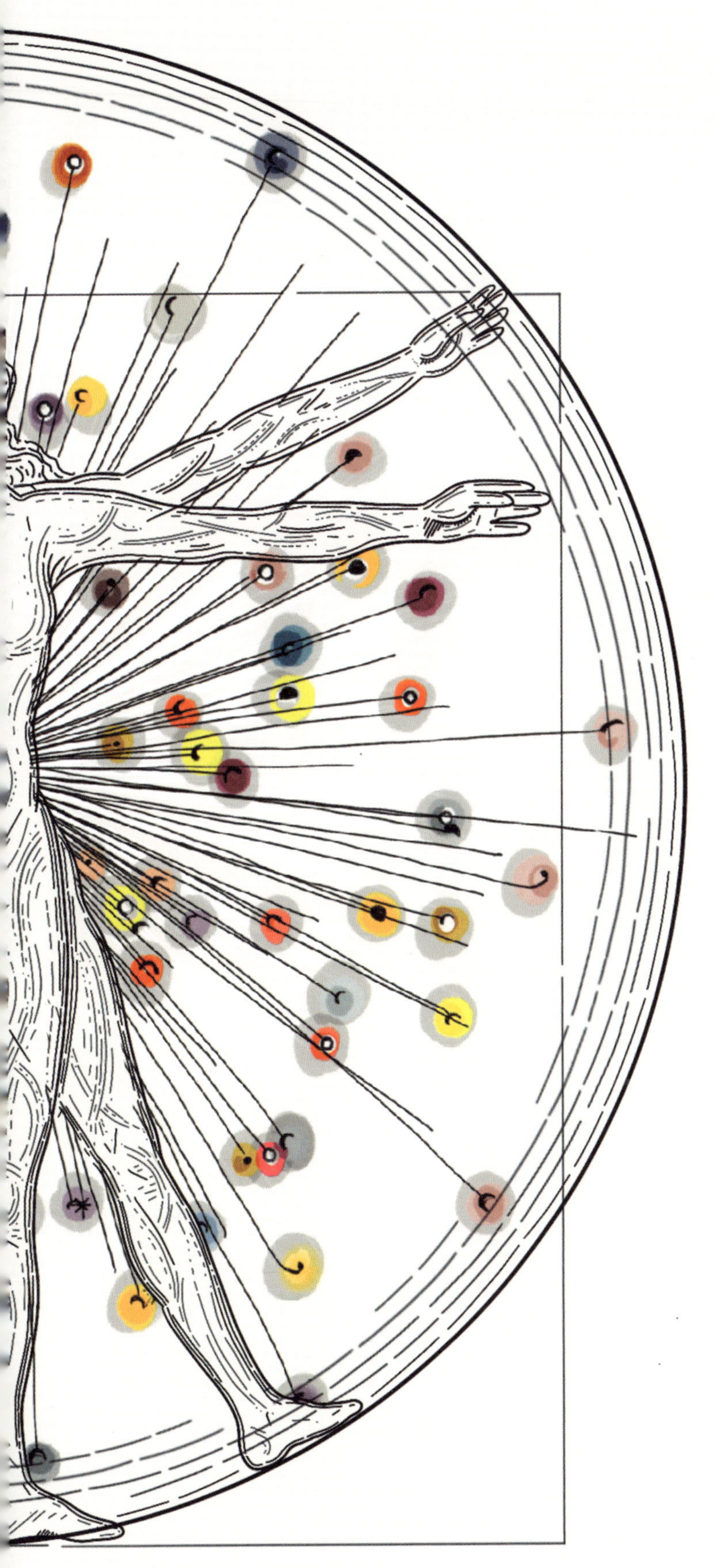

Acknowledgments

Thank you to our teams, collaborators, and clients—past and present—who have helped envision a future where a more humanistic approach to data might thrive.

From Giorgia
Thank you to Gabriele Rossi, Simone Quadri, Stefanie Posavec, and Paolo Ciuccarelli for helping to shape many of the ideas and concepts in this book. Thank you also to all my partners at Pentagram for the constant inspiration. And thank you to my mom, Ehren, and Melinda for the many conversations that helped me reflect, refine, and see things from new angles.

From Phillip
Thank you to my family, Daniel, Caroline, and Rob.

We thank the following individuals who contributed to the projects highlighted in the preceding chapters:

MethaneSAT
Giorgia Lupi, Abbott Miller, Michelle Brown, Phillip Cox, Madeleine Garner, Ed Ryan, Gabrielle Merite, Paul Lenaers

Nobels, No Degrees
Giorgia Lupi, Simone Quadri, Gabriele Rossi, Davide Ciuffi, Federica Fragapane, Francesco Majno

Data ITEMS
A Fashion Landscape: Giorgia Lupi, Gabriele Rossi

Connecting the Dots
Giorgia Lupi, Sarah Kay Miller, Ting Fang Cheng, Phillip Cox

Equal Is Greater
Giorgia Lupi, Phillip Cox, Sarah Kay Miller, Talia Cotton, Ting Fang Cheng

***Vote* poster**
Giorgia Lupi, Phillip Cox, Talia Cotton

Mindworks
Giorgia Lupi, Abbott Miller, Luke Hayman, Kirsty Gundry, Lindsey Petersen, Michelle Brown, Ting Fang Cheng, Sarah Kay Miller, Phillip Cox, Shigeto Akiyama, Janny Ji, Katie Lovins

Peninsula Talks
Giorgia Lupi, Simone Quadri, Gabriele Rossi, Giovanni Marchi, Marco Bernardi, Marco Vettorello, Paolo Corti, Luca Falasco, Giovanna Silva

Triennale Milano
Giorgia Lupi, Phillip Cox, Ed Ryan, Julia Saimo, Zach Schienfeld, Rachel Crawford

Bruises
Giorgia Lupi, Kaki King

Dear Data
Giorgia Lupi, Stefanie Posavec

What Counts
Giorgia Lupi, Ting Fang Cheng, Phillip Cox, Sarah Kay Miller, Tommaso Renzini, Gabriele Rossi, Melisa Altinsoy, Serena Girardi, Luca Falasco

Bulletin of the Atomic Scientists
Giorgia Lupi, Talia Cotton, Phillip Cox, Ting Fang Cheng, Sarah Kay Miller

Friends in Space
Giorgia Lupi, Simone Quadri, Gabriele Rossi, Alex Piacentini, Marco Vettorello, Francesco Merlo

Building Hopes
Giorgia Lupi, Gabriele Rossi, Alessandra Zotta, Giovanni Magni, Elisa Spigai, Vito Latrofa, Luca Mattiazzi

Plastic Air
Giorgia Lupi, Talia Cotton, Phillip Cox

Incroci
Giorgia Lupi, Ehren Shorday

& Other Stories
Giorgia Lupi, Mara Pometti

The illustration on pp. 266–67 is based on an earlier design by Julia Saimo.

The essay "Vital Signs" is based on the op-ed "1,374 Days: My Life with Long Covid," written, designed, and developed for *The New York Times.* Thank you to the teams at Pentagram (Phillip Cox, Madeleine Garner, Gabrielle Merite, Jacopo Poletto, Tommaso Renzini, Julia Saimo) and Decimal (Guillermo Brotons, Nathan Gordon, Gabrielle Harlid, Kirsten Holland, Nate Minnick, Alex Muñoz, Chérif Zouein), as well as to editor Jeremy Ashkenas.

Image Credits

15 Aldo Soligno
18 Jacob Hand
34 Nick Fancher
46 Jamey Stillings
56 Courtesy of Advocates for Trans Equality
70 Cover of Bulletin of the Atomic Scientists, public domain
71 Data visualization by Charles Joseph Minard, public domain
78 Brian Bloom
110 Julia Ruiz Pozuelo
132 Courtesy of Icahn School of Medicine at Mount Sinai
142 Stefen Chow/Fortune
176 Cath Muscat
186 Carson Lund and Kenny Kelly
196 Efsun Erkılıç
214 Courtesy & Other Stories
215 Courtesy & Other Stories
218 © 2021 The Museum of Modern Art, New York. Photo: Peter Ross
228 Kris Graves
250 Alex Kwan